THE RECLAMATION OF
EXMOOR FOREST

The village created by John and Frederic Knight. Simonsbath today

THE RECLAMATION OF EXMOOR FOREST

C. S. ORWIN and R. J. SELLICK

DAVID & CHARLES: NEWTON ABBOT

ISBN 0 7153 4959 7

The Reclamation of Exmoor Forest was first
published by Oxford University Press in
1929. This second revised edition contains
substantial new material.

Set in Garamond eleven on thirteen point
and printed in Great Britain
by Latimer Trend & Company Limited Plymouth
for David & Charles (Publishers) Limited
South Devon House Newton Abbot Devon

To E.

'In Travelling thro' *England*, a Luxuriance of Objects presents itself to our View: where-ever we come, and which way soever we look, we see something New, something Significant, something well worth the Travellers stay, and the Writer's Care; nor is it any Check to our Design, or Obstruction to its Acceptance in the World, to say the like has been done already, or to Panegyrick upon the Labours and Value of those Authors who have gone before, in this Work: Whoever has travell'd *Great Britain* before us, and whatever they have written, tho' they may have had a Harvest, yet they have always, either by Necessity, Ignorance or Negligence pass'd over so much, that others may come and glean after them by large Handfuls.

'Nor cou'd it be otherwise, had the Diligence and Capacities of all who have gone before been greater than they are; for the Face of Things so often alters, and the Situation of Affairs in this *Great British* Empire gives such new Turns, even to Nature it self, that there is Matter of new Observation every Day presented to the Traveller's Eye.'

'The Country is called *Exmore*, Cambden calls it a filthy, barren Ground, and, indeed, so it is.'

DANIEL DEFOE (1661–1731)

CONTENTS

LIST OF ILLUSTRATIONS

PLATES

MAPS

PREFACE

The story of the reclamation of Exmoor Forest by the Knights, father and son, should have something more than a local interest. Every student of economic history is familiar with the general procedure upon the inclosure of land during the Hanoverian period and is aware that large areas, hitherto unproductive, were brought under cultivation in those times, but very little has been recorded of the steps by which the work was done, of the persons to whose initiative it was due, of the difficulties they had to overcome, and of the results achieved by these pioneers of agricultural progress. Although the inclosure and settlement of Exmoor Forest presented problems of exceptional difficulty, the venture is typical, in many ways, of the enterprise of men of wealth, all over England, during the industrial revolution, directed towards the development of the resources of the soil. The subject is an absorbing one for all who are not content to accept the things they see around them in the countryside as natural phenomena; but the information needed for some account of the synthesis of agricultural expansion is singularly scanty concerning the days when progress was most active, when the growth of urban and of rural industry was going on side by side, and when farming in England was a business which really mattered to the nation.

No area could provide a better illustration of such work than Exmoor, and moreover, it is the last big piece of land reclamation that has taken place in England. Except for one small farm its twenty thousand acres was a complete waste, untouched by man. Except for the one farmhouse there was no habitation upon it; except for a few ancient trackways it was untraversed. It was unfenced, its confines being marked by stones, barrows, trees, and streams; it was extraparochial, and it possessed no social institutions of any kind except the Swainmote Court and the innkeeper's licence held by the tenant of the farm.

From the construction of the boundary wall and the metalling of the old trackways, the story of its reclamation proceeds to the breaking of the soil, first with ox-teams, then with horses, and later with steam tackle. There were vain attempts at corn-growing in an impossible climate, by the owner; later, at mixed farming and dairying by tenants from the more fertile farmlands of the midlands and southern counties, who took up the new farms and homesteads created on the Forest. They came and went, and the development of Exmoor went on, by the process of trial and error, till the time arrived when a farming system adapted to the potentialities of the locality had been evolved at last, and native farmers came in to occupy the holdings created by others at an expenditure of so much toil and money. There is the foundation of a great sheep-ranching enterprise—probably unique in England—on the unimproved portions of the Forest. The building of a village is seen, and the evolution of a civil and ecclesiastical parish, the largest in Somerset, out of what was once a wilderness. There is also a brief interlude during which it was sought to develop the resources of the property in minerals.

Materials for the history of the reclamation are not complete, but sufficient remains to make it possible to construct a picture which is exact in most of its details. By the kindness of Major Eric A. Knight, access has been had to the records and papers preserved at Wolverley House; and the information they contain has been supplemented by him in many important directions, filling in some of the gaps disclosed. Without these materials, and his ready assistance, it would have been impossible to complete even so much of the picture of Exmoor land reclamation and settlement as is given here, particularly as regards the earlier years. Second only to his help has been that afforded so freely by Earl Fortescue, who made available for the purpose in view his own records as owner of the Forest in its later years, and his experience of a lifetime of its changing fortunes. Whatever success has attended this attempt to trace the history of a great agricultural adventure during a hundred years is due, in the main, to the kindly interest they have shown and to their very practical assistance.

It is a pleasure, too, to acknowledge the ready help of the late George Cobley Smyth-Richards, who, succeeding his father as agent, first for the late Sir Frederic Knight and then for Earl Fortescue, had an intimate knowledge of the locality extending over a long lifetime. It is a matter of regret that he has not lived to see this acknowledgement, so gladly made.

In particular matters much help has been given by many people: Mr E. T. MacDermot, author of the exhaustive history of the Royal Forest; Capt E. C. Lloyd, secretary of the Devon and Somerset Staghounds; Mr Arthur F. Brown, agent for the Blathwayt estates; Mr A. B. Rodger, fellow and tutor of Balliol College; Mr F. R. Huxtable, of the *Yorkshire Post*, and his brother Mr John H. Huxtable, of Challacombe; Mr George Molland, the steward at Simonsbath; Mr D. B. Toye, of the Ministry of Agriculture; Professor R. G. Stapledon, of the Welsh Plant Breeding Station, Aberystwyth; Mr F. J. Prewett and Mr D. Skilbeck, my good colleagues; my sons, Robert, John, and Francis; and Mr Alfred Vowles of Minehead, many of whose photographs of Exmoor have been used as illustrations.

Certain information has been obtained from such of the old rate-books as are still in existence, including the earliest of all, that for 1858, but many of them have been lost. There seems to be no responsibility for the care of such records, but obviously they should be in public custody.

As to the assistance obtained from published sources, practically nothing has been found prior to 1850—that is to say, concerning the period in which John Knight was directing, in person, the reclamation enterprise which he had originated. After that date, and for the next thirty years, when farming rather than equipment was the principal feature, a good deal was recorded in contemporary journals, particularly by Sir Thomas Acland, the eleventh of his line; Robert Smith, for thirteen years agent on Exmoor; William C. Little, one of the Assistant Commissioners appointed under the Royal Commission on Agriculture, 1879 (the Richmond Commission); and Samuel Solomon, an agricultural journalist who assumed the name of Sidney, under which he wrote. All of them appreciated the immensity of the task and some of them, dealing more, perhaps, with promise than with fulfilment, may have been unduly optimistic in their comments. This tendency is certainly corrected in the works of the many more modern writers on Exmoor, most of whom have gone to the other extreme, and have failed to see the real achievement through the haze of costly experiment and misdirected effort.

C. S. O.

Agricultural Economics Research Institute,
Oxford
June 1929

NOTE TO THE SECOND EDITION

In the forty years that have elapsed since this work was first published, there have been greater changes on Exmoor than at any time since the pioneer reclamation. While this has necessitated bringing the story up to date, Dr Orwin's historical research was such that he has still no competitor, and indeed subsequent published accounts have been largely pillaged from his pages.

Though the second edition contains various additions and corrections to the original text, Chapters I to VIII, XI and XII are still largely as Dr Orwin wrote them and a number of the amendments are his own; some made as a result of suggestions by E. T. MacDermot. This has been achieved through the kindness of Mrs C. S. Orwin, who has made available her husband's notes and correspondence, and I am most grateful to her. I am also indebted to her and to Mr R. J. S. Orwin, OBE, for their help and advice.

Apart from the additions and amendments the original text has, wherever possible, been left unaltered, and thus for instance, the wording of Chapter VIII (dealing with the Forest as Orwin knew it) remains in the present tense, while his references are to 1929. To cover the period since then, I have added two new chapters, IX and X, and also included in this new edition is an appreciation of Dr Orwin, a list of the properties owned by the Knights in Devon and Somerset, and an edited version of William Hannam's 'history' of his experiences as first tenant of Cornham Farm.

It is only right that the original acknowledgements should be retained, and in turn I gratefully acknowledge the help of the succeeding generation of those connected with the Forest. Both Lady Margaret Fortescue and Sir Bernard Waley-Cohen have kindly granted me facilities on their respective estates and by their courtesy I have been able to consult the Fortescue Estate records and the farm records at Honeymead.

Wherever possible, I have endeavoured to go back to original sources and, though some of the papers consulted by Dr Orwin cannot now be traced, certain new material, not available in 1929, has come to light. The main sources of information are in the Knight papers (some of which are retained by the family and others at Kidderminster Public Library), the Fortescue Estate records (now at Devon County Record Office), and the Dowlais Iron Company correspondence (at Glamorgan County Record Office). Other material has come from the Somerset County Record Office, the Blathwayt papers in Gloucestershire County Record Office, the Clerk to the Dulverton Licensing Justices (Mr R. W. Halse), the Somerset County Surveyor, the North Devon Athenaeum, the *North Devon Journal-Herald*, the *West Somerset Free Press*, the Ministry of Agriculture, The Royal Agricultural Society, the Royal Meteorological Society, the Public Record Office, the Registrar General and the British Museum Newspaper Library, and I am indebted to all those concerned for their unfailing courtesy and help. I must particularly thank Mrs Enid Teague-Knight for making available to me the family papers which are in her possession. Mrs Dorothy Waddon has very kindly made available the notes on Exmoor mining, compiled by her late husband, Mr Jack Waddon, and I should also like to thank Mr M. H. Jones, who drew my attention to the plan of inclines at Porlock in the Dowlais papers. Mr R. A. Lewis and Mr Norman Mutton for advice on the early history of the Knight family; the Rev R. J. Fuller; Mr George Jarrett for information on subsoiling and Mrs R. Fasnacht of the Oxford Agricultural Economics Research Institute.

I gratefully acknowledge the invaluable experience of Mr F. G. Smyth-Richards, now eighty-one and the ready assistance of Mr E. R. Lloyd at Honeymead. To Mr John Hayes, manager of the Fortescue Farm, I am especially grateful for the benefit of his knowledge and advice. His family, long connected with the Forest, included one of the first cattle drovers at Cornham and his subsequent untimely death is a great loss to Exmoor. Many local people have borne with my questions, but in particular I must mention Mr G. Comer-White of Williton (an ex-chairman of the AEC) and Mr Brian Duke of Warren. My daughters Charlotte and Sarah have been cheeful companions on my visits to the Forest and without my wife's patience in visiting, listening, advising and proof reading, this edition could not have been completed.

Bridgnorth, Salop   R. J. S.
December 1969

ILLUSTRATIONS

Where possible the general plan of the original illustrations has been followed in this edition, but there have been changes. Some portraits are missing, or have deteriorated and in spite of the help of Mr R. Kingsley Tayler, who took over his business, many of Alfred Vowles's original photographs cannot now be found.

The illustrations therefore include some of the original photographs, some in substitution of those missing and some additions. In one or two cases it has been necessary to copy the illustration from the first edition. Whilst this has inevitably slightly reduced the quality of reproduction, this was felt preferable to leaving out an important picture.

The portraits on pages 49 (*below*), 50 and 157 are by kind permission of Mrs Enid Teague-Knight and that on page 176 (*top*) by courtesy of Mr F. G. Smyth-Richards. Photographs on pages 67 (*top*), 103 (*top*), 104, 122 (*top*), 139, 175, 176 (*below*), 193 (*top*), 194 (*top*), 229 (*below*), 230 (*top*) and 248 (*below*) by Alfred Vowles and those on pages 158 (*below*) and 248 (*top*) are by permission of Mr R. Kingsley Tayler of Minehead. Those on pages 211 (*top*) and 212 (*top*) are by Mr S. H. Bath of Barnstaple, and on page 140 (*below*) by the late J. Guttridge Barber and that on page 158 (*top*) is from the Borough Museum, South Molton. Those remaining are by R. J. Sellick.

The map on pages 40–1 is from E. T. MacDermot's *History of the Forest of Exmoor*, that inside back cover from the Ordnance Survey and on pages 184–5 and 202–3 by courtesy of Mrs Teague-Knight.

B

C. S. ORWIN AND EXMOOR

Although innumerable books have been written about Exmoor, there are still no rivals to the two great histories of the Forest, E. T. MacDermot's *History* and C. S. Orwin's *Reclamation*. Indeed, on Exmoor the names MacDermot and Orwin are so closely linked with the history of the Forest, that it is often forgotten that both authors are equally famous in other fields. MacDermot's *History of the Great Western Railway* is a classic of transport history, while Orwin, Director of the Oxford Agricultural Economics Research Institute, was a national authority on agriculture and a prolific author on rural subjects.

Charles Stewart Orwin was born in Sussex on 26 September 1876. Though his rural background gave him his lifelong love of agriculture and the countryside, his family were not farmers and in his own disarming phrase: 'My grandfather was a doctor, but my father never did anything at all.' He went to school at Dulwich College and, having set his heart on a career in agriculture, entered the newly formed Wye College in October 1895. Here he studied under A. D. (later Sir Daniel) Hall, whose pioneer enthusiasm for farm costings aroused Orwin's interest in agricultural economics, the two men becoming lifelong friends.

For a short time after leaving Wye, C. S. Orwin worked with a land agent at Tunbridge Wells and then with a City firm, but in 1903 he returned to the college as lecturer in estate management, where he was able to do research and widen his knowledge, particularly of forestry, which he studied on holiday in Germany. His reputation for original thinking reached Christopher Turnor, who in 1906 offered the thirty-year-old Orwin the post of agent to his 25,000 acre estate in Lincolnshire. Here was a unique chance to put his ideas into practice, to run a vast estate as a business, and he accepted the challenge. For seven years, as he later described, he was 'administrator, surveyor, builder, valuer, accountant and farmer' of nearly forty square miles of farming enterprise, and he still found time to devise simple systems of farm accountancy by which ordinary farmers could find how their different farming activities were paying. It is a measure of his achievement that we now take such costings for granted.

In 1912 it was decided to set up an Institute for Research in Agricultural Economics at Oxford, and with his ideas and experience it was not surprising that C. S. Orwin was appointed the first director, taking up his duties on 19 January 1913. His task was twofold, to establish a basis for costing the varied types of British farming all over the country, and even more daunting, so to gain the confidence of a fundamentally suspicious farming community, that it would supply the information needed and use the results he could provide. No such cost analysis of British farming had ever taken place on this scale before, and the work of Orwin and his enthusiastic few young assistants proved invaluable when agriculture came under government direction during World War I. His reputation spread and in 1917 Orwin was appointed a member of the Agricultural Wages Board; in 1921 President of the Agricultural Section of the British Association, and in 1922 agricultural assessor to the Agricultural Tribunal of Investigation.

From 1920 onwards Orwin was responsible for building up at the institute a team of research workers in what was still an entirely new field of research in Britain. New techniques had to be worked out and applied and the results presented to an initially unreceptive industry. In this he was helped immensely by his flair for picking good men and giving them a free hand to get on with their chosen field of work, while at the same time keeping the institute working as a team. Many of these men later filled high academic posts at other universities, while others gained distinction in quite different fields. From a very modest beginning the reputation of the institute grew to become known internationally, and with it, that of its director.

Amongst all this activity, Orwin still managed to devote time to writing—in his concise, lucid, style, so well exemplified in this book. In addition to the steady stream of surveys and reports coming from the institute, under his direction, he was from 1912 to 1927 editor of the *Journal* of the Royal Agricultural Society, and his books ranged over every aspect of farming and the country-side. Works such as *Farm Accounts* were to be expected, but histories including *The Open Fields* (with C. S. Orwin), *The Tenure of Agricultural Land* (with W. R. Peel), and *A History of English Farming*; books on agricultural policy, such as *Back to the Land* (with W. F. Darke), *Speed the Plough*, and *The Future of Farming*, and on rural planning, such titles as *Problems of the Countryside* and *Country Planning*, show the breadth of his interests.

In 1902 Orwin had married Elise Cécile Renault, of Cognac, and they had six children, three boys and three girls. His uncle, Dr W. A. Orwin, had left him the house Periton Mead at Minehead in 1913 and it was here, in the holidays with his family, that he got to know Exmoor well and in the process formed a close friendship with E. T. MacDermot. At this time the Forest was regarded as Knight's folly, a monument only to the obstinacy of a Worcester-shire ironmaster and his son, who had wasted a fortune on what any West Countryman could have told them would prove a fruit-less adventure. Orwin was immediately attracted by the heroic scale of the Knights' enterprise in attempting to reclaim 25 square miles of inhospitable moorland, and the absence of any accurate account of this work provided a challenge to him both as an agricultural economist and historian. Each summer would bring Orwin and his family to Exmoor, not just to seek written evidence of the past, but to get to know every part of the Forest and those who farmed there. Sadly his wife died in 1929 and the house at Minehead was later sold, but the result of his work, *The Reclamation of Exmoor Forest*, was published that year, and in the apt words of *The Times*, it was 'a book written *con amore*'. It brought esteem, but not financial success, agricultural history not then being fashionable, and was eventually remaindered, but Orwin had the satisfaction of later seeing it listed at high prices in booksellers' catalogues.

The man himself was huge, 6ft 5in tall and weighing 16 stone, his size accentuated by 'the typical flourish of what appeared to be a good square yard of red silk handkerchief'. Sometimes quick tempered, yet with great courtesy and a delightful sense of humour, he inspired not merely respect but friendship. Politically he has been described as of the left, and certainly it is some indication of his stature that an advocate of land nationalisation and a champion of agricultural workers was so highly regarded by farmers and landowners to whom these views were anathema. In fact, he was not politically minded (he once said that 'If you can see both sides of a question you can never be a whole-hogging politician') and his advocacy of land nationalisation was not dogmatic, but on the practical grounds that, in the depressed thirties, only the State had the resources to re-group and re-equip farms into economic units and so provide the tenants with an adequate living.[1] A convinced Free Trader, he had a bust of Cobden placed in the Institute library. Orwin's second marriage, in 1931, was to Christabel Susan Lowry, secretary and librarian of the institute, and the resulting identity of initials has often confused the unwary, for she not only collaborated in writing with her husband, but is an agricultural historian in her own right.

At Oxford, Orwin had been a Fellow of Balliol since 1922 and since 1926 Estates Bursar, and he was also a joint founder of the Oxford Trust, a modest forerunner of the Oxford Preservation Trust, one of his pleasures being to farm part of the land the Trust had saved from development. An MA, a Chartered Surveyor and a Chartered Land Agent, he was made a DLitt by the university in 1939, and was also an Hon Fellow of Balliol, a Fellow of Wye, a Freeman of the City of London, and a governor of St Hugh's and of the College of Tropical Agriculture, Trinidad. Because of the war, his retirement was delayed until the end of 1945, almost thirty-three years after he had founded the institute, and he moved to Blewbury on the Berkshire Downs, where, characteristically, he promptly founded a Village Produce Association.

When he died at Blewbury on 30 June 1955 obituaries appeared in publications ranging from *The Times* to *The Countryman*. Perhaps the tributes which would have pleased him most were a memorial service of his friends in Balliol College Chapel, the subsequent naming in 1963 of the new Department of Agricultural Economics building at Wye as 'Orwin House', and a resolution passed by the Witney District Committee of the National Union of Agricultural

Workers proposing that he be posthumously elected an honorary member 'for his services to agriculture in general and, in particular, for his championship of the farmworkers' struggle for better monetary, domestic and social standards'.

I

PIONEERS OF AGRICULTURE

The making of the land of England has been, for the most part, a slow and often a painful process. Following the days when men moved over the country with their flocks and herds, tilling a few patches of land as they went, cultivation began as communities settled, here and there, on the more favourable spots, and it was extended and developed, first of all, just so far as the growth of population required. 'Land' was added to 'land', and 'furlong' to 'furlong', to provide sustenance for the self-sufficing local communities which went to make up the nation before the dawn of industrialism and the advent of farming for profit.

With the spread of the inclosure movement and the allotment of the common lands in the later eighteenth and early nineteenth centuries, coinciding as these changes did, very largely, with a prolonged spell of high prices for agricultural produce, consequent on the disturbed state of Europe and the demands of the growing urban population, the reclamation of the waste lands of England came more and more to be dictated by the chances of profit, and to depend less and less merely upon the needs of an increasing rural community. No doubt the two processes went on simultaneously, the small, slow, and laborious inroads into the wild by the peasant cultivator seeking to increase the family food-supply, of which ocular demonstrations are provided in every hill-district of England, and the larger, more ambitious, better-directed schemes of the greater landlords for the exploitation of large areas formerly regarded as below the margin of profitable cultivation; but it was through the latter, rather than the former, that production from the soil was made to keep pace during, say, the century following the year 1750, with the need created by the rapid development of a great, non-agricultural, consuming class. In very many districts large areas of heath and moorland were brought into cultivation, and in others the drainage of tracts of waterlogged land put a great acreage of potentially fertile soil under the plough. Thus much of the sandlands of Norfolk and Suffolk; the great tract of light limestone between Sleaford and Lincoln which constituted Lincoln Heath; the chalk formation in the Lincolnshire and Yorkshire Wolds; much of the wet lands of the Fen counties; these and many other stretches came first into productive use in agriculture at this time. The increase and spread of knowledge of new methods of cultivation, of new crops and of engineering, leading to drainage and to the successive steps of paring and burning, of claying and marling, root-growing and sheep-feeding, and to the four-course system of farming, perfected, in Norfolk, by the invention of the drill and the horse-hoe and the use of crushed bones and rape-cake, to which the economic conditions generally prevailing applied the stimulus of self-interest, all these things combined to bring about results, during this period, which have no parallel in agricultural history before or since.

Some of these great works of land reclamation are well known, both in themselves and in association with the names of those to whose enterprise they owe their achievement. Thus the dukes of Bedford will always be remembered in connection with the drainage of the Ouse valley, and everyone today has heard of 'Coke of Norfolk', afterwards Lord Leicester, who made a great agricultural estate, and inspired others to go and do likewise, where formerly was only 'one blade of grass and two rabbits fighting for that'. As regards other pioneers, the study of contemporary literature brings to light many works of improvement carried out all over the country, and it comes with something of a shock to realise how recent, historically, most of them are, and how very little is known of the men to whom they are due. Roads, fences, drains, ploughland, grassland, woodland, homesteads and cottages, all of which are accepted today without arousing a single curious thought, owe their being, in many cases, to the courage and enthusiasm, no less than to the business acumen, of landlords and farmers hardly a hundred years dead—makers of rural England who have gone to their graves unhonoured and unsung except, sometimes, in obscure or ephemeral literature. 'The owners of property, fortunately for themselves, for the cause of improvement, and the benefit of the country at large, co-operated with their spirited tenants. . . . The money which was made by farming was again eagerly applied, under the encouragement of leases, to the reclaiming of waste lands and the promotion of agricultural improvement. Section after section of the outfield land, so-called, was brought into productive cultivation.' Often their reward, in a financial sense, cannot have been forthcoming, and in some cases the results of their efforts have not been permanent; either these were wrongly conceived or they could be justified only if the economic conditions prevailing at the time of their inception had enjoyed a permanence which was not destined to be theirs. Thus there can be seen today tens of thousands of acres of permanent grassland showing the marks of more intensive use, at some earlier period, in their ridge-and-furrow formation; other grassland areas, similarly marked, which are now given up largely to bushes and brambles; a few again, which have reverted completely to the natural thicket or scrub forest from which they were first evolved; though much which had reverted, has again been reclaimed within the last thirty years. In other cases, the farming lands and homesteads created by the enterprise of these stout-hearted pioneers still exist, to gladden the eye, to provide employment, and to add their quota to the wealth of the nation, but with the probability that, if measured only by the return on the capital staked, the ventures must be regarded merely as failures.

In England, during the period under review, there is no doubt that much of the land reclamation and development yielded a full measure of compensation to those concerned in it, but it is equally sure that, here and there, the time, thought, and money spent upon such works brought an inadequate financial return. The subsistence-farmer, eating slowly into the waste outside his boundary, took no thought of the cost of his work, nor could this be expressed in terms of money; it represented to him so much additional pasturage for his stock, so many extra crop-acres, gained at an expenditure not of his capital but of his labour, and of this he was, by necessity, prodigal. The capitalist adventurer was in a different case, for with whatever public-spirited motives he may be credited—and such may fairly be conceded in many cases—the mainspring of his operations was, quite naturally, the prospect of gain.

Records of the cost of small ventures were never kept, and those of the larger enterprises are almost unknown. Either they have been destroyed, or else they lie, for the most part, buried and forgotten, in the estate offices and muniment rooms of such of the older estates as have survived the national indifference to the agricultural industry between the two world wars. Today, the value of reclamation and improvement can be judged only by the results that have survived, and who can establish a standard by which to measure them? In many cases satisfactory returns, on a strict financial basis, must have accrued to the improvers; in others, the border-line cases, it may be asserted that if the returns to the landlords were not of the order of 5 per cent, the joint returns on the capital of landlord and tenant together, considered over a term of years, have been enough, probably, to justify the work. In the last case, the one in which the balance of probability is definitely against any adequate financial return on the capital outlay of the original improver and his first tenants, the lot of these men has been no other than that which falls, commonly enough, to the pioneer. 'While the field laughs with grain, it is more than possible that the owner groans at the cost of its artificial fertility. Too often he must feel it would have been better to have left the down unbroken, the copse ungrubbed, the gorse and heather to bloom in peace, the sullen clay undrained, the boulders where they lay on the moor and the grand homestead in the architect's office.' Nature is an intractable steed, and her surrender to those who seek to guide and control her is sometimes dearly bought. But who will venture to equate the cost and the value of work such as these men accomplished? And who can look upon productive fields and comfortable homesteads, making their contribution both in men and material to the welfare of the State today, and say that they have not been worth while? It may well be that, as the State is the ultimate gainer by them, the State should have borne the cost, and indeed today it does so contribute, but despite the absence of such assistance the past history of achievement in agriculture affords an impressive example of the enterprise, the skill, and the capacity of the English agricultural improvers, both land-lords and farmers, of days gone by. 'Side by side with social progress the ameliorating changes have been advanced, not by the silent operations and development of Nature or by the natural increment of value, but by the dogged effort which the land-owner, as a rule, has ever put forth in the making of the land, and at any cost fitting it for the practice of improved husbandry suited to the progress of civilization and the modern wants of the people.'

Of this class was John Knight, with whom originated the making of Exmoor Forest as it appears today. He came of a family distinguished both in industry and the arts. He was the fourth in succession from Richard Knight, of Castle Green, Madeley, Salop, but though there is a family tradition that he was descended from a family which included several Bailiffs of Shrews-bury, evidence is lacking, and this may have been an attempt to justify the assumption of arms. Richard Knight's second son, also Richard (1659–1745), born at Castle Green, was the first sub-stantial ironmaster in the family, though his brother Francis was in the trade and his father may have been also. He began work at a forge at the lower end of Coalbrookdale, then moved to More-ton, in Shawbury parish, and about the year 1698 he took a twenty-one years' lease of Bringewood Forge, near Ludlow, from the Earl of Craven, and he himself acquired the Downton estate in that neighbourhood. Before the expiration of his lease he had bought the property, and during the first thirty years of the eighteenth century he added to it other lands in Herefordshire. By 1730 he had two furnaces and several forges in Shropshire (in-cluding Charlot, Bouldon and Willey), a forge in Staffordshire, besides the furnace and forge at Bringewood. He died in 1745, and was buried in Burrington Church, with a slab of cast iron for his tombstone. He left a large fortune which passed eventually to his grandson, Richard Payne Knight (1750–1824), elder son of his second son the Rev Thomas Knight (1697–1764), rector of Bewdley and Ribbesford, Worcestershire.

In Richard Payne Knight the genius transmitted by his forebears took on a new expression. He was a delicate boy who was not at

PEDIGREE OF THE FAMILY OF KNIGHT, OF SHROPSHIRE AND WORCESTERSHIRE

Richard Knight, of Castle Green, Madeley, Salop.

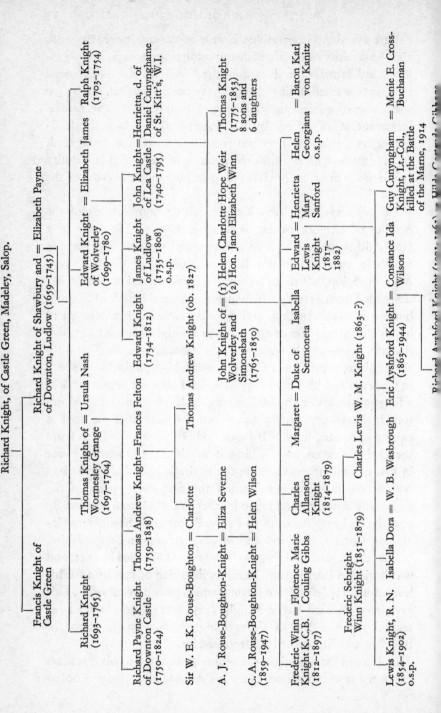

any university, but much of his youth was spent abroad, where, no doubt, he first acquired his taste for classical art, as a connoisseur of which he was pre-eminent in his day. He cared little for sculpture, but he made a fine collection of bronzes, coins, and gems. He wrote much on Greek mythology and art, but he was opposed to the national acquisition of the Elgin collection, and told Lord Elgin at a dinner party that he had 'lost his labour' in bringing over the Parthenon marbles. Goethe published a translation of his diary, in his life of Hackert, the German painter, with whom Payne Knight had travelled in Sicily.

On inheriting the Downton estate of some 10,000 acres, he built the castle on it, and he sat in Parliament, first for Leominster, and then for twenty-two years for Ludlow (1784–1806), but he made no particular mark in the House. At his death he left his collections to the British Museum upon the sole condition of the appointment of a perpetual 'Knight family Trustee', which was arranged by an Act passed in the year of his death[1]. His portrait was painted in 1792 by Sir Thomas Lawrence, and is now the property of the Society of Dilettanti.

Richard Payne Knight died unmarried, and was succeeded by his brother, Thomas Andrew Knight (1759–1838), a man equally distinguished in another sphere. He had been educated at Ludlow Grammar School, and matriculated in February 1778 at Balliol College, Oxford, but it is said that 'close application was not one among the characteristics of his College life'. He was early distinguished, however, as a sportsman, farmer, and horticulturist. He became a correspondent of the Board of Agriculture on the nomination of Sir Joseph Banks, and conducted many experiments at his home, at Elton, in raising new varieties of fruit and vegetables. In fact, he was the first man to undertake scientific hybridisation and cross-breeding among fruit trees, and was one of the forerunners upon whose work Darwin founded his great generalisations. At least four of the cherries he raised are still largely grown, including 'Waterloo', and he contributed also to the creation of the modern strawberry. In 1795 he was the reader of a paper before the Royal Society on grafting and the inheritance of disease among fruit trees.

He was an original member of the Royal Horticultural Society (established 1804), of which he was President from 1811 until his death, and he contributed to every number of its *Transactions* from their first publication in 1807. In 1806 he was awarded the Copley Medal of the Royal Society, and in 1836 the first Knightean Medal of the Royal Horticultural Society, founded in his honour, bearing his own portrait by Wyon. In 1805 he was elected Fellow of the Royal Society and, in 1807, Fellow of the Linnean Society.

Thomas Andrew Knight married Frances, daughter of Humphrey Felton, of Woodhall, near Shrewsbury. He lost his only son as the result of a shooting accident, and with his own death in 1838 the elder branch of his family ceased. The Downton property passed, after a protracted lawsuit, to his second daughter, Charlotte, wife of Sir William E. K. Rouse-Boughton, with whose descendants, who added the name of Knight, it still remains.

This accounts for the family and fortune of the elder branch. In the meantime Richard Knight's third son, Edward (1699–1780), had established another line of the family with extensive interests in the iron industry in Worcestershire. Many of the old corn mills on the river Stour, which had been converted into ironworks in the latter part of the seventeenth century, were now acquired. Wolverley Forge was obtained in 1727 from the Jewkes family, then the principal family in Wolverley parish, near Kidderminster. Cookley Mill, nearby, had for some years been in the hands of the Knights, and between 1731 and 1748 a controlling interest in Wolverley Mill was purchased by members of the family, from, amongst others, William Rea and Samuel Jewkes. Edward Knight, 'a capitol Iron Master' according to Abiah Darby, and one of the best customers for Coalbrookdale pig iron, settled at Wolverley and managed the ironworks there, including Cookley Mill, Lord's Mill in Debdale, and Bouldon Furnace near Ludlow. He was a prominent ironmaster in the Stour district, and in 1757 gave evidence before the Committee on the Petition of Merchants and Ironmongers and several other petitions relating to the manufacture of iron, in the course of which he said that he made about 1,000 tons of bar iron per annum for the use of nail ironmongers, 'but at present meets with great complaints from them for want of demand for same, and he has lately seen great stocks of nails lying in the warehouses. . . . Mr. Knight said that he knew of his own knowledge that in the County of Salop woodlands have been stocked up and more land used for tillage than before 1718.'

He was succeeded by his eldest son, also Edward (1734–1812), who, dying unmarried, bequeathed his fortune to John, the elder son of his youngest brother, also John (1740–95), and it was to him that the Exmoor reclamation enterprise was afterwards due.

This was the stock from which John Knight descended, a family which, before his time and after, maintained an unbroken connection with one of the fundamental industries of the country during some two hundred years, and contributed also, through some of its members, to its artistic life and rural development. From his mother's family, too, he may have derived some of the qualities which were disclosed in his career, for she was the daughter of Daniel Cunynghame, of St Kitt's, one of the pioneers of the sugar plantation industry in the West Indies.

John Knight, the maker of Exmoor, was born in the year 1765. It was a generation of agricultural improvers, and the agricultural revolution in England was yearly gathering force. 'Farmer George' was on the throne; Arthur Young was at the height of his activity as a writer; the Board of Agriculture was first constituted when Knight was twenty-six years of age. It is recorded of him that he was already farming largely in his native county, and that he had had a share in bringing under cultivation large tracts of its heathy commons before the time of his purchase of Exmoor. It is said that he had made a study of the methods by which Thomas Coke had turned Holkham from a rabbit warren into a fertile estate, and that he had been a guest at the Woburn sheep-shearings. When it is realised that agricultural experience of this extent was combined in him with force of character, tenacity of purpose, inherent familiarity with 'big business', and financial resources ample to stand the strain of a great adventure, some comprehension of the man and of his motives is obtained, and it is not difficult to understand that his imagination may well have been stirred by the opportunity, or it may have been the challenge, of an estate still in virgin condition—without roads, unfenced, without woodlands, untouched by the plough, and virtually uninhabited. Fairly judged, he stands out as one of the pioneers of his day, notwithstanding that his efforts may have met with no financial success and that their results were not realised in his own lifetime. Those, today, who laugh at some of his more extravagant schemes, know nothing of his journeys of hundreds of miles by coach to buy cattle to stock his land, of his eager search for lime with which to sweeten the sour soil of Exmoor, of his experiments to improve the livestock of the district, of the long process of trial and error by which the appropriate farming system was at length evolved. His letters disclose a knowledge and an enthusiasm equalled by few and excelled by none of his class today.

John Knight married, first, Helen Charlotte, daughter of the Hon Charles Hope-Weir of Craigie Hall, West Lothian, who died without issue, and, second, the Hon Jane Elizabeth Winn, daughter of the first Lord Headley, of Aghadoe, Co Kerry. By her he had three sons, Frederic Winn, Charles Allanson, and Edward Lewis, through the last-named of whom the family continued at Wolverley, where it remained until the death of Major Eric Ayshford Knight in 1944; and three daughters, Margaret, Isabella, and Helen Georgiana.

After his purchase of Exmoor, John Knight made Lynton his headquarters, living at what is now the Castle Hotel. It is said that his coach-and-four was the first ever driven up the old road there. About 1830 he took up his residence at Simonsbath House, the only habitation on Exmoor Forest before his acquisition of it, until, in 1837, he removed to Trinity Manor House, in the island of Jersey, on account of his wife's health. Two years later the family went to Rome, where they lived in the Palazzo Bracci, Via Rassella. Mrs Knight died there in 1841, and John Knight continued in Rome until his own death, in 1850. His eldest daughter, Margaret, married the Duke of Sermoneta, the head of a Roman family tracing its descent from classical times, and his third daughter, Helen Georgiana, married the Baron Karl von Kanitz, who was Prussian Minister at Rome at this time.

Frederic Winn Knight, the eldest son, upon whom was to devolve the task of completing the work begun by his father on Exmoor, was born in 1812. He was educated at Charterhouse, and much of his early life was spent at Simonsbath, he and his brothers entering fully into the social life of the very sporting community which inhabited North Devon in their day. All of them were noted men to hounds, and as such are commemorated in many stories and songs of the West. Frederic and Charles were members of the select fraternity who composed the South Molton Hunt Club and made its headquarters at the George Hotel for a fortnight in each season, during the fifties, to hunt the district with several packs. At this period the opening meet of the Staghounds was always held at Simonsbath House. Charles Knight, too, kept a pack of foxhounds, in Rome, for many years during his father's residence there.

Frederic Knight was a man of great determination and almost boundless energy. At a comparatively early age he had to assume control of his father's work on Exmoor, at a time when much still remained to be done and the prospect was obscure. 'I am 29 to-morrow', he wrote to his mother, at Rome, in May 1841, 'and my father has given me the entire management of the Forest.' At first he employed no agent, managing the property entirely by himself, as his father had done, and when the increasing calls upon his time, together with the forward policy which he decided to adopt in regard to Exmoor, made the task too great and he found it necessary to appoint an agent to assist him, he continued to retain a most active personal control. In the same year as that in which he took control of the Forest, he was elected member for West Worcestershire, the seat since held by Prime Minister Stanley Baldwin, which constituency he continued to represent in Parliament for forty-four years, the seat being contested on two occasions only during that period. He does not seem to have made any great mark in the House as a speaker and he never held any high office, but it is evident that he was recognised as a man of parts, and he was Parliamentary Secretary to the Poor Law Board in 1852, under Lord Derby's administration, and again in 1858-9, under Lord Palmerston.

He found time, also, to engage in commercial life in the City of London, becoming, in 1856, a director of the Bank of London and National Provincial Insurance Association. In this capacity he fell foul of some of his co-directors and officials as regards their financial dealings, and his circular to the shareholders on this occasion, extending to twenty-six printed foolscap pages, is a refreshingly frank and unrestrained document, full of the most pungent criticism and giving evidence of his own capacity for business.

He was an enthusiastic supporter of the Volunteer movement, being associated with Lord Elcho in this matter, and the KCB with which his public services were recognised in 1886 was due largely to his work in this connection.

Throughout the whole of his life, following the death of his father, Frederic Knight was hampered by the want of adequate financial resources. He had been brought up in the expectation that the great fortune of his cousin, Thomas Andrew, of Downton, would eventually be his, but the Courts interpreted the will otherwise. Under his father's dispositions he found himself possessed of broad acres and little money, while substantial fortunes were the lot of his younger brethren, as happened not infrequently to the eldest sons of agricultural magnates in the nineteenth century. Many of the farms on Exmoor were coming in hand, and the estate was producing no net revenue; it had been heavily charged to raise money for the works of reclamation and improvement;[2] there were large legacies to be paid and no liquid assets. There is no doubt that the energy with which he threw himself into the search for ironstone about this time, and his uncompromising insistence on his legal rights under the contracts with his mineral tenants, even after the uneconomic character of the venture had been pretty clearly established, were due to the paramount need for making the Forest a paying proposition.

Frederic Knight married, in the year 1850, Florence Marie, daughter of Edward Adolphus Couling Gibbs. She was more than twenty years younger than Frederic Knight who is reputed to have fallen in love when he first saw her as a girl of sixteen in her father's picture gallery in Wardour Street. They had one child, Frederic Sebright Winn, born in 1851, who died in 1879. It is said that his father's great interest in his work on Exmoor declined rapidly from that date, and in 1886 he parted with the reversion to the estate though he lived to enjoy it for another eleven years. He is remembered as a strict landlord and master, but he was just, and showed kindness and consideration in cases of need. 'If once he had confidence in a man, the world would not shake it,' and Mr W. C. Little, writing of the agricultural labourers of West

Somerset and North Devon in the report of the Royal Commission on Agriculture published in 1882, refers to him as 'their old friend'. All the time that he could spare from his other activities was spent at Simonsbath House, and he and his beautiful wife were always about the estate together. It is said that some of the cottages were built from Lady Knight's designs, and she seems to have shared to the full his deep interest in the estate and its development.

Frederic Knight died at Bath in 1897, six days before his eighty-fifth birthday. He was buried at Simonsbath in the grave in which his son was buried, and three years later Lady Knight was laid to rest beside them.

The tendency has been to criticise, if not to ridicule, the steps by which the Knights, father and son, attempted to reclaim the Forest, and to belittle the results that they achieved. Certainly this was not the attitude of their contemporaries, who knew them best, and who were best able to judge of the problem they undertook to solve. Throughout West Somerset none have stood higher in the public estimation, both as landlords and farmers, than the successive heads of the family of Acland, and as lessees and wardens of the Forest for three generations prior to its inclosure, they knew it as few others can have done. 'He will long be remembered', wrote Mr T. D. Acland (afterwards 11th bt) in 1850, on hearing of John Knight's death, 'as the first person who had the spirit to commence a great agricultural work which Mr. Billingsley foretold fifty years ago. . . . There are doubtless many difficulties in this, as in all great undertakings, and more than lookers-on are willing to allow. The present proprietor [Frederic Knight] is in a position not of his own choosing, but he wants neither the energy nor the will to do his duty in it, and to bring the Forest into a condition which an English gentleman may look upon with well-grounded satisfaction.'

But the reclamation of Exmoor by the Knight family falls definitely into the category of schemes the value of which cannot be measured by their profit to the entrepreneur. They found a waste, and they and those who followed after them have established, in the place of it, a community of farmers as prosperous today, probably, having regard to the capital they have at stake, as any in the country. The Knights made roads, bringing this great tableland into communication with the surrounding country; they enclosed fields, built houses for those who should till them, and planted shelter-belts to provide 'succour' from the strong winds. They were responsible for the formation of the largest parish in Somerset, and for the erection of a church, parsonage, and school. They attempted other things which proved, some of them, to be unfruitful, others impossible—the erection of a great house, the utilisation of storage water, the exploitation of minerals, the construction of a railway to the coast. Even the farming, successful as it is today, was the outcome only of many years of fruitless experiment directed towards the growth of crops which could not ripen at these altitudes and towards the maintenance of a class of livestock unsuited to the rigorous climate of Exmoor.

Still, the Knights' monument, *aere perennius*, stands out today clearly enough for those who have eyes to see it, in the homesteads and farmlands which they spread along the southern-facing slopes of all the deep valleys intersecting the Forest; Tom's Hill and Larkbarrow; Warren; Pinkery, Driver, Titchcombe, Duredon, Simonsbath Barton, Cornham, Winstitchin, and Picked Stones; Cloven Rocks, Honeymead, and Red Deer; Emmett's Grange, Wintershead, and Horsen. It is by these that the contribution of father and son to the social and economic development of this part of West Somerset must be judged, rather than by the tale of their frustrate efforts and costly failures in other directions. To quote one of the older of its inhabitants, who can recall the later period of development, when the mining and other extravagant ventures had passed and only the active prosecution of agriculture remained—'Exmoor misses Sir Frederic Knight to this day.'

(See pp 295–9 for notes)

II

INCLOSURE AND SALE OF THE ROYAL FOREST AND THE BEGINNING OF RECLAMATION

The story of the reclamation of Exmoor begins with the Act for its inclosure, passed in the year 1815. As a royal forest its existence extends backwards from this date, for a thousand years or so, into the time when records cease, and their place can be supplied only by conjecture. Its history has been twice told, first by Mr E. J. Rawle, and fully and finally by Mr E. T. MacDermot, from whose work have been derived the brief notes that follow, concerning the happenings between the inclosure enactment and the conveyance of the Crown allotment to John Knight.

For some two centuries the Crown had granted the Wardenship of the Forest on the system of lease and renewal on payment of a fine. One Robert Siderfin, of the Middle Temple and of Croydon, in Carhampton, was lessee and warden in the early part of the eighteenth century, and it may be of passing interest to agriculturists to record that he married, for his third wife, Anne, daughter of Sir John Wittewronge, first baronet, of Rothamsted, Hertfordshire, who was the great-great-grandfather of Sir John Bennett Lawes, founder of the Rothamsted Experimental Station.

Siderfin was followed, first, by the son and, next, by the grandson of Prime Minister Walpole, and in 1767 the grandson, the third Lord Orford, sold his interest to Sir Thomas Dyke Acland, seventh baronet, with whose descendants the wardenship remained until 1 August 1814, when the current lease expired. Before this date the then lessee (the tenth baronet and the third Sir Thomas) had made application, on two occasions, for a new reversionary lease, suggesting in the alternative, that it might be more advantageous to the Crown to dispose of the freehold, in which case he hoped to become the purchaser.

The administration of Crown Lands at this time was in a state of flux, but in 1810 Parliament had passed the Act by which the Commissioners of His Majesty's Woods, Forests, and Land Revenues were brought into being, and it fell to them to deal with the application. Their first step was to cause a survey of the Forest to be made, and they presented their first report on 30 June 1814, two months before the expiration of the Acland lease. It is full of information on the condition of the Forest at that time; the stock agisted, and other income; the outgoings on rent, taxes, and wages (no other expenditure had been incurred in the previous six years); the rights claimed by individuals to depasture stock, to cut fuel and litter, etc; the ownership of the tithes. The Commissioners concluded their report by summarising the alternatives open to the Treasury as to the future of Exmoor, namely:

1st.   Whether to grant a new Lease of it to Sir Thomas Acland, upon terms founded on the above-mentioned valuation of Mr Hawkins, the effect of which would probably be to continue the Forest in its present unimproved state, to be used for depasturing sheep, cattle, and horse thereon, as heretofore.

2nd.   To dispose entirely of the Crown's Rights and Interests in the Forest, either by private contract to the present Lessee or by public auction . . . Or,

3rd.   To endeavour to procure an Act for the Inclosure and Division of the Forest, stipulating for an adequate allotment thereof to the Crown, in severalty, in lieu of His Majesty's Rights and Interests therein, such allotment, or such portions thereof, as may be found to be adapted to the growth of navy Timber, to be afterwards appropriated to that purpose, or to be disposed of by Sale, and the Money appropriated to the purchase of other Land for the growth of such Timber, as may be then considered to be most advisable.

The Commissioners gave a clear indication that they themselves inclined to the third alternative, and it is of interest to note that they say that local opinion round Exmoor was not only in favour of inclosure, but also expecting it. Sales of land which carried rights on the Forest, they state, had taken place at figures based on this assumption.

The Treasury adopted the inclosure suggestion, and in 1816 the Commissioners reported that, acting on this, they had 'proposed terms to the several noblemen and gentlemen principally interested', and that, after a meeting at South Molton to discuss them, it was agreed to introduce a bill by which Inclosure Commissioners should be appointed to survey and value the Forest, and, after setting out lands for the repair of roads and watering-places for cattle, to allot the remainder to His Majesty, to Sir Thomas Acland, and to such other persons who had made good their claims to rights on the Forest. The King, it was agreed, was to have an allotment equal in value to twelve twenty-second parts, and Sir Thomas Acland, the owner of the tithes of the Forest, which his father had bought in 1790, one of one-eighth part in lieu thereof, leaving, approximately, one-third part for all the other parties.

The Commissioners added that the Act to give effect to these proposals had already been passed,[1] and such progress made as to enable the Inclosure Commissioners to set out the various allotments by the summer following (1816). Under the Act, the Commissioners for the inclosure were to settle and define the boundaries of the Forest, to set out the public highways, quarries for their maintenance, and watering-places for common use by stock belonging to future occupants of land upon the Forest. They were next to value the whole of the Forest, and to allot the portion accruing to the King 'as near to the centre of the said Forest as conveniently may be'. They were then to prepare their first award, which was made in October 1817. This done, the Act directed that they should allocate to Sir Thomas Acland one-eighth part of the whole in lieu of his freehold tithes, and this allotment was to be as near to his other property in the neighbourhood as possible. The free-suitors of Hawkridge and Withypool were next to be considered, and the residue of the Forest was to be divided between the other suitors, owners of the old-inclosed tenements in the several parishes named in the preamble to the Act (twenty-seven in all), who had been accustomed to depasture sheep upon the Forest at less than the full toll of fivepence per head.

The second and final award, dealing with these allotments, was made in the spring of 1819, and with it Exmoor ceased to exist as a royal forest. The survey made under the Inclosure Act had disclosed its total extent as being 20,014 acres, contrasted with the

SCALE—One inch to a mile.

Forest Boundary ... ...   ————————
Allotment Boundaries ...   ---------

Note.—Allotments Nos. 15-31 (Watering Places and Quarries)
and Nos 282-296 (Private Roads) are omitted. Nos.
108-110 (John Sanger) were among the Free Suitors'
Allotments Nos. 43-76.

Exmoor Forest at the time of Inclosure, 1819.

The shaded area shows the boundaries of the Knight's ownership

Ordnance Survey figure of 20,344 acres for the present Parish of Exmoor, which is co-terminous with the inclosed Forest.[2] This was exclusive of Simonsbath Farm, of 108½ acres, which was reserved, under the Act, from the jurisdiction of the Commissioners, so that the discrepancy is reduced to 222 acres. The King's Allotment was 10,262 acres; Sir Thomas Acland was allotted 3,201 acres in lieu of tithes, and the only individuals other than certain of the free-suitors to receive allotments of more than 100 acres were: Sir Charles W. Bampfylde, 1,880 acres; Thomas P. Acland, 560 acres; Mrs Blathwayt, 365 acres; Earl Fortescue, 248 acres; Lord Clinton, 183 acres; Lord Morley, 183 acres; John Lock, 163 acres. Free-suitors receiving allotments of more than 100 acres were: T. Thornton, 511 acres; the Earl of Carnarvon, 246 acres; John Hill, 133 acres; Federata Cutliffe, 127 acres.

Before the appearance of the final award, the Commissioners of Woods and Forests had taken action on the first award by the sale of the King's Allotment. In June 1818 they advertised that:

> Such persons as are desirous of purchasing an extensive tract of WASTE LAND are hereby informed that the Allotment made to His Majesty on the FOREST OF EXMOOR, in the Counties of Somerset and Devon [*sic*], consisting of about 10,262 Acres, together with an inclosed Farm 108a. 2r. 0p., will be DISPOSED OF by Public Tender for the Highest Price offered for the same, above a certain sum to be previously named and deposited under a sealed cover to be opened at the same time with such tenders as may be received. And Persons who may be desirous of becoming Purchasers of the Lands in question, are requested to send in their Tenders to the said Commissioners on or before the 23rd day of July next, sealed up and indorsed 'Tenders for purchasing the Exmoor Allotment', and stating in words at length the sum they are willing to give.

Tenders were to be opened at the offices of the Commissioners on the date named above. Seven tenders were received, but the names of all those tendering and the amounts they offered are not now recorded, though it is commonly reported that Earl Fortescue was the second highest bidder (Sir John Fortescue, writing in *Country Life*, 1930, gave the figure as £30,000), and that Sir Thomas Acland, who was the last lessee of the Forest and who had acted as forester on behalf of the Crown since the termination of his lease in 1814, put in a bid of £5,000. The highest tender was that of John Knight, of Wolverley Hall, Worcestershire, and 52

Portland Place, London, who offered £50,000. His purchase was recorded in the local press in August 1818:

> Mr. Knight of Worcestershire has purchased the allotment (10,000 acres,) given in right of the Crown, on Exmoor Forest, for £50,000. The property is near Simonds-Bath; and the greater part is to be inclosed by a wall, in the centre of which a handsome residence is to be built. The spot affords great facilities for this purpose, and will, under the judicious plans in contemplation, become an enviable possession.

The conveyance of the Crown estate was not completed until 15 March 1820. Simonsbath Farm was conveyed separately from the rest, out of which, 12 acres, already staked out, were reserved to the Crown, in accordance with the Inclosure Act, as provision for a church, churchyard, parsonage house and homestead, if and when the Forest became inhabited and the necessities, spiritual and temporal, of its inhabitants required it. The Forest was extra-parochial, and the Act provided that on the erection of a church and parsonage etc, the district should become a distinct parish of itself, to be called by the name of the Parish of Exmoor. These things all came to pass in 1856.[3]

The stage was now set for the reclamation and settlement of the Forest, and it is interesting to note how this step had been anticipated for some time in the locality. There is the evidence contained in the first Report of the Commissioners of Woods and Forests in 1814, quoted above, to the effect that the inclosure of Exmoor was generally desired and expected on the termination of the Acland lease, and inclosure was generally the prelude to improvement. But twenty years before this, the possibility had been foreseen by John Billingsley, when engaged upon his survey of Somerset for the Board of Agriculture. 'A very large proportion of the whole', he says, 'needs but the spirit and fortune of some one or more of our wealthy gentlemen of England, whose attention, if turned this way, sanctioned by the royal proprietor, would render the Forest of Exmoor in a few years as fair a prospect as the surrounding country, and not a useless and void space in the map of the County of Somerset. Excepting for a few willows and thorns by the sides of the rivulets, not a tree or a bush is to be seen on the whole Forest, but plantations of most kinds need no more shelter nor better soil than is met with here. Let there be a small town or village erected near the middle, suppose by Simonsbath, which should form proper residences for artificers and husband-men employed in building farm houses and enclosing many a considerable estate around them.'

Billingsley was right as to the treelessness of Exmoor, for the Commissioners' survey, made in 1814, disclosed only thirty-seven trees, all of them growing round Simonsbath House. But he was overstating his case when he described the Forest as a useless and void space. For long years it had been the practice to depasture sheep, in large numbers, and a few cattle and ponies on it during the summer season, and this constituted its only value beyond anything which it may have been worth for sport. At Simonsbath, a house and homestead had been built and a few fields inclosed along the Barle, in or about the year 1654. The house came to be the residence of the deputy-forester and to be licensed as an inn; the farm attached to it extended to 108 acres. No other house had been built, nor any further inclosures made up to the sale of the King's Allotment to John Knight, but from about Lady Day onwards, in every year, flocks of sheep were to be seen converging slowly on Exmoor, for the summer grass, by every road and trackway in North Devon. They came from more than half a hundred parishes, to the number of many thousand head. In Sir Thomas Acland's last annual account, 1816–17, for the years during which he acted as forester for the Crown after the expira-tion of his lease, the number accounted for is just short of 25,000, exclusive of flocks belonging to the free suitors. North Molton, with a total of 3,609, furnished the largest parish contribution, whilst a Somerset farmer, Thomas Rawle, of Porlock, with a flock of 569, made the largest individual entry. Almost every well-known name in North Devon and West Somerset is to be found in the record. There are Buckinghams, Clatworthys, Comers, Crangs, Goulds, Huxtables, Mogridges, Muxworthys, Passmores, Ridds, Shoplands, Sladers, Sloleys, Tamlins, Thornes, Webbers, and Westacotts, whilst some of the neighbouring clergy, who farmed their glebes, availed themselves also of the Forest grass, amongst them the Rev J. Blackmore, rector of Charles, uncle of the author of the great Exmoor epic.

MacDermot relates that it was the custom for flockmasters to enter their sheep with the deputy-forester at the various markets around the Forest, in the early part of the year. They remained on Exmoor until June, when they were taken off, by their owners, for shearing, and tellers were appointed to watch the roads and take a count of the sheep as they passed. The various owners, the numbers of their sheep, and the parishes to which they belonged were then entered up, and the sums payable for agistment by each was calculated. The sheep were returned to the Forest after shearing, and remained until autumn, when they were driven off to the farms whence they had come.

There were no boundary fences round the Forest, its borders being identified by watercourses, boundary stones, barrows, and such-like landmarks. Thus, the sheep were apt to range on to the adjoining commons, and these were driven, from time to time, to round up the strays. The standard charges, for the season's agistment and for such services, were 5d per sheep for ordinary persons, 2½d for sheep the property of Forest borderers, whilst those belonging to the free-suitors paid nothing. Similarly, the fees for ponies were 4s, 2s, and nil, but in numbers these were relatively few. The accounts for the season 1817, the last, or the last but one, before John Knight took possession, which were presented to the Commissioners by Sir Thomas Acland on 5 October 1818, run as follows:

FOREST OF EXMOOR

'Acc^t of Willm Lock, Deputy Forester, concerning Sheep and Colts Ent^d to pasture on the Forest of Exmoor, beginning Lady Day 1816 and ending Lady Day 1817.'

There follows a complete statement of the farmers entering sheep and colts, the numbers entered, and the numbers told, all grouped under the parishes from which they were sent. The total amount due and received for the pasturage is carried to a Receipts and Payments account, the balance of which gives the net income of the Forest for the year (see page 47).

The net income of £259 11s 6d is somewhat lower than the estimate of the Commissioners' Surveyor made in 1814, and there seems no doubt that the numbers of sheep entered to pasture in 1817 were lower than oftentimes before. MacDermot gives figures for earlier times which run up to 30,000 sheep, 177 beasts, and 102 colts, exclusive of animals belonging to the forester and to the free-suitors. But Sir Thomas Acland's tender of £5,000 for the King's Allotment, on the inclosure of the Forest, was based, evidently, on the net income according to the last account, capitalised at twenty years' purchase.

By the spring of 1819, John Knight was making his arrangements for the development of his property, and while his first works of reclamation were in progress it is evident that he continued to make the Forest available for grazing. An advertisement in the *Taunton Courier* of 22 April 1819, signed by him, notified the times and places at which attendance would be given for receiving and entering names, and numbers of sheep. The price for each sheep was raised from the old rate of 5d, at which it had remained since 1655, to 1s.

Exmoor Forest

Notice is hereby given to all persons who intend to Depasture Sheep on the Royal, and Sir Charles Bamfylde's Allotments, that attendance will be given at the times and places following, *viz*

Simon's Bath,	Wednesday April 28*th*	
Golden Lion Inn, Barnstaple,	Thursday 29*th*	1819
Bamfylde Arms, Northmolton,	Friday 30*th*	
George Inn, Southmolton,	Saturday May 1*st*	

For the purpose of receiving and entering the names of such persons, the number of their sheep intended to be depastured and a figure of their sheep mark. The price for each sheep will be one shilling per head, from the 1*st* of May, 1819, to the 24*th* of March, 1820. The respective owners of the sheep will receive a ticket from the office of Messrs. Wood and Strong, signed by the Proprietors of the pasture; and no sheep will be permitted to be Depastured without the production of such ticket. All ponies found trespassing on the above Allotments after the 1*st* of May next, will be impounded, except such as bear the mark of Sir Thos. D. Acland, Bart.

JOHN KNIGHT
52 Portland Place, London.

The purchase of the Crown Allotment was completed on 15 March 1820. Twelve months before this, John Knight had bought Sir Thomas Acland's allotments of 3,298 acres, while also in 1820 he acquired the adjoining manor of Brendon, which carried with it the owner's (Sir Arthur Chichester's) allotment on Exmoor. The

FOREST OF EXMOOR IN THE COUNTIES OF SOMERSET AND DEVON

The Account of Sir Thomas Dyke Acland, Baronet, the Forester as to the Rents and Profits of the Said Forest from Lady Day 1816 to Lady Day 1817.

CHARGE.

	£	s.	d.	£	s.	d.
1818						
Received for Pasturage of sheep	388	17	4½			
Deduct as usual for Tithes at the Rate of 4s. in the Pound	77	15	0	311	2	4½
Received for Pasturage of Colts	0	10	0			
Deduct as usual 1s. 8d. in the Pound for Tithes	0	0	10	0	9	2
Chief Rent				3	7	8½
Amerciaments				0	9	0
A year's Rent of Symonbath House and Lands				35	0	0
				350	**8**	**3**

DISCHARGE.

	£	s.	d.
1818			
Expenses of drifts and driving the Commons adjoining the Forest. (No Voucher.) Same as in preceding year	8	18	6
Tellers	10	10	0
Helpers. (No Voucher.) Same as in preceding year	2	18	9
Poundherd, a year's Salary to L. Day 1817	2	0	0
Repairing Pound Wall	1	4	0
Repairing Roads on the Forest	10	1	0
Expenses of Forest Court			
Repairs of Simonsbath House	4	14	6
Wm. Lock, the Deputy Forester, 1 year salary to Lady Day 1817. (No Voucher.) The same as in preceding years	40	0	0
Mr. John Day two years Salary for holding Swainmote Court, receiving and transmitting Rents, Postage of Letters, and Carriage of Parcels to Lady Day 1817	10	10	0
	90	**16**	**9**
Balance	**259**	**11**	**6**
	350	**8**	**3**

following year Sir Charles Bampfylde's 100 allotments totalling 1,881 acres were conveyed to him. Only three were in possession, but John Knight had patiently succeeded in purchasing ninety-two of the tenants' life interests, though at prices which increased the longer they held out. Several of the smaller allotments were later bought, and in all he acquired over 16,000 acres formerly part of the old Royal Forest. (Details of these purchases are given on page 292.)

Lastly, Mr Knight applied to the Commissioners of Woods and Forests to treat for the rights of the Crown to any mines or minerals which might be under Sir Charles Bampfylde's and Sir Thomas Acland's allotments, such rights being reserved, as they were in all similar cases, to His Majesty. The Commissioners, after inquiry, decided correctly, as has since appeared, that these rights were of merely nominal value, and sold them to Mr Knight 'for one year's rent of the land, which has been reported to us to be about 3s. per acre'. They were not conveyed, however, until long after his death, that is to say, in 1855, when his son, Frederic Knight, was engaged in an attempt to develop the mineral resources of Exmoor. The question was also raised as to whether there had been any reservation by the Crown of the minerals under the King's Allotment, but it was decided to treat them as being included in the conveyance to John Knight.

The process here was similar to that which must have occurred all over England upon the inclosure of wastes. The stages by which the small allotments to many individuals, in lieu of rights of various kinds, became assembled into farms of every size, equipped with homesteads, fences, etc, and the farms themselves into the great estate, giving rise to the landlord-and-tenant system of land tenure as it manifests itself today, have never been traced, in particular cases, to illustrate that which is known to have occurred. There is ocular evidence of the aggrandisement of farms and of estates which took place during the period, and the causes of it, if not the processes by which it was achieved, are pretty clearly established. 'The social advantages of landownership continued with high profits to give land a fancy value. Yeomen consulted their pecuniary advantage by selling their estates; capitalists gratified both their tastes and their speculative instincts by buying

Page 49 (left) Richard Payne
Knight 1792. From a portrait by
Sir Thomas Lawrence, PRA

(right) The Hon Mrs John
Knight

Page 50 (left) Frederic Winn Knight c 1835

(right) Lady Knight 1853

land. The purchasers were not yeomen, but neighbouring squires or successful manufacturers. Everywhere large landed properties were built up on the ruin of the small landowner.' What was true of the yeoman, in many cases, was even more general in the case of the recipients of small allotments of land upon inclosure, as in many instances the utility of their new possession bore no relation to that of the one formerly enjoyed, even though the money values were identical. Thus, the right to graze a cow upon a common found no equivalent, in utility, in the allotment of an acre or two of land, always unfenced and often remote, and it is no wonder that purchase and absorption by larger neighbours was the rule. The large tenant farmer and the labourer replaced the yeoman and the tenant of the common lands, while the profits of industry and commerce found an outlet for investment in the assembly of large estates built up out of the ruins of the old land system.

Although the Royal Forest of Exmoor bore little resemblance to the more fertile fields of rural England, it affords an example of the consolidating process which was going on all over the country. The free-suitors' rights to depasture stock were met, upon inclosure, by the allotment of Forest land of the average extent of 31 acres to each, and the rights of the owners of the old-enclosed tenements were satisfied with even less, but it must be obvious that a plot of this size was no equivalent for the right of the allottee's flock to range the Forest at large, and Exmoor shared the common experience, in such cases, through the sale or abandonment of the useless exchange. The fences to be erected between neighbour and neighbour were never made, and the private occupation roads, fifteen in number, of a width of 20ft each, set out in the Award of 1819 'for the exclusive use, convenience and benefit' of the allottees, were not needed, nor was their construction undertaken.

'Except that the prices of labour and livestock were low, the moment did not seem favourable for a great reclamation scheme. The long wars that sprang out of the French Revolution of 1789 had been closed at Waterloo; war prices for corn had only been temporarily sustained by two bad harvests; but the War taxes remained, and threatened to be increased by an approaching return to cash payments. Wheat brought 5*l.* a quarter in 1814, and was only 40*s.* in 1822; while beef in Newgate Market was quoted from 2*s.* 4*d.* to 3*s.*, and mutton at 2*s.* to 2*s.* 10*d.* per stone.'

In Devon John Knight continued to run the Manor of Brendon in the same way that Sir Arthur Chichester had done before him; as a tenanted agricultural estate, and it was to his Somerset possessions that he turned his reclaiming energies. The earliest work set on foot was the construction of the boundary wall with which John Knight encircled the whole of his acquisitions upon the Forest. It has a total length of about 29 miles, and it must have been completed before the end of 1824, for in November of that year 'Nimrod', writing of Exmoor, remarks that 'a gentleman of Worcestershire, by the name of Knight, having purchased it on a speculation, he has built a high wall round it, which somewhat obstructs the stag-hunting'.[4] Although several of the allotments subsequently purchased adjoined the boundary wall, they clearly form a separate field pattern, added to the original inclosure. Several of the old boundary marks of the Forest seem to have been absorbed or converted in its construction, being regarded, no doubt, as obsolete.[5]

Another work taken in hand at once was the construction of roads. Like all the improvers of his day, John Knight was a great road-maker. The obstacles to development of the countryside presented by difficulties of communication, even so late as his time, are not always realised. The writings of Arthur Young and of his contemporaries are full of references to the evil condition of the roads, and many villages were practically cut off from communication with the outside world, so far as concerned the transport of goods, for six months of the year. 'Food', Lord Ernle has recorded, 'rotted upon the ground in one parish, while in the next there was a scarcity.' Most of the main roads had been put in order by the end of the eighteenth century, but the parish roads remained, for the most part, impassable except for horsemen, during the winter months, until long after this date. 'People now living', wrote Albert Pell, in 1899, 'may have seen decaying under the walls of a parish church the enormous wooden plough, girt and stayed with iron, which, as spring approached, was annually furbished up and brought into the village street. For this the owners and their tenants, acting in concert, made up joint teams of six or eight powerful horses, and proceeded to the restoration of their highways, by ploughing them up, casting the furrows towards the centre, and then harrowing them down to a fairly level surface for the summer traffic.'

There were no roads on Exmoor at the time of the disafforestation. The Inclosure Award was accompanied by a map, which set out a number of roads following, in almost every case, the trackways already existing. No obligation was imposed on those obtaining allotments, nor on the purchaser of the King's Allotment, to make these roads, nor have all of them been made to this day, but John Knight set to work, and metalled those at Sandiway and from Exford to Simonsbath, and thence towards South Molton and Brendon. Not only this, but he stirred up the farmers and others in the country round Exmoor to do likewise, convincing them of the advantages to themselves of better means of communication, and so his own good roads were linked up with the main arterial highways in the low country, and access to his moorland estate was secured. The new road leading to Lynmouth (the Brendon Road) is mentioned in a record of a run with the North Devon Staghounds, in September 1828. The road over Challacombe Common was not taken seriously in hand until some twenty years later, when Frederic Knight, as agent for his father, was getting large quantities of lime from the Combe Martin kilns, and sought to reduce the cost of transport by making up the road. Mr A. G. Bradley, writing of the early sixties, and commenting on the excellence of the Challacombe–Simonsbath road, describes John Knight as 'the most famous faddist and experimenter that the West-country ever knew', and says that the only useful marks left by him on Exmoor were the roads he made, which had never been called upon to carry any traffic to speak of. But this view seems to overlook the immediate object of this road, and also the conditions of transport and communication in general, off the main roads, in the early part of last century—not to mention the ultimate value of the land reclamation initiated by John Knight and completed by his son, which could not have been realised without the roads.

One of the ancient trackways, which came from the Midlands, through Gloucester and Bristol and so to Bridgwater, over the Quantocks, on to Exford, Simonsbath, Barnstaple and into Cornwall, may still be traced on the Forest in a portion rendered obsolete by the construction of the Simonsbath–Challacombe road. This length starts opposite to Driver Cot, crosses the Barle and continues by Great Vintcombe to Mole's Chamber, whence it goes on as a parish road. In the illustration on page 68 the alternative tracks may be discerned, a new one being made as an older one became impassable, and they give some idea of the difficulties of travel little more than a hundred years ago.

Altogether about 22 miles of public roads were made by John Knight within the Forest. It is to be inferred that his plans for developing the estate were made, to a large extent, before the purchase, for the announcement of his acquisition of the King's Allotment in the local press was accompanied by the statement of his intention to build a residence in the centre of it, and by other indications of works subsequently carried out. He spent much of his time on Exmoor, living, as already related, first at Lynton and later at Simonsbath House, and superintending all the operations in progress. The mansion was begun, at the back of the old house, and there is a story in the family that it was his intention to dismantle Wolverley House to provide timber and fittings for it, but it had not been completed when he left Exmoor to reside in Rome, and it stood for more than sixty years in the condition in which it appears in the illustration on page 158. It was pulled down in 1899. As an appendage to the house, though not immediately adjacent to it, a large deer-park was inclosed adjoining the South Molton road, and numbers of fallow deer were enlarged upon it.

A work much more difficult to understand was the construction of Pinkery Pond. John Knight dammed up the headwaters of the Barle, at the foot of the great bog known as the Chains, making a reservoir some 7 acres in extent and some 30ft in depth at its lower end. There is no record nor any positive tradition of the purpose of this storage water, and Mr A. G. Bradley mentions that so long ago as the sixties of last century no one could tell him of the object with which the pond was made. A small leat runs from it down the valley towards the present Pinkery Farm, and a much larger channel, the so-called canal, can be found starting near the pond, though never connected to it, which runs, carefully contoured, across the country for a considerable distance in the direction of Simonsbath. That this canal was intended for the conveyance of water from the pond is obvious, but the use to which this water was to be put remains uncertain. This was an age of great activity in the construction of canals, as well as of roads— the Tiverton branch of the Grand Western Canal, for example, was opened in 1814—but it is difficult to believe that John Knight had serious thoughts of providing water transport from this comparatively insignificant source. Nor is the suggestion that the pond was intended as a source of water power, for mining, much more probable; the only iron ore known to exist in his time was never worked, and it occurs lower down the river, where, except in a long summer drought, power would have been available at much less expense. A more likely suggestion is that Pinkery Pond and the canal were constructed to provide irrigation water for the long stretch of land from Pinkery Farm to Honeymead, but that its peaty nature made it unsuitable for this purpose and led to the abandonment of the project. The work of construction was carried out by a party of 200 Irish labourers. The story has been handed down in the family that the canal, or drain, was never connected to the pond because they worked to the wrong levels, and, if completed, it would have tapped the pond too high. Although the line of the canal is below the top of the dam, it is well above water level, and the difficulty may have been that the dam was not strong enough to impound the pond to the originally intended height: it covers less than half the intended 7 acres.

It is stated, sometimes, that John Knight engaged in mining on Exmoor. It is true that he had acquired the mineral rights of the Crown, and, as an ironmaster himself, he might well have been interested in such a venture, but he made no attempt to exploit the minerals on the estate, though a few years before his death, and long after he had retired from Simonsbath to Rome, he granted a mining lease to a small syndicate.

As regards work more definitely agricultural, the boggy nature of so much of the land, due to a thin, clay-iron pan just below the surface, at once suggested the need for drainage. As will presently appear, the effective solution of the drainage problem was found in subsoil ploughing, to break the pan, but John Knight and, more particularly, his son, attempted the removal of water from large tracts by cutting surface drains. On Great and Little Buscombe, Trout Hill, East and West Pinford, and The Chains—to mention some of the areas—many miles of these drains were cut, and, though they failed completely in their purpose, they remain to this day, to the discomfiture of the unwary staghunter who attempts to cross them. Most of this work, however, belongs to the period following John Knight's management.

John Knight seems never to have realised the effects of the great elevation of Exmoor on its climate. Almost the first steps in any works of reclamation should have been the formation of woods and shelter-belts, to break the force of the wind and give protection to livestock and crops. But very little planting was done in the early years, the 26 acre plantation known as Birch Cleave being the only one formed prior to the year 1840.

(See pp 295–9 for notes)

III

1820-41 DEMESNE FARMING

The progress of farming on Exmoor is divided into periods, more or less sharply defined, by the changes in policy which experience necessitated from time to time. As already mentioned, John Knight continued the old practice of taking in lowland stock for summer grazing on Exmoor, after his purchase of the property, but he had not acquired the Forest for the purpose of carrying on no more than the traditional pastoral industry. Farming on a large scale was his object. He was his own agent, organising and superintending the works of reclamation upon which he resolved, and at a very early date he had begun to plough the land, with the object of bringing it into rotation farming. Exmoor may be described as a great tableland, which is traversed by four considerable valleys, running, for the most part, from west to east. Near its southern border there is the valley through which flow Kinsford Water and Sherdon Water; north of this is the valley of the Barle, a wide and deep depression which runs from one side of the Forest to the other; north again is the valley carved out by the Exe, above Simonsbath and Honeymead Allotment; finally, the headwaters of Badgworthy Water, flowing in the opposite direction but still following, more or less, a course east and west, have opened out a valley near the northern border of the Forest. If any cultivation was to be done it was natural that the southern slopes of these wide valleys would suggest themselves for the purpose, and John Knight selected the widest and longest of them, that of the river Barle, for his first operations. There were already at Simonsbath old inclosures of some 108 acres, which formed the farm attached to the only house on the Forest, and east and west of these, at Honeymead and Cornham, he began to break the

57

ground. All this land consisted of 'forest grass' (principally Purple Moor Grass—Molinea Caerulea), for it is a remarkable thing that there is practically no heather on the Forest, and the boundary, which was a purely arbitrary one judged by all surface indications, marks almost to a yard the division of the sedge land from the heather. No positive explanation of this fact can be given, but Professor R. G. Stapledon writes that 'it is a fact that under grazing, particularly by cattle, heather is destroyed to a considerable extent, and if destruction were started many years ago, even though intensive grazing be not maintained, the ecological balance having been once upset would have let in the grasses, altered the whole trend of competition, and left an effect for a long time. It is an ecological fact that grass-heath tends to arise, in substitution for heather-heath, when heather-heath is used as fairly intensive grazing land.' Thus, it may be that the regular yearly stocking of the Forest through two centuries or more, in contrast with the casual grazing of the adjoining commons, may have resulted in the difference in the character of the herbage which is so notable today.

The forest soil is of two types. About one-half of it, which is naturally dry, consists of a brown loam covering a deep, yellow subsoil, the debris of the soft Devonian clay-slate rock which underlies it. An analysis made at a later date (about 1850) by J. C. Nesbit showed the following composition:

Exmoor Dry Land

	Per cent.
Moisture	28·16
Organic matter	11·90
Siliceous matter (insoluble)	55·74
Oxide of iron and alumina, with trace of phosphoric acid	3·89
Lime	0·12
Magnesia	0·12
Soluble alkaline salts	0·07
	100·00

Nitrogen (equal to) 0·56 per cent.
Ammonia   0·68 ,,   ,,

Some five and twenty years later, the 'dry' soil of Exmoor was analysed by Dr Voelcker, his figures differing from those of

Nesbit partly for the reason that his sample was dried at 212°
before analysis:

Exmoor Dry Land

	Per cent.
Organic matter and water of combination	14·11
Insoluble siliceous matter . . .	82·45
Oxide of iron and alumina . . .	1·43
Phosphoric Acid	0·29
Lime	0·19
Magnesia and Alkalies	1·49
Sulphuric Acid	0·04
	100·00

This soil, which occurs for the most part on the sides of the
valleys, has a natural drainage, and requires nothing more than
the addition of lime to make it fertile.

The other half of the Forest is covered with a thin clay-and-iron
pan, quite impervious to water, on which the growth of centuries
has laid a shallow layer of peat. For the greater part of the year
these peat soils are saturated with water, like a sponge, and they
form a strong contrast to the dry Exmoor land, by which heavy
rain is absorbed almost as quickly as by a New Red Sandstone
soil. Where the pan exists, the water cannot penetrate to the
pervious subsoil. Dr Voelcker's analysis of the soil and of the pan,
both dried at 212°, was:

Exmoor Wet Land and Pan

	Wet Land.	Clay Pan.
Organic matter and water of combination	28·40	9·90
Insoluble siliceous matter . . .	69·50	86·01
Oxide of iron and alumina . . .	0·97	3·38
Phosphoric Acid	0·15	0·14
Lime	0·05	0·08
Magnesia and Alkalies	0·90	0·47
Sulphuric Acid	0·03	0·02
	100·00	100·00

Bullock-teams, in yokes of six, supplied the power for the
cultivation of the land, which had never before been moved by
man. The first operation performed was 'spading', which consisted in paring off two or three inches of the top layer of turf with

a broadshare. 'Burning' followed, this top layer being got together in heaps, burnt, and then spread. The next step was 'liming', for John Knight well knew the virtue of this aid to soil improvement, and he recognised, from the first, that these acid soils, full of the vegetable accumulations of centuries, could never become productive without liberal dressings of lime. Three tons to the acre was the amount applied in later years, but there is no record of the quantities used in the early days. Then came the first ploughing, known, from the method of execution, as 'halving'. The bullock-teams were put on to plough every alternate furrow-width, the furrow-slice being turned over on to the unploughed strip beside it. As to the depth of the furrow, this was determined by the depth of the soil, and where there was no pan the general instruction was to let the plough in 'till the soil turned up yellow'—to secure that the yellow subsoil was reached. Where the thin clay and iron pan prevailed, the plough was followed by subsoiling, only every alternate furrow being so treated, as the disturbance thus created was found to suffice. The land was then left, in the low ridges formed by the half-ploughing, until the following spring, when it was ready for spring cultivation and sowing.

The effect of this work on the drainage and the texture of the soil was immediate and permanent. It is well illustrated by the condition of the land today in many places, as, for example, on either side of the South Molton road, by Emmett's Grange. On the south side of the road the land was first reclaimed, by processes similar to those described above, in or about the year 1848—on the north side it remains in its native unreclaimed condition. When examined in 1929 during a wet autumn spell, the natural land overlying the pan, on the higher side of the road, was standing in water, whilst the improved field, at the lower level, was no wetter than the recent rainfall would have rendered any land. Seventy-five years before, the same spot had been examined by an earlier visitor, who remarked that 'wild moorland and high cultivation may be found divided only by the carriage way—on the one hand fields of crops worthy of the Lincolnshire Wolds, on the other the brown and purple moor'. By common consent, land that has once been broken never reverts to sedge, and white clover comes naturally on Exmoor after liming.

How much land was broken and brought into cultivation in this way by John Knight, during the period under review, has not been determined, but it was very considerable, and 2,500 acres is the figure mentioned by Frederic Knight, in 1845. Homesteads were built at Cornham and at Honeymead at an early date. A correspondent of the *Sporting Magazine*, in 1824, mentions 'the disafforestation of Exmoor and the enclosure and cultivation of very large tracts of country' as a cause of shortage of deer, and mention occurs of Cornham Farm in an account of a run with the North Devon Staghounds, in September 1828, during which the stag 'crossed Mr. Knight's farm to Cornham House, where he was headed by some farm people'.[1] What is certain is that his object in cultivating these parts of the Forest was to introduce the improved courses of husbandry with which he had made himself familiar in the Midlands. Having pared and burnt the surface, limed the land, and broken the pan, where necessary, he proceeded to farm on the four-course system, and right away up to the year of his death the attempt to grow barley and wheat, with the help of turnips and sheep, under the impossible climatic conditions of Exmoor, continued. 'We have magnificent oats, fine turnips and barley and spring wheat—winter wheat rather a failure'—wrote Captain Lewis Knight, from Simonsbath, to his father in Rome, in August 1849, but the number of seasons of which so much could be said must have been few.

The greatest expense, probably, was the provision of lime. Without it, any cultivation was useless, and a diligent search was made on Exmoor for local sources of supply. In 1829 it was thought that limestone had been found, and Lord Headley, having been notified of this discovery, so important to the development of the Forest, replied that it gave him 'great pleasure to hear that it had been found in such abundance. I hope it is near the fuel or turf—in case it is, you may say the Peat is the most valuable part of the purchase—but having found lime at all in any large quantity in my view doubles the Value of the Property'. At another date Lord Headley told his nephew, Frederic, that he was looking out 'for three labourers for your father to take over [from Ireland] to the Forest, who were accustomed to burn lime in running kilns. We have 120 Lime Kilns of the description your father wishes to introduce, namely to be used with Turf.' But the discovery was illusory. 'I am very sorry to tell you', wrote John Knight to his wife some little time later, 'that everything goes on but badly here—and the Lime seems altogether a perfect delusion. I now believe I shall never have occasion to build a kiln.' In the meantime, supplies were being obtained, at considerable expense, about 20s per ton, from Combe Martin, and from a kiln belonging to John Williams, at Newlands, between Simonsbath and Exford. Some twelve years later (1841) another discovery appeared to have been made, and Frederic Knight writes that he has great confidence of being able to burn lime in the Warren. 'The rock breaks at the top with 94 per cent. of lime and is precisely like the heads of the best lime rocks at Combe Martin. I have been several times at Combe Martin to make my bargains, and they are now putting lime on my fallows at Cornham 6s. per ton cheaper than Mr. Williams delivered. When the road is made over Challacombe Common, which I will do very soon, I shall get it cheaper.' But once more, expectation was not realised, though in 1848 a kiln was built and some lime was burned at Bale Water.

It may be of interest to note that the winter labour force employed at Cornham at this time comprised two carters, each at 1s 9d per day; two ox-men, each at 1s 6d per day; their two drivers, at 1s per day each; and one labourer, who was paid 1s 4d per day. There were fifteen oxen available for the bullock-teams. No particulars of the staff at Honeymead have been found.

All the time that reclamation by tillage was proceeding, John Knight was hard at work enclosing large areas within his boundary for grazing purposes. Mention of the Deer Park between Blue Gate and Prayway Head has already been made, but other large enclosures were stocked with sheep and cattle. Most of these were bought by John Knight himself, and he was at great pains to secure the best stock of its class, even though it may have proved ill-adapted to his purpose.

On the journeys undertaken by him to buy stock he was keenly observant of the conditions of agriculture and of the people in the districts through which he passed; one of them may be described, as being typical of many. On an evening early in October 1826, he left Bristol by the mail coach and drove for two nights and a day, stopping only once to drink tea and eat bread and butter, and reaching Carlisle on the morning of the second day. He remarked upon some recent heathland reclamation, by the Duke of Portland, between Appleby and Carlisle, and everywhere he was astonished at the extent of road-making in progress. The people, he records, were for the most part in employment and comfortable. After a night in 'a little dirty room' at Carlisle, he proceeded north a further 120 miles to Falkirk Fair, where he bought 'about 400 most beautiful West Highland Bullocks' and 'missed 80 others by not knowing the ways of the market'. He notes the arrangements of the Fair—'a considerable plain covered with immense herds of cattle standing separately, and tended mostly by persons in a variety of Highland dresses and all kinds of music, but the Bagpipe left the other but little chance of being heard. A long row of very large seats, full of whisky, divided in the middle of the plain the Highlanders from the Angus or Lowland cattle.' Leaving Falkirk he proceeded to Edinburgh, from which city he wrote to his wife for news of the Dongola Arab mares which he had just imported; remarked that 'many of the Scotch women still go without stockings', and regretted that he would not have time to see the steam-coach. Hearing of a water-meadow, near the city, which was let at £62 per acre and gave at least six cuts of grass every year, he went to see it. From Edinburgh he journeyed home, via Hereford, 'making a capital purchase of 95 Herefords. They appear cheaper than any cattle I have ever had'. So much impressed was he with this bargain, that he returned to Hereford a fortnight later 'and marched out with 200 of them at low prices'.

In the space of a month, he had travelled, by coach, about 1,000 miles, and had bought, in the course of his journey, some 700 head of cattle. All of them were sent down to Exmoor, but they did not exhaust the resources of the Forest, and John Knight determined to husband his capital and increase his returns by taking in more horned stock at agist. All the family were following his work with interest. 'I was so glad to hear', wrote Lord Headley from Paris, to his sister, Mrs Knight, 'about the plans for the Forest. I mean that of taking in young Stock, which I should think would answer well, as the place seems adapted for it and it supersedes the necessity for so large a capital being invested in a perishable commodity. I shall not regret the scarcity of Veal, knowing that it arises from so auspicious a cause.'

The Scotch cattle acclimatised very well on Exmoor, and the large herd must have presented a fine picture on its hills. They fed well, and in the local markets they seem to have roused but little of that prejudice against strange stock which is still to be encountered in some places. Writing to his sister at Rome, on Christmas Day 1838, Charles Knight relates that eighty steers had been sold at the rate of 11s per score, when other fat beasts in the market were making no more than 10s per score; and that two of the old cows sold out by his father in the previous year had been fattened, and sent to Tavistock Fair, where 'they carried off the Ribbons. This from the Devonians in the midst of their own country, who think no cattle can be good without a fine skin and small bones, is a great deal.'

But although they did so well in their new quarters, the Highland cattle were not a success. They could not live on the Forest in winter without artificial food. For some reason, too, they proved very intractable, and their reputation for wildness still lingers. 'All were wild and some were wicked.' Frederic Knight has described an extraordinary experience with a small lot which were ready for the butcher in the spring of 1841. 'Bennett [the farm manager at Cornham] fatted 20 of our Scotts, but could not tame them, for when they tried to drive them to market, they started in different directions across the country, tossed and gored everybody they met, and were shot in fields all over the country. I have got a short summary letter from him, detailing these events and giving a list of the wounded.'

In course of time the Highlands and the Herefords gave place, and the Devon Rubies and Shorthorns came into their own again. It must be remembered that Exmoor had been summer-grazed almost exclusively in the past by sheep, and in attempting to increase its capacity as an all-the-year-round cattle country, John Knight had little local experience to guide him. This business assumed considerable importance before it gave place in later years, the sales of cattle in 1840, for example, exceeding £7,000 in value.

Sheep had always been the characteristic and almost the only feature of Exmoor farming, and to them John Knight early turned his attention. Agistment during the summer grazing season fell off as the inclosure of the Forest proceeded and as the substitution of bullocks increased, but he himself kept large numbers, both for grazing and to consume the root crops on his newly broken farm lands. He began with the local Exmoors, but had much difficulty in securing them of the quality at which he aimed. 'Alas for my sheep', he writes, in 1836, to Mrs Knight, 'which are still very shabby, and my wool I cannot sell at my price which is merely the market price—but as wool is improving in price every day and the manufacturers have "no Gauds in House", I have still hopes.'

For a few years he continued in the effort to improve his Exmoors, and in 1838 he notes the passing of an Act for the inclosure of Bratton Down, which would compel the farmers to sell their sheep, and he looked forward to obtaining a flock of the best quality. This, presumably, was a case similar to that of Exmoor itself, where the allotment of a parcel of land upon inclosure was no real equivalent for the right to range the Common at large, and flocks had to be dispersed.[2] At the same time he was experimenting with other breeds. Those who know Exmoor today are aware that the Cheviots have long been established there, but it is not generally known that their first introduction dates back to before 1840. There is no record of how they were obtained, but it is likely that John Knight bought them himself on one of his journeys to Scotland. He seems to have had no more success with them than with the Exmoors, in the early days. Great difficulties were experienced in getting good shepherds in this remote district, and John Knight's predilection for the employment of single men can have done little to promote the closer settlement of the country. Moreover, the district being extraparochial and on the county boundary, it had always borne a reputation for lawlessness. 'On account of being stolen, killed by dogs and disease and lost by bad shepherds', he writes of his Cheviots, 'I could produce an account sufficient, I should think, to frighten the young Gents who are going to Australia with a certainty, as they suppose, of making great fortunes, if they had but once established a small flock.'

So serious were the thefts of sheep and deer, the shepherds

themselves being particularly bad offenders as regards the latter,[3] that he formed a guard of Irishmen for the protection of his property, under the guise of gamekeepers, to whom he promised large rewards for the detection of the thieves—'but I find these Potato-eaters must all come from the same part of Ireland or they will do nothing but fight.' Even the farmers of the district were stated to have 'taken every possible means of obtaining my breed of sheep', and their character for enterprise is borne out, further, by a note that 'Lord Ebrington has just found out that 1,800 sheep have been pastured on Lord Fortescue's land at his expense, by his Steward Belmont and Farmer Crang, his favourite, for many years. Belmont fled; Crang remains to enjoy his newly-exposed character, and the sheep are to be sold for want of pasture.'

Disappointed with the Cheviots, in 1840 John Knight tried the rather remarkable experiment of a flock of Merinos, exchanging some Scotch bullocks for 100 ewes of this breed. A married shepherd was imported from Wiltshire, 'and a clever boy. They are likely to be of great use if I can prevail with the shepherd to put up with the solitude, of which I almost despair. I am doing my best to fit up the White Rock Cottage for this family, but society I cannot provide; indeed, several servants have lately left my station for want of company. The shepherd has three children and Wilts overstocked with such families. Bennett says we shall be able to get others if this one settles comfortably. He is quite different from the wild race I employ here. I hope the Merinos will answer better than the Cheviots.'

Exmoor, even at this date, may well have been a solitude. It is said that John Knight did little in the way of cottage-building, believing that married men were out of place on the Forest. Single men were employed, accommodated on the Scotch bothy system, and sleeping in hammocks. Besides the White Rock Cottage mentioned above, and cottages at Cornham and Honeymead, the only dwellings built by him were at Limecombe, Warren, Bale Water and Cloven Rocks, with the range at Simonsbath known as Pound Cottages, and that at right-angles to it, facing the Inn, since demolished. The estate staff in November 1841 consisted of five grooms, two carpenters, two blacksmiths, three carters, three herdsmen, three gardeners, three labourers and twelve 'Irishmen'.

67 Inclosing the Forest: (*above*) the boundary fence at Brendon Two Gates c 1925; (*below*) an internal fence at Trout Hill

Page 68　Exmoor roads as John Knight found and made them: (*above*) Great Vintcomb
(*below*) Drybridge

The numbers varied from time to time, and at different seasons carters would turn ploughmen or levellers, while the 'Irishmen' included both labourers and 'keepers'. All were paid rather better than most agricultural labourers at this time, doubtless to entice them to so remote a workplace, and boys received 6d per day, most men from 1s 8d to 2s, and craftsmen (carpenters and blacksmiths) 2s 6d per day. A steward, Osmond Lock, managed the day-to-day running of the estate until 1840, when he was succeeded by John Litson.

Exmoor is not a pig-breeding district. In 1929 there were, probably, not half a dozen sows kept for breeding, and the few pigs that were fed were for home consumption. It is unlikely that there were any at all in the pre-inclosure days. Whether John Knight made an attempt to establish them has not appeared, but he certainly tried an experiment with Westphalians. His brother-in-law, Lord Headley, had imported some into Ireland, but having decided not to keep them he forwarded them, in August 1835, to Exmoor. As illustrative of the transport difficulty in those days, these pigs were sent by road from Aghadoe, Co Kerry, to Cork, shipped thence to Bristol, thence by another steamer to Ilfracombe, to the care of the bank there, whence they had to be conveyed by cart to their destination. 'They are a hardy sort', wrote Lord Headley, 'admirable for bacon, and I think would do well wild in the Brendon Woods. The young you will easily ascertain are thoroughbred by the curious stripes.' What became of these pigs is not recorded; there have been none in the Brendon Woods in living memory.

The inquiry as to the Dongola mares in the letter quoted from John Knight to his wife (page 63) has reference to another early enterprise. Exmoor, of course, had for long been the home of a native race of ponies, and it is said that there were some 400 of them at the time of the inclosure of the Forest, the largest herd being that of the Warden, Sir Thomas Acland. Most of these were removed to the neighbourhood of Winsford Hill, but Sir Thomas left a small stock for John Knight. As with all else that he found, his desire was to improve them, and hearing a good account of the big Arab horses of the Dongola district, he joined with a few of his friends, Lords Headley, Morton and Dundas, in the expense of

E

importing some. In colour they were black, with very fine skins, Roman-nosed, short-backed, and very good quarters. On the other hand, they are described also as being rather flat-ribbed, with drooping croups and rather high on the leg. The portrait of one of the stallions, 'Mahmoud', painted by James Ward, RA, in 1828, when the horse was getting old, brings out both the qualities and the defects.

Two of the Dongola stallions and three mares arrived at Simonsbath, where John Knight had set up a considerable stud, consisting of some thoroughbred sires, seven or eight thoroughbred mares and some thirty well-bred mares of the Cleveland coaching type. To these, at this time, the Exmoor ponies formed only a secondary consideration, but a dozen twelve-hand pony mares were included. From this large and varied assortment, numbers of hunters, hacks, and harness horses of every type were bred and sold, and it is recorded that at one time twenty-eight horses from the Simonsbath stud were going as the best hunters with the neighbouring packs, besides those selected for the use of the owner and his family. The Dongola horse left some good stock, and Frederic Knight had some of the blood so late as the seventies. Two of his own breeding, Tory and Commodore, were successful steeplechasers.

As regards the ponies, the intention was to increase their size and quality by the use of thoroughbred sires. The Dongola horse was first tried, and he was followed by English thoroughbreds of the best blood—Pandarus, by Whalebone; Canopus, by Velocipede; Old Port, by Beeswing. Though there was no difficulty in securing the desired improvement, none but the mares of the old stock could endure the winter fare and climate of the open Forest, and those of the first cross could only rear their foals if wintered on the inclosed and improved pastures. In the early days the ponies were not numerous, but the stock was gradually increased, particularly after the Highland cattle experiment had been abandoned.

All through the period of time under review, the surplus produce of the stud, including the ponies and all the draft animals, were disposed of privately. The public sales were not established until after John Knight's death.

To sum up this account of the first steps towards farming on Exmoor, three primary objects are manifest in the first twenty years or so of the work.

To begin with, as regards policy, it was clearly John Knight's intention to exploit the property at first-hand, and to organise a great agricultural enterprise under his own direction; there is no evidence at any time during this period that he contemplated the creation of a tenantry, holding farms under him, as the ultimate object in view. As the land came under cultivation, the necessary buildings for live and dead stock were erected, but there was no attempt, as yet, to carve out farms, to equip them with home-steads and so to settle the estate, step by step, in the most expeditious way.

In the second place, as regards reclamation for purposes of agriculture, he believed that large portions of the Forest, lying for the most part on the southern slopes, could be brought under the plough, and farmed under one of the established crop rotations of the recognised arable districts, for the production of corn and meat—regardless of the limitations imposed by the high elevation and heavy rainfall. Frederic Knight used to say that his father expected to farm on Exmoor, at an elevation of 1,200ft, as he had been wont to do in the Midlands, a little above sea-level. The steps by which he proceeded to convert land in a state of nature into tillage were skilful and economically sound, but he failed to realise that this process should have been followed by the evolution of a crop-rotation adapted to the climate and soil, and he persisted in his attempt to establish something like the four-course system long after the impossibility of the task had been demonstrated.

In the third place, as regards the improvement of the pastoral industry, John Knight sought to increase the value of those parts of the Forest which were unfitted for tillage, or which, at least, he was not then ready to till, by the introduction of livestock of other than the indigenous breeds, and, particularly, by increasing the cattle stock. As has been shown already, Exmoor before inclosure was utilised, in the main, for summer grazing by the local breeds of sheep. Some cattle were grazed, and the ponies were there summer and winter, but the sheep were the mainstay of the business. John Knight experimented with other varieties of sheep, and though he met with little success at this time, important results emerged at a later date, as will presently appear. As to cattle, he originated the business of summering stock from the lowland districts on the unreclaimed portions of the Forest, which grew, ultimately, to very considerable proportions.

For the rest, he seems to have had no idea, at this time, of colonising the Forest, and herein lay one of his fundamental mistakes. A family of five was resident at the house at Simonsbath at the time of his acquisition of the property; otherwise the place was an uninhabited waste, nor had the locality surrounding it a very good reputation for law and order. By 1842 he had built two farms and about sixteen cottages, and his only tenant was the innkeeper at Gallon House, Red Deer. The best chance for successful reclamation lay in the settlement of the estate, and its equipment with homes and the means for some sort of social life, as speedily as possible, and not a few of John Knight's difficulties and failures, so far as his farming was concerned, arose from neglect of this necessary accompaniment of his task in its earlier years.

(See pp 295–9 for notes)

IV

1842–50   LANDLORD AND TENANT

John Knight was now an old man. He had carried on the heavy work of organisation and management long after an age when most men would have been content to stand aside and leave the task to others. In 1836, being then seventy years of age, he had written from Simonsbath to his wife, who was visiting her brother in Ireland: 'I am full of my plans as usual—perhaps when you return you will find too many of them executed.' But eighteen months later he was complaining that his locomotive powers were so fallen off that he was no longer capable of the active management of the work in hand, which he had been compelled to delegate to his second son, Charles Knight, then about twenty-five years of age. At the same time, it is clear that for another few years he surrendered little beyond the personal superintendence of the farming and estate work, and that he still directed the policy.

In 1840 he had suffered a severe disappointment through the alienation of the great fortune of the elder branch of his family, the Knights of Downton, to a female line. He had been brought up to believe that it was settled to follow the male line, in which case he would succeed, and to a lay mind the settlement would seem to bear that interpretation, but the Courts decided against his claim. Whether it were the loss of this expected accession of financial strength, whether it were merely the result of advancing years, or whether it were due to both these causes, John Knight decided in 1841 to give up the management of the Forest, and he handed over the sole control to his eldest son, Frederic. The following year, being then seventy-six years of age, he retired to Rome, where he died in 1850, but up to the end he was kept

73

closely in touch with the progress of Exmoor reclamation, and his interest in it never flagged.

The period now to be considered is marked by a definite change of policy. For a short time Frederic Knight had to carry on as before; he travelled to Scotland to buy sheep, and the four-course farming continued. But the idea of letting off the land to tenants was already in his mind, and in the letter to his mother in which he tells her of his assumption of the management, he mentions also inquiries he had been making in this direction, from which he concluded that he would 'be able to get tenants from Wiltshire, who will cultivate farms and give good rents'. His determination to let arose from his conviction that he could never make the farming pay. 'I am going to try to let Honeymead and Cornham, with allotments of the Forest, for what I can get for them. If no one will have them I do not see what I can do.'

Honeymead was let at Lady Day 1842 to Henry Matthews. It seems to have included, as well, most of the land now occupied as Cloven Rocks, Picked Stones, and Winstitchin farms, with their buildings and six cottages, as well as Honeymead Allotment. The total extent was 2,100 acres, the rent £740 per annum, and the term of the lease twelve years. A house had been built at Simonsbath Barton, and this farm of 1,030 acres with buildings and two cottages, was let, a year later, to Edward Godwin, at a rent of £439 5s 6d per annum, likewise on a lease of twelve years.

The next farm to be let was Emmett's Grange, the boundaries of which were set to contain 1,300 acres. The tenant was Richard Hibberd, who had been farming previously at Tisbury in Wiltshire, and in September 1844 he took a twelve years' lease at a rental not recorded. The house had not been built at this date, but the buildings were in course of erection, and Frederic Knight on behalf of his father covenanted to complete the buildings, to erect a dwelling-house, two cottages for labourers, a granary, and a milk house and cowsheds sufficient for thirty-five cows. He covenanted also to erect fences to divide the land into eight enclosures, and all this work was to be carried out during the twelve months following. In the subsequent year some minor buildings were to be erected, together with a further sub-division of the land, dividing it into fourteen fields in all.

To continue the story of the early lettings, in 1844 tenants were found for Wintershead, Horsen, Crooked Post and Cornham farms. This last was let to William Hannam on a twelve years' lease from Lady Day 1845, at a rent of £244 13s, this figure to be increased by one-third at the middle of the term, and was to consist of a house, homestead, three cottages, and 545 acres. Hannam's account of his life on the Forest is related on page 240.

On paper, at all events, Frederic Knight had already secured an annual gross income, under the new policy, of some £1,400 from Honeymead, Simonsbath Barton and Cornham alone, and he was well satisfied with this result. Reporting progress to his sister Margaret, at Rome, in the autumn of 1844, he wrote: 'The letting of the farms has, however, gone on better this year than I had reason to expect. I have no doubt that my Father still thinks the price very low, but it is impossible to get people of capital to change their country without offering them what they consider to be a certain advantage: and people without capital would do me no good. I believe I could not have a better lot of tenants if I may judge from all I hear. No one who has come to look at the Forest from any other part of England would hear of taking a forest farm under twenty-one years. Mine are all twelve years.'

The process of enclosing large fields of 50 acres or so had been going on steadily all the time. Fences were made, consisting of stone and earth, turfed over and surmounted with a beech hedge protected on either side by 'wreath'—a strip of wattle fencing necessary to make the walls sheep-proof—and there were now large tracts in all the valleys equipped as to boundary walls in this way, some of the land being already under cultivation. Frederic Knight's success in letting the first farms had led him to go forward vigorously with his scheme for developing the tenant-farming system, by the division of this land into further large farms which he was prepared to equip with houses and buildings as required by the tenants. The idea was to follow the system which had been so successful in other parts of the country—for example, in the Lincolnshire Wolds and on Lincoln Heath—of letting the farms on long leases at very low rents in a state practically unimproved except for the buildings, a certain amount

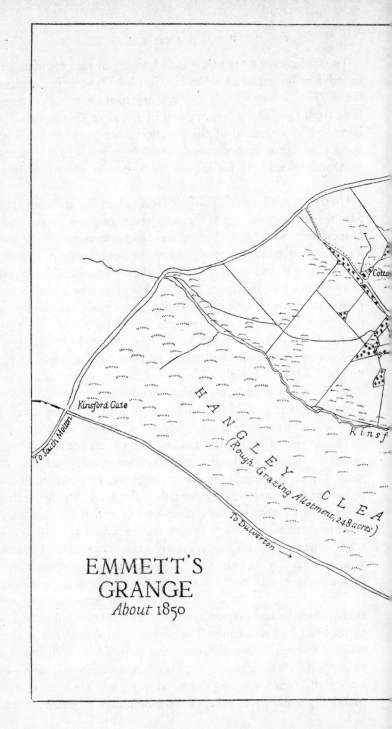

Cotto

Kinsford Gate

To South Molton

HANGLEY CLEA
(Rough Grazing Allotment, 248 acres)

Kinsf

To Dulverton →

EMMETT'S
GRANGE
About 1850

From Simonsbath

From Cornham Ford

Blue Gate

To Wintershead →

ter

of fencing, and here and there some breaking of the land, with a liberal scale of tenant-right allowances for improvements subsequently to be effected by the tenants, combined with a progressive rent to stimulate their execution.

Customs for the compensation of tenants for improvements effected by them on their holdings and unexhausted at the time of quitting, originated in the eastern counties. This was natural, these being the areas most predominantly arable, where developments in farming practice calling for the expenditure of the tenant's capital on improvements of a more or less long-term character were occurring more rapidly than in the parts of England predominantly grass. The 'Lincolnshire Custom' for compensation on quitting was the best known; it spread through many other districts and it formed the basis of the first statute regulating the relations of landlords and their farming tenants, the Agricultural Holdings Act, 1875. The idea of arable farming, on an extensive scale, on Exmoor, still prevailed; but this apart, farming there of any kind, at this date, called for the outlay of much capital on fencing, subsoiling, liming and so forth, and the tenant had to be secured in his expenditure if he were to be called upon to make the improvements.

To get a picture of the estate at this time, all the farms, with the exception of Honeymead, Simonsbath Barton, and Cornham, were in a condition approximating to that of Titchcombe today. They had been laid out, and certain enclosures made within the boundary fences, and so they remained—ready for equipment with house, homestead, and cottages, and for cultivation and improvement, so soon as the policy of landlord occupation gave place to that of tenant farming.

Frederic Knight now had as his agent, or steward, J. Mogridge, of Molland, a member of a well-known Devon farming family. With his assistance he set to work to equip the farms which he had partially enclosed and made, and for which tenants had been found. During the winter of 1844, work was started on farmhouses and buildings at Emmett's Grange, Wintershead (200 acres), Horsen (400 acres), Warren (700 acres) and Crooked Post (350 acres), and on a new house at Cornham to supplement the cottages already there. Though delayed, by bad weather, all were finished during 1845, but by then several tenants had had a change of heart.

Richard Hibberd at Emmett's Grange had sent cattle and horses to the farm, which had to be wintered in the straw-yards of other farmers, and by March 1845 he had given up his farm at Tisbury and arrived on Exmoor. The house was not completed when he arrived, nor were all the buildings ready for occupation, and for three months Frederic Knight gave him the use of Simonsbath House. He was a dairy farmer, and dairying on Exmoor was his object, but before his first summer was out, he was so much alarmed at the prospect that he made overtures to Frederic Knight for a surrender of his lease. The terms he proposed were unacceptable. A distress for rent was levied, the amount taken being £120, and finally an ejectment was ordered and Frederic Knight resumed possession. The final scene was enacted at Bridgwater Assizes, in 1847, when cross-actions were brought—on Hibberd's part, for breach of covenants as to the erection of buildings, and on the landlord's part, for bad cultivation.[1]

Hibberd was not alone, and the tenants of Wintershead, Horsen and Warren also took fright and never occupied the new houses and buildings. Horsen and Warren remained un-let until 1849 and 1850, by which time two new tenants had come and gone at Wintershead. This left only Henry Matthews at Honeymead, Edward Godwin at Simonsbath Barton, William Hannam at Cornham and James Coombes at Crooked Post, the last being 350 acres of detached land at Litton, purchased from Earl Carnarvon and others between 1829 and 1839.

Houses and buildings were erected at Duredon (900 acres) in 1846 and at Driver (400 acres) the next year, but though the tenant found for Duredon in 1847 stayed but a few months, part of Driver was let that year to John Hedditch, for £160. Hedditch came from Dorset, and dairying for cheese was the system of farming he introduced. Pinkery (400 acres), Titchcombe (557 acres) and Cornham Hill (600 acres) were also designated farms at this time, but they had not yet received their building equipment, and the extent of each of the holdings, at this time, was evidently quite tentative, remaining to be determined by the tenants' requirements. Larkbarrow had been let in 1846, but the tenant continued to live at Exford and only two cottages were built there.

The slow letting of his farms and instability of many of his tenants was a great worry to Frederic Knight, who, denied the anticipated family inheritance, was now critically short of money. By September 1847 the interest on the mortgage of the Royal Allotment was more than three months overdue and the mortgagees were threatening to take possession—'A forced sale or rather robbery of the Royal Allotment would be entire ruin—I know not what to do.' To add to his difficulties there was a recession in the iron trade and the Wolverley ironworks had to close for six weeks in November and December for lack of orders, and though later that month the family's Bromsgrove estate was put up for auction there were no bidders. 'I have been an idiot to remain in Parliament, give dinners, keep hunters, and live like a man of fortune, when I should have been keeping quietly at Simonsbath on the small establishment of a country parson.' The grand scheme of reclamation came desperately close to collapse, and though fortunately he was able to come to terms with the mortgagees, lack of capital was to remain a problem, and was doubtless one reason for the stern treatment of the luckless Hibberd.

Frederic Knight is said to have been his own architect, and certain sketches and notes for houses and cottages support the statement. All the work was done direct, by local labour, and local stone was used, but the prejudice against home-grown timber seems to have been as strong then as now, and a note at the foot of one of the specifications runs—'No English fir for me.' Slates were brought across from Wales to Lynmouth Harbour. The houses vary but little in design, and they are planned quite reasonably well, but by their unrelieved severity they serve to contribute to the grimness of Exmoor at some seasons, rather than to mitigate it by their suggestion of human occupation. But this appearance could be changed at any time by an application of colour-wash in any one of the shades which give the appearance of warmth and comfort to the farmhouses and cottages of the surrounding district. This was subsequently done on the Honeymead properties.

In 1848 a notable change in the management of the estate took place, by the appointment of a new agent to succeed Mogridge. He left at Lady Day, but due to his disagreements with the tenants he had not dealt with the lettings for nearly three years, these being handled by Frederic Knight and his Worcestershire agent, Combes. This change followed, almost necessarily, upon the change in the policy. All the farm tenants found up to this date had come from afar, and it was recognised that if the rest of the new farms were to be let, their tenants would have also to be imported. North Devon and West Somerset then, as now, were districts of small farms, occupied by men whose labour formed a large part of their capital; moreover, the local belief was strong that Exmoor was of no use except for summer grazing. So Frederic Knight resolved upon the appointment of a man, as agent, who should come from a country where improved farming on a large scale was understood, and he found him in Robert Smith.

Smith was a member of a well-known East Midland farming family. His father, William Smith, farmed first at Stoke Doyle, near Oundle, where Robert, the fourth son, was born in 1809, and then at Postland in the parish of Crowland, Lincolnshire. In due course Robert Smith had taken the Home Farm on the Burley Estate, near Oakham. Here he soon made a name for himself as an agriculturist, and he became noted as a breeder of Shorthorn cattle and Leicester sheep. He was one of the founders of the Rutland Agricultural Society, and was elected a member of the Council of the Royal Agricultural Society before he was forty at a time when vacancies were filled, not by the votes of the general body of the members, but by the Council itself, and the honour was very carefully bestowed. After migrating to Exmoor he became a member also of the Council of the Bath and West of England Society, and for many years he contributed articles to the *Journals* of both societies. These afford ample evidence of outstanding ability; he had a scientific mind, a philosophic outlook, and a wide range of knowledge on matters pertaining to his craft. He was, in particular, an authority on irrigation, and Philip Pusey went to see his Exmoor water-meadows. Above all, he was a farmer. 'His writings are the results of his experience, instead of his farming being the result of other people's writings. At Burley he carried the Leicester sheep to perfection, and at his sale, previous to removing to Exmoor, he realized twelve hundred guineas for sixty rams. He is, in fact, a farmer of the modern school, who, used to agriculture from his earliest years among the Lincolnshire men, has found it worth while to study earnestly the science and theory of his profession.'

Robert Smith was appointed agent at Lady Day 1848. His salary was £400 per annum, and he lived at Emmett's Grange, where he occupied the farm of about 670 acres, as an ordinary tenant of the estate. What induced him to forsake his fertile farm in the Midlands for the strenuous task of land reclamation, at a small salary, in this distant country, is not apparent, but there is a story that he had been practically ruined by protracted litigation with another exhibitor who had committed some illegality in the showing of a beast at the Rutland Show, and he may have been under the necessity of seeking some salaried appointment.[2] Or it may be that his active and resourceful mind was attracted by the opportunities for experiment and creative work presented by the Forest in its condition at this time. 'Robert Smith's coming here', wrote Charles Knight to his father, 'has occasioned a great talking in his country, and Exmoor is very much talked up in those parts . . . he goes on very well and understands perfectly how to manage the farmers, and has no wish to spend money unnecessarily.'

Robert Smith went to Emmett's Grange when the house had just been built, and when the farm, except for the boundary fence and a few inclosures inside it, was still as Hibberd had left it. The policy of the estate, as regards the equipment of new farms, was to build the house when the tenant was forthcoming, and to let him into possession to begin the reclamation of the land while the erection of the farm buildings proceeded. As regards the land, Robert Smith himself has described the principles upon which he went to work. 'In the laying out of a hill farm', he says, 'which shall be chiefly dependent upon its own resources, it is found best to divide the lands into three distinct classes. First, the hill-top and other rough land should be set out, if possible in one block, as summering ground for young cattle, store sheep, colts, ponies, &c., to be subsequently improved by surface drainage, similar to the Scotch plan of "Sheep-drains"—an inexpensive process, yet found of infinite value. [But not on Exmoor.]

'The second, or middle class of land to be set out is the portion lying immediately below the rough, wet ground, or situated upon a southern aspect; these lands are intended for arable culture.

'The third class consists of the flats and marshes in the valleys, together with some portions of the adjacent hill-sides, which should be laid out for pasture and water-meadows.'

As regards buildings, in the case of new farms a bargain seems to have been made with the prospective tenants that the landlord should spend a sum equal to £2 per acre on house and homestead, and figures have been provided by Robert Smith of the details of the expenditure on thus equipping one of the Exmoor farms—not named, but possibly Tom's Hill—in the year 1850. The farm extended to 300 acres, without the allotment of rough grazing.

Cost of erection in 1850

					£	s.	d.
Total cost of building farm-house	.	.	.		177	9	2
,,	,,	,,	,,	calves' houses and piggeries	46	13	4
,,	,,	,,	,,	barn, stable, and cart-shed .	160	15	3
,,	,,	,,	,,	open cattle-sheds and turnip house	50	8	4
,,	,,	,,	,,	cowsheds, stable, corn, gig, and coal houses . .	58	15	0
,,	,,	,,	,,	stone walls, gates, &c. .	18	13	4
					512	14	5

By 1848 the prospect of letting much of the land had made the question of fencing a serious one as regards expense, and it was decided to make the tenants responsible, they being given material, which they had to cart themselves, and being allowed to deduct 6s per chain from their rents in respect of all fences built. 'Wreath' was to be abolished as a coping, and wire substituted—a single wire for interior fences and two wires for the boundary fences. 'There are 4 farms with buildings upon them (Duredon, Warren, Wintershead, and Horsen), but they are not yet let. The thickest wire used for fences costs £4 per mile, and if the farms are let 15 miles will be wanted this winter. It will take the first year's rent to let in the new tenants, but they will have to pay their rent

almost in time for the outlay.' The fences are earth banks, faced
with stone on each side to a height of 4ft and finished with 2ft of
grass sods, making the fence, when complete, full 6ft high. It was
then planted with a double row of beech plants upon the crown,
protected on either side, at first by 'wreath', and later, as mentioned above, by strands of wire. The full cost of such a fence was
about 30s per chain at this time, and the labour, including carriage
of materials, accounted for about one-third of the total. For some
of the interior fences earth banks covered with turf or sown with
grass seeds and surmounted with beech were used, so saving the
cost of stone facing. The beech alone represented a considerable
expense. Many of the plants were bought, but probably most of
them were grown at Simonsbath, where there was a considerable
nursery and a full-time nurseryman. In one year alone (1850) no
less than £16 was paid for beech nuts.

As to the cultivation of those fields which were to be broken up
after fencing, the cost depended upon the need, or otherwise, for
subsoiling. Robert Smith has recorded the operations necessary,
and their cost, in either case. 'The system adopted upon my own
farm is, first to pare the land by manual or horse labour, according
to circumstances; then to burn the furrow as it lies upon the
surface; the ashes are then ploughed in as thinly as possible, and
from 2½ to 3 tons of lime per acre spread upon the surface to
decompose the vegetable matter; after which the whole is mixed
by the harrow, &c., the cost per acre being as under:

	£	s.	d.
Paring, if by manual labour . .		12	0
Burning upon the land . .		1	6
Ploughing, harrowing, &c. . .		8	6
Lime and labour . . .	2	10	0
	3	12	0

Should the furrows have to be thrown in heaps for burning, and
the ashes spread, the cost will be 3s. 6d. per acre more.

'On the peaty soils requiring to be subsoiled, I find it best to
prepare the land in the autumn for the succeeding spring, by
paring and burning upon the land, half-plough the land into
ridges, and sub-soil between them, the subsoil plough following

Page 85   (*above*) Pinkery Pond; (*below*) the Canal at Pinkery

Page 86 The Forest as John Knight found and made it: (*above*) Little Tom's Hill; (*below*) Emmett's Grange from Hangley Cleave

the teams every other furrow. By this plan the ashes are preserved
for early use and the land left perfectly dry and exposed to the
winter frosts. This is succeeded by a cross ploughing in the spring,
and the whole is complete for harrowings, sowings, &c., at an
early period. The cost will stand thus:

	£	s.	d.
Paring and burning		13	6
Half-ploughing into narrow ridges (2 horses) . .		4	0
Subsoiling every other furrow (4 horses, man and boy,			
2 acres per day)		8	0
Cross-ploughing		6	0
Harrowing, &c.		3	6
Lime and labour	2	10	0
	4	5	0

This process may be followed by any crop, either corn or roots.'

The prices given are for horse-labour, but Robert Smith preferred to use bullock-teams of six oxen. Not only were they
particularly adapted to the heavy tasks of ploughing this fibrous
soil and then subsoiling it, but he found them a more economic
proposition on the farm than horses. There was very little winter
work for team-labour, and horses had to be kept in idleness; on
the other hand, the yoke-oxen could be tied up, when the autumn
work was over, and converted into beef.

It was obvious that much of the task of the making of the land
was to fall upon the tenants under Frederic Knight's proposals.
They were to be given the occupation of land still, for the most
part, in virgin condition, and they were to bring it into cultivation
at their own expense. So Robert Smith drew up for him a form of
lease and a scale of allowances for improvements which should be
attractive to tenants; in fact, Sir Thomas Acland said that he
deserved 'the credit of being the first to introduce into the far
West the Lincolnshire principle of compensation to tenants for
durable improvements made at their own expense, from which
they have not had time to reap a profitable return'. The leases were
to be for twenty years, divided into periods of four years, with
rents beginning at very low figures, and rising at the end of each
period of four years, the lessee having the power of determining
his lease at the end of eight or sixteen years, on giving twelve

F

months' notice. Thus, in the case of Wintershead, let, as will appear, to Gerard Spooner, at 5s per acre for twenty years, 300 acres were to be improved and the rent of this portion was to rise to 7s after four years, to 9s after eight years, and to 11s after twelve years and for the rest of the lease. These principles, upon which the landlord-and-tenant farming system was to be developed, and the nature of the tenant-right to be created, have been recorded by Robert Smith himself, and they cannot be described better than in his own words.

'The letting of moorland upon equitable terms embraces an extensive range of topics for consideration.

'First, we have the "lord of the soil" to consult, and next to find a suitable tenant for the work to be done. These parties either do or should meet upon equitable terms, in the character of two men meeting to make a bargain, the result being, "If you will do this, I will do that."

'The first business will be to arrange the general principles of the bargain. The landlord will probably agree to erect suitable buildings, fences, to make roads, &c., and to perform all drainage, the tenant paying a proper percentage for this latter outlay. The tenant will then have to reclaim all lands and wastes (worthy of cultivation) under suitable covenants.

'The carriage of materials is usually thrown upon the tenant, or in other words it forms a part of *his* agreement towards the matter. This is a stipulation which I have long thought, at least upon this class of farms, objectionable, and it would be well at any rate to postpone bringing it into operation, for the tenant will have enough to do with his teams, during the first few years of his tenancy, in reclaiming these rough and rugged lands.

'In after years this subject may be more fairly pressed, and thus made agreeable to both parties, by the tenant doing the carriage for future permanent improvements, and so encouraging the landlord to keep pace in his outlay with the progress of land cultivation.

'With such an understanding clearly defined, every possible and prudent encouragement should be given to the tenant. First, by a long lease with breaks in it, to allow the tenant to quit at the end of a certain number of years, should he wish it. Second, by a proper tenant-right for unexhausted improvements at the end of either term, to prevent the farm being run out towards the end of the term. Third, by the adoption of the plan of a "scale of rents", commencing at the lowest possible figure in the outset, and increasing every four years to the end of the term, as the farm improves in value.

'To illustrate this last point we may suppose a case, viz.—that a farm is let for 20 years; that the tenant may quit at the end of 8 or 16 years, and that the average value of the farm for the whole term is 10s. per acre; the scale of rents in this case would run thus:

		s. d.	
1st 4 years, average		6 0	per acre.
2nd ,,	,,	8 0	,,
3rd ,,	,,	10 0	,,
4th ,,	,,	12 0	,,
5th ,,	,,	14 0	,,

'Thus, should the tenant quit at the end of the first terms of his lease, he will only have paid the lowest rents during the period of making his major outlay.

'In illustration of the second point—compensation for durable improvements—I subjoin a copy of a Memorandum which I have found highly satisfactory to the tenants on the property of which I have the care as resident agent.

Memorandum

In order to encourage the tenant to cultivate the farm in the highest possible manner, the said   hereby engages on behalf of himself and his representatives, owners of the farm let to the said   , ON CONDITION of the foregoing covenants having been fulfilled and kept by the said   , his executors or administrators, that when the said   , his executors or administrators, shall quit the said farm, either at the expiration of the lease for   years under which he holds it, or at the expiration of   years, as by the said lease provided, and not otherwise, the said   or the incoming tenant will allow to the said   or his executors, administrators or assigns, for such improvements made on the said farm, subsequent to the date of this memorandum, and within the stated period before quitting, as are contained in the following list, and are marked and enumerated with the figures
        ; that is to say, so much of the amount of such expense as

shall be in the given proportion, in each case, to such a number of years as the said   , his executors, administrators and assigns, shall fall short in the occupancy of the said farm, after incurring such expense; IT BEING EXPRESSLY STIPULATED THAT THE TENANT IS TO GIVE AN ACCOUNT EACH YEAR of such outlay as he proposes to make in DURABLE improvements, in order to obtain the owner's sanction in writing to the proposed expense, SUCH SANCTION BEING NECESSARY IN ORDER TO CLAIM OR BE ENTITLED TO ANY ALLOWANCE from him; and shall also render an account of such disbursements within each year,—such account to be examined and signed by the landlord, or his accredited agent, and to serve as a voucher for the sums so to be recovered by the said tenant; and that non-payment of rent (if the same shall have been demanded, and afterwards remain unpaid for the space of six months) or non-fulfilment of covenants shall FORFEIT any claim or right to such allowance for improvements.

The proportion of the proposed conditional allowances to be regulated as follows:

1st.   If the tenant drains the land at his own expense, with the consent and subject to the inspection of the landlord or his agent, an allowance to be made for the materials and workmanship, for (*eight to fourteen years as the case may be*) years, so that the allowance shall yearly diminish in equal proportions, and be cancelled by   years' enjoyment of the improvement.

2nd.   For lime used on the land, with like sanction; the allowance to extend in like manner for FOUR years.

3rd.   For bones used on the land, with like sanction; the allowance to extend in like manner for THREE years.

For other manures, as the case may be.

4th.   For subsoiling peat-lands, with like sanction; the allowance to extend in like manner for FOUR years.

5th.   For making and planting new fences, with like sanction, the same being left in a good and growing state; the allowance to extend in like manner for FOURTEEN years.

6th.   For making water-meadows, with like sanction, the same being left in a good and tenantable state; the allowance to extend in like manner for (*four to eight years as the case may be*) years.

7th.   For buildings erected on the land, with like sanction, the same being left in a thorough repair; the allowance to extend in like manner for TWENTY years.

And the said   and hereby mutually agree that if any dispute shall arise between the said   , their executors and administrators, upon the said   quitting the said farm, or upon the state of cultivation or condition thereof, such dispute shall be settled by two referees, one named by each party, or their umpire; and in case one party refuse to nominate a referee within ten days after notice has been given in writing by the other party, the referee of the other party alone may make a final decision.

If two referees are appointed, they are to nominate an umpire before proceeding to business, and the decision of such referees or umpire, as the case may be, shall be final.

WITNESS the hands of the parties.

'The landlord should reserve, at least on strata deficient in lime (as one of his conditions), that no land shall be broken up from its original or natural state without being properly and sufficiently limed, that is, with at least $2\frac{1}{2}$ to 3 tons of lime per acre, upon which the landlord will stipulate to pay his proportion, according to the annexed memorandum.

'In the event of the tenant commencing upon a small yet eligible site for additions, as had been previously named under the head of "Buildings", it should be agreed that only a certain amount of money should be spent in buildings each year, that is, just so fast as they are required for use, instead of erecting a *mass* of buildings in the outset, many of which must remain unoccupied until the farm shall have so far advanced as to require them.

'The enclosure fences to be erected by the landlord should all be properly specified in the agreement and upon the plan of the farm, leaving all subsequent divisional fences to be agreed upon as the work proceeds; as so much depends upon the turn things may take for and against the farm. In the carrying out of these subsequent agreements there need not be the least difficulty, provided that both parties meet on the footing of having a mutual interest in the progress of improvement as fast as their respective capitals can be laid out with a prospect of reasonable returns; and that the consideration of these two distinct interests is regulated by mutual confidence and goodwill. *In no instance* should a new fence be erected until the land is required for cultivation, as it would be absurd to enclose rough lands (or a whole farm) before they are actually wanted for improvement. The cost of fencing is a high charge upon "open lands"; but with an increasing population, and consequent increased consumption of food, we have a good guarantee before us that our increased produce will find a ready and remunerating market; so that the investment to be made by the landlord, coupled with that of the tenant, may fairly be classed amongst the safe calculations of the day, and a proper return of interest for his outlay may be expected. In saying this I must, however, add, that the outlay should be judiciously adapted to local circumstances, and that too much should not be expected at first, as the value of the "fee simple" of the estate will be steadily increasing (as shown by the scale of rents), if a tenant is well and efficiently encouraged, and may ultimately warrant even a more extended outlay in permanent improvements for the further development and beauty of an estate. There is no safer investment than well-directed capital in permanent improvements; and far better would it be to improve a property already in hand than to extend the acreage by purchase of additional lands.'[3]

With the farms delineated and conditions of tenure settled, Robert Smith proceeded to make them known, and the following advertisement appeared in *The Lincolnshire Chronicle* and in other papers circulating in the East Midlands:

Farms to Let upon Improved Principles

Mr. Robert Smith begs to inform the Public that he has two Farms to Let upon the Forest of Exmoor, the property of F. W. Knight Esq., M.P., one consisting of 740 acres, the other of 1000 acres.

Also several smaller Farms, the property of other noblemen [*sic*], varying in size from 100 to 600 acres.

Emmett's Grange, South Molton,
14 August 1849.

And again a year later:

Farms to Let on Exmoor

Several more farms of various sizes are now ready for occupation, some of which are partly cultivated, have excellent model buildings upon them, and will be let upon liberal terms to enterprising tenants.

The tendency of these new soils to the growth of roots, etc., is remarkable, hence especially adapted to Sheep and Stock Farming. The property is extra-parochial.

Every particular as regards Rent, Lease, Tenant-right, character and capabilities of the soil, etc., may be had on application to Mr. Robert Smith, Emmett's Grange, South Molton, Devon.

16 August 1850.

Five farms were quickly re-let from Lady Day 1849—Horsen, with 763 acres, to Robert Searson, Robert Smith's brother-in-law, who was farming also at Market Deeping in Lincolnshire, and who ran the Exmoor farm through a bailiff; Larkbarrow, with 600 acres, to James Meadows, who came from Leicestershire; Wintershead, to 'a prepossessing young man (Chambers) from Derbyshire—he takes down his newly married wife with him'; a new holding at Pinkery to Groves; Tom's Hill to Stribling. Warren was let the following year with 540 acres to George Allen Harold, but by then the tenants at Wintershead and Tom's Hill had flown, and soon after the unfortunate Groves shot himself.

In 1850 John Knight had died, and Frederic Knight had become owner as well as manager of the Forest. As a result of the advertising campaign the leasing of land went on, and by Lady Day 1852 Simonsbath House had been let for the first time, with 584 acres, to Charles Le Blanc, of Epsom. Also on this date new tenants took over five other farms—Driver (vacated by Hedditch), let to John Allen with 450 acres; Duredon, with 540 acres, let to John Bullas; Simonsbath Barton (which Edward Godwin had left in 1850), let with 400 acres to Charles Popple; Wintershead, with an allotment on the South Forest (still known as Spooner's allotment), in all 1,200 acres, to Gerard Spooner, a Scotsman; the Inn at Red Deer with 124 acres (vacated six months before by a tenant from Castle Cary, Joseph Biggin), to John Mills. Tom's Hill had been briefly re-let in 1851, but was now in hand once more.

During the years 1851–2 Robert Smith drew £69 11s 6d for 'entertaining gentlemen seeing farms', and his success in letting holdings seems to have outstripped the estate's capacity to put them in good order. William Howchin, writing to Frederic Knight in May 1852 (mainly about the letting of summer grazing for which he was responsible) added: 'I think the best tennant is at Duredon. He is a hard working, industrious man and *hauling Lime* on his farm well, that is what I like to see going on—but he is dissatisfied with not having his Gates put up as Mr. Smith promised to have done and his premises put in order, and unless it was done as he could wish and without delay, he told me last night that he should soon prepare to leave, as he could not put in crops and have stock running all over it would not answer.' The work, however, must have been carried out soon after, for Bullas remained at Duredon for nine years.

By this time the policy decided upon ten years before, when, apart from the old Simonsbath Farm, only Cornham and Honeymead farms were made, had resulted in the formation of eleven new holdings, which together with these three extended to over 9,000 acres and produced, when fully let, a gross revenue of some £3,500. This achievement had not been without serious setbacks for the estate and often ruin for the tenants. The Rev Thornton recorded that 'the lowness of the rents per acre had attracted broken-down farmers from afar' and many of the early tenants, with little capital, did not realise until too late the cost of the improvements they had contracted to undertake, and the rigours of farming at that altitude. Some of the farms had changed hands two or even three times and only Honeymead and Cornham retained their original tenants.

To Gerard Spooner, although he remained at Wintershead only for six years, belongs the credit of having introduced a system of farming on the Forest which was one day to be its most permanent and important feature. His farm was 'occupied as a Scotch sheep farm, with flocks of Cheviots and black-faced sheep. It is well known that the Cheviots thrive best where the grass is green; the blackfaced will do where there is little but heather. This tenant, who has Scotch shepherds and Scotch collies, is endeavouring to introduce the Scotch system of selling off his lambs every year in the autumn. The total ignorance of the surrounding people of the existence of any sheep except their own native breeds is a great obstacle to this plan; but if he succeed, it will be a capital thing for the country.' Frederic Knight was, naturally, much interested. At this time he estimated that he had some 6,000 acres of open land unoccupied. 'If Mr. Spooner's plans answer'—he noted, on some calculations he was making, in 1852, as to the potential income from the Forest—'this will soon be let.' Once more his expectations were disappointed, but though a failure at this date, the plan was tried again some twenty years later with every success, and it continues in operation to this day. The shepherd brought down with the sheep was John Scott, and he became a stockman or herd to Frederic Knight when Spooner gave up.

To an experienced farmer, such as Robert Smith was, the impossibility of growing wheat and barley on Exmoor was quickly apparent, (if Hannam is to be believed, he gained this experience the hard way, following the failure of his crops at Emmett's Grange), and he realised that the development of farming there depended on intensifying its long-established capacity to carry stock. Thus, root-growing and rotation grasses became the main objectives, though it is a tradition that the tenant at Larkbarrow grew wheat during his brief occupation of the farm. Oats were only grown to be chaffed as winter feed for horses and cattle. As to the utilisation of the crops, sheep and cattle raising and feeding were practised, but several of these early tenants attempted dairy-farming for cheese-making, and their cheese-presses remained for many years in some of the farmhouses. A reference by Mr Acland (as he then was) to the 'excellent Stilton cheese' of one of the tenants is quoted on the next page, and Lewis Knight wrote, in January 1850, 'I have got a cheese, a Stilton, made on the Forest, which Frederic thinks will be rich and good.' These were the produce of Larkbarrow. 'All the farms on Exmoor are store-farms, with some dairies. The cattle most in favour, and deservedly, are the Devons, which can be fed to great advantage on the moor in summer, and on the reclaimed land in winter.'

There is no doubt that the Forest at this time must have presented a very attractive appearance to the eye of the land-improver. All down the valleys were signs of activity; inclosures were being fenced, buildings were going up, plantations were being made, bullock and horse teams were breaking the Forest soil. It was just now that the work was visited by Sir Thomas Acland (as he became later), and that which he saw impressed him very much. 'Good hedges are rising and the farmhouses are being surrounded with plantations, which will give them an air of comfort and respectability. Once furnished with "succour", the natural capabilities of the Forest may be turned to account. These are a soil and climate favourable for the growth of grass and of root crops; for the breeding and rearing of stock; natural springs and convenient slopes for water-meadows; ample streams for water-power, and lime close at hand.

'Since Mr. Smith's agency commenced he has let 4,000 acres to highly respectable tenants, in addition to land previously occupied. It is a real pleasure to witness the success of manly and enterprising farmers on new ground. Mr. Hannam [of Cornham], from the neighbourhood of Wincanton, has a herd of yearlings, crossed between Devon and Hereford, in as beautiful condition as any one would wish to see; and makes very good cheese, like Cheddar. Excellent Stilton cheese is made on the north side of the Moor [at Larkbarrow] by Mr. Meadows, from Leicestershire. But one of the most remarkable sights on the moor in November last [1849] was a field of 60 acres of purple-topped turnips, which, after a tour through Lincolnshire and Norfolk, I thought were the finest I had seen within the year. They were on Horsen farm, rented by Mr. Searson, who is still in occupation of a large farm near Market Deeping, in Lincolnshire, and wishes to have two strings to his bow in these times; and if corn fail him, to fall back on roots and stock. 700 sheep, a cross between Exmoor and Southdown, were folded on these turnips, and made the hill look like Lincoln Heath. On the pastures outside was a breeding flock of Exmoor ewes with a Leicester ram, intended to drop their lambs as late as April. The turnips were grown on newly-broken ground dressed with lime.'[4]

Altogether the estate incurred an expenditure of £16,800 on buildings, roads, and fences during the period under consideration, apart from the money laid out by the tenants themselves for which the landlord had a contingent liability under the terms of their leases. The estate office work, under Robert Smith, was of the highest order. Nothing was undertaken without the preparation of estimates of cost, both of labour and materials, in the fullest detail, including an analysis of the latter to show 'materials in stock' and 'materials required'. The clerk, John Southwood, was paid £150 per annum and a house, but after his death, in 1852, there seems to have been no new appointment. Most of the building had been finished by that date.

Full details sufficient for the compilation of a statement of the total cost of the building equipment of the Forest farms are not now available. On many holdings the steading was not built all at one time, and it is evident from the accounts preserved that considerable alterations were made from time to time, for the convenience of successive tenants. Some idea of the expenditure may be got from accounts of the cost of the buildings at Warren, Horsen

and Larkbarrow, which amounted to £331, £434 and £267 respectively. But it is possible now to make some computation of
the cost and of the financial result of land reclamation, at this
date, on Exmoor. John Knight had paid £5 an acre for the land,
and taking the case of the 300 acre farm already given as an
example of building costs, and allowing for an allotment of about
300 acres of unimproved grazing to accompany the improved
land, the total cost of the farm would be as follows:

	£
Purchase of 600 acres at the average price paid for the King's Allotment, viz. £5 per acre . . .	3,000
Erection of House and Buildings at £2 per acre . .	600
Subsoiling, liming and cultivating 300 acres at £4 5s. .	1,500
Fencing—say 400 chains at £1 10s.	600
Making road, say	80
Total cost of Farm	5,780

To give a return of 5 per cent on the cost, a rent of £290 would
be required. Now the unimproved grazing on the Forest was
estimated to be worth 4s per acre, in fact it realised this, through
agisted stock; so deducting £60 as representing the annual value
of the 300 acres of allotment, then £230, or some 15s per acre,
would be needed as a fair return on the cost of the improved
portion of the farm. Nor does this take account of the general
estate expenditure apportionable amongst the various holdings—
public roads, plantations and shelter-belts, boundary-fences, etc—
both their construction and maintenance.

On the whole, the rents secured under Frederic Knight's leases
to his first tenants approximated sufficiently closely to a fair return
on the capital legitimately accountable—that is to say, omitting
amenity and luxury expenditure and the cost of some of the more
fantastic experiments. Had the rents reserved proved themselves
to be payable, the finance of Exmoor reclamation would have
made a fair showing, but events were quickly to prove that in
expecting returns from the land of this order, the capacity of the
Forest had been overestimated.

(See pp 295–9 for notes)

V

1851–61 CHEQUERED EXPERIENCES

John Knight's death brought about but few changes in the administration of the Forest. As noted already, his house was let, together with a large block of farming land, and the hunter breeding stud was sold by auction, realising £945 15s 10d. Frederic Knight took up his residence at Lynton, and, for the rest, the policy of development and farming at second hand was continued. The number of the farm holdings created was completed by the equipment of Pinkery; the pony stud was maintained at about 400, though the efforts at improvement by out-crosses were given up, and only pony sires were used; large numbers of cattle were taken in from the surrounding country for the summer grazing on the undeveloped lands, and a revenue of some £1,000 per annum was derived from this source alone.

Although the income from the Forest had now reached a considerable figure, the expenses of maintenance absorbed the

Receipts.	£	s.	d.	Payments.	£	s.	d.
Rents . . .	1,812	17	7	Buildings and Repairs . .	1,791	6	1
Keep of Cattle and Ponies . .	962	5	2	Establishment .	572	2	3
Bark . . .	85	0	0	Taxes . . .	420	5	10
Dairy Produce .	24	14	10	Farms in hand .	420	1	3
Grass and Hay .	20	10	0	Fences . .	367	12	4
Corn (from Goat Hill) . .	11	8	6	Nursery . .	172	0	4
Sundries . .	24	15	2	Deer and Game .	99	3	4
				Challacombe Lime Rock . .	11	5	0
	2,941	11	3	Simonsbath School	6	4	8
Excess of Payments over Receipts	933	12	0	Petty Cash . .	15	2	2
	3,875	3	3		3,875	3	3

whole of it, as the summary shows on facing page; the period covered is from 16 January 1850—the date of John Knight's death —to 25 March 1851.

This summary takes no account of an item of £745 6s od paid to Frederic Knight, of which no particulars are furnished, but which seems to have been in respect of services and expenses in connection with the executorship.

In April 1850, Charles Knight had written: 'There is about £1,400 to be laid out in buildings this summer in the Forest, after which the expenses entirely cease, with the exception of Smith's salary, the taxes, Harriet to take care of the House, a carter with two horses, and two labourers. So that the Forest will begin to pay from next October.' Events were shortly to prove, however, the truth of 'the old saying that land is capital without interest'— which he himself quoted in another letter before the year was out.

The Knight family were clearly disappointed with the financial position of the estate, which contributed to the difficulty of Frederic Knight and his co-executor in the payment of the legacies under John Knight's will, and a Chancery suit, which led to the appointment of a receiver, was the result.[1] There is nothing to show that this step had any effect on the work on Exmoor, and arrangements were made, by 1862, by which the parties were satisfied and the receiver discharged.

Things were still going badly with the tenants of the new farms. 'If the prices of live-stock and dairy produce had kept to the scale of preceding years, on which these men had made their calculations, some of them would probably have succeeded. But the groundless state of panic and consequent fall in the price of corn, meat and live-stock, which took place after the passing of Sir Robert Peel's Free Trade measures, cleared Exmoor of most of the strangers who had first settled down under Mr Frederic Knight's low rents and liberal leases.'

In 1851 the tenant of Larkbarrow, who made the Stilton cheese which Mr Acland praised, had failed, and a distress had been taken for his arrears of rent (this farm has never been re-let); the same year the tenant of Crooked Post also became insolvent, and the farm was taken in hand until 1854, when Robert Sharpe took 275 acres of it only to abscond after twelve months, when it had to be let in allotments. In 1853 a new tenant, William Minett, had to be found for Driver, and George Avery Gould succeeded Popple at Barton the following year. Horsen changed hands in 1857 and Warren came in hand for eighteen months until let to Richard and Thomas Crick in 1859. (George Harrold had apparently under-leased Warren farm to a Mr Wood in 1855: see Hannam.) An achievement was the re-letting of Tom's Hill, with 207 acres, 'only 115 fenced', for twenty years from 25 March 1857 at a rent of 6s per acre, rising by increments of 1s after each four years, to 10s, but the tenants, William and Ford Dixon, left before the rent reached 8s. In 1858 Simonsbath House and farm, Cornham, and once more Horsen, changed hands, while Driver came in hand again and a tenant was not found for a year, at which time Wintershead had to be re-let.

Pinkery was let again in 1859, as a holding of 250 acres, at a rent of £62 10s, to Richard Ridd. As he covenanted to pay 6¾ per cent on the sum of £400 to be expended by the landlord on house and buildings, it may be surmised that the farm was not fully equipped during its previous letting. In 1860 Simonsbath House and farm was vacated once more; Duredon changed hands in 1861; Honeymead was given up that year by Henry Matthews, who had farmed it since 1842, and it was split into three holdings by cutting off Picked Stones, with 385 acres, and Winstitchen, with 407 acres.

William Howchin, who was factotum both to John and Frederic Knight, throws a side-light on the condition of farming on Exmoor about this time, in a letter written to his master in April 1852, which reveals the hand-to-mouth system of some of the new tenants. 'I am sorry to find that nearly *all* your Tenants are red-hot for taking in cattle to summer on their Farms, being told by some individuals here that it will pay better than anything and their money is certain. Consequently, last Saturday handbills came out by hundreds to keep cattle. Mr. Popple [Barton], Mr. Allen [Driver], Mr. Harrold [Warren], and others get what they can by the sly. All this may be very well as far as it go, but the light I see it in, if carried to extent, is this, your land will not get improved but very little, as they will not go to the expense to break it and *Lime it*, and by not doing so they will not pay themselves nor you.

'I do not know the provisions of your Leases as to breaking and

Limeing, but I have been told that one of the new Tenants has been sowing oats without Lime. . . .

'I find that Mr. Smith is not much interested in the stock *you* take in, no further than he is obliged to be in his capacity. The Advertisement he put in the paper, and by which I had my bills printed, I found out was half of it wrong, that is, the dates I was to be at different Fairs and Markets. I went to Barum [Barnstaple] and saw the Editor of the paper. I have made it all right now and got my bills correct, but it has put you to an extra expense of 18s. I have three great Markets to attend this week. I hope to have good luck against my *Radical Opposition*.

'I went to look at the Gallon House Farm [Red Deer] to see what grass there were. I found the gates all open last Thursday and in the different fields were 137 sheep . . . I walked away very vexed. I told Mr. Smith what I had seen, who told me he expected to let the Farm [which he did]; if he cannot let it there had better be a Boy daily with a Dog, and to keep fast the gates. . . .

'Mr. Meadows sale [the tenant of Larkbarrow] is tomorrow.'²

The up-country farmers who had responded to Robert Smith's advertisements could not stand the strain involved in reclaiming these Forest holdings. It may be that they were inexperienced in the work involved, or it may be true, as has been reported, that they were men of insufficient financial resources who were attracted to Exmoor by Frederic Knight's liberal leases and low rents, without realising that these were arranged in contemplation of the expenditure entailed upon the tenant. Anyhow, several of them did not see their first rotation through, and few of them survived a second. 'They came in their po'chaises and went in their dung-carts.' Thus the native farmers of the locality summarised the experience of their migrant neighbours.

During the ten years 1852–62, the rents accruing amounted approximately to £49,000. Of this sum, about £6,300 was allowed to the tenants for making fences, breaking and liming land, draining, damage by deer, losses of livestock in the severe winter of 1852–3, and, in the case of the Gallon House Inn, for 'loss of custom'. These allowances reduced the amount payable to the landlord to £42,700, of which only £31,500 was actually received, so that the arrears of rent, all of which had to be remitted, amounted to no less than

£11,000—or nearly 25 per cent of the sums secured under the contracts of tenancy. Either the capacity of the Forest for improvement had been assessed too high, or these early tenants were lacking in the ability to handle so difficult a proposition.

Certainly Robert Smith was successful, and he has left a full account of his experience. 'The first ground selected for culture was naturally near the house and yard, that some few small fields may be quickly broken up for roots and subsequent crops for the yet small but varied stock of the farm. Paring and burning the surface of the soil is the first step (in the right direction) towards improvement; then followed the usual ploughings, harrowings, dressings, etc., for a root-crop, which is invariably a good one. The ashes resulting from the burning of the thick coating of indigenous plants are found to be powerful agents for the production of roots, but little good is really effected without the aid of lime to mix with the fibrous earth, beyond the growth of a turnip of inferior size. By way of testing these matters I determined to try certain experiments with varying quantities of lime, which was the more important to me as I had decided that the amount of money to be expended in the purchase of artificials should be laid out in lime, the *great essential* for newly broken-up land.

'The turnips have usually been drilled fourteen inches on the flat, with a few loads of ashes per acre (collected in the same field), and the crops have fully realized my expectations. In the earliest stage of cultivation and progress, some portion of the turnip land has to be sown with oats for the use of the yard; this should be done in the month of March, and upon land that was first cleared of its roots, the later eatage of roots being upon those lands that are intended to be sown down with artificial grasses, without a corn crop.

Experiments upon One Acre of Land

On Natural Soil, without Ashes or Lime.	With Native Ashes alone.	Native Ashes and 1 ton of Lime.	Native Ashes and 2 tons of Lime.
Came up weakly and died away again.	Produced 6¾ tons of turnips.	Produced 12½ tons of turnips.	Produced 18 tons of turnips.

Page 103 (above) Emmett's Grange; (below) Cornham

Page 104 Driver 1929: (*above*) an Exmoor kitchen;
(*below*) cheese presses

Native Ashes and 2½ tons of Lime.	Native Ashes and 3 tons of Lime.	Native Ashes and 3½ tons of Lime.
Produced 20½ tons of turnips.	Produced 22½ tons of turnips.	Produced 23 tons of turnips.

Time of Sowing, June 1.

'When the farm is sufficiently advanced, I much prefer the following course of cropping:

'*First year.* To pare and burn the natural herbage for a root crop, and apply 2½ tons of lime per acre, mixed in with a moderately thin furrow of soil, say 2½ inches; this will produce 20 tons of turnips per acre at a cost of £4 10s. 0d.—say £5—per acre.

'*Second year.* My present plan is to seed out all lands after a turnip crop with proper artificial grasses, omitting the corn crop at this stage of culture, and until the new fibrous soil shall have its frolic and become more fixed and consolidated for the growth of corn. When the grass-seeds are sown, it is both desirable and profitable to add half a dressing more lime (1½ ton), for their enjoyment and that of the farm stock when depasturing them; still, it is an extra outlay of capital that must be considered with reference to other expenses when so many other works are waiting to be performed, and these alike with tenants' capital.

'Thus, after the turnips are consumed (chiefly upon the land), the land is carefully ploughed, cleaned, and sown with artificial grasses and rape-seed, commencing the first week in April. These young grasses will be ready to stock by the end of June, and, if allowed to get well established, they will usually fatten full ten sheep per acre, and if care be taken to clear them occasionally, so that they sweeten and recover themselves, they will prove of infinite value up to Christmas. If they remain clear from the end of September for the ewes and lambs, which is a still better plan, they give a help over the inclemency of the months of March and April, after which they become first-rate pastures for the fattening of any class of stock, and maintain their comparative goodness for several years.

'This plan of farming in an elevated country goes very far to conquer the climate and to enable the farmer to maintain a large

G

and healthy flock of sheep; in fact, it may be said to form the *keystone* to the whole structure—without it, the building is in danger. If any practical man will take into account the newness of the soil, coupled with the preceding management, according to which *no corn crop* will have been taken out of the land, I leave it to him to judge what comparative return may be fairly expected from stock in after years in a hill country remote from corn-markets, but where all animals can readily be fattened and *walk* to market, with the produce of the farm upon their carcasses.

'The grasses to be sown should be those which have the quali-fications for quick and abundant growth. During the last few years I have sown the following quantities and qualities, at an average cost of:

	Per Acre.	
	s.	d.
2 pecks of Pacey rye-grass, at 6s. per bushel	4	6
1 peck of Italian rye-grass, at 6s. 6d. per bushel	1	7½
4 lb. of Timothy grass, at 6s. per stone	1	9
2 lb. of cow-grass, at 9s. 6d. per stone	1	4
4 lb. of white clover, at 10s. per stone	2	10
3 lb. of rib-grass, at 6s. per stone		5
Small quantity of parsley-seed		8½
	13	2

'While I believe it is admitted that corn is liable to be lodged and spoiled upon new land when sown after the first root crop, it is equally worthy of note that *no land* can well be too rich for the growth of succulent grasses. However luxuriant these may be, they can at all times be overtaken by good management, and kept in good and respectable order; and, as time goes on, these pasture lands may be safely and profitably cropped with corn, especially oats, and afterwards renewed again by roots, &c. These pastures remain good about four years, and then require to be broken up for oats, thus completing a seven years' course of cropping. Then follows the usual rotation again, viz:

	Acres.
1st year, roots—say	30
2nd year, rape and grass seeds	30
3rd, 4th, 5th, and 6th years—pasture	120
7th year—corn	30
	210'

In brief, roots and rape-pastures for the feeding of stock, grown with liberal dressings of lime, comprised his scheme of reclamation, and little has been discovered by way of improvement upon it.

Robert Smith was an expert in the construction and management of water-meadows, and the hillsides of Exmoor gave him full scope. 'The red deer are certain to bow their antlered heads before Mr. Robert Smith and his water-sluices', wrote the 'Druid' on the occasion of a visit to Exmoor in 1860, but it is the latter rather than the former which have given place. There was nothing, probably, in the work here to differentiate it from the practice in other districts, so that it need not be particularised, but, as an example of his thoroughness, some tests made by Robert Smith to find out if the effects of irrigation were due in any way to the temperature of springs may be quoted. He remarked that several springs were known by the old men as 'warm-springs' and were said to be hot in winter and cold in summer. 'This assertion, together with the striking effects produced by certain springs, first led me to an inquiry as to their prevailing merits, and hence I determined upon testing their temperature, as also the rivers Barle and Exe, at the foot of the hills upon whose summit the springs in question are situated.

		25 *June* 1854.	4 *Sept.* 1854.	19 *Dec.* 1855.
Temperature of	Picked Stones Spring, at point of issue . . .	$47\frac{3}{4}°$	$49°$	$47\frac{3}{4}°$
,,	,, Picked Stones Spring, at point of junction with River Barle, 110 yds. below	$45°$	$57°$	$38°$
,,	,, River Barle at same point .	$42°$	$65°$	—
,,	,, Spring above River Exe, at point of issue . . .	$46°$	$46\frac{3}{4}°$	$46°$
,,	,, Spring above River Exe, at point of junction with the river, 254 yds. below .	$40\frac{1}{4}°$	$61\frac{1}{4}°$	—
,,	,, River Exe at same point .	$40°$	$64°$	—
,,	,, Stagnant bog-water .	$39\frac{1}{2}°$	—	$33°$
,,	,, Air	$40°$	$65°$	$30°$

'The average temperature of the Exmoor springs may be written at 46° to 46½°; and such is the importance of warmth that before testing a spring an experienced hand will decide upon the degree of heat by the verdure or quality of the grasses springing at their edge and onward course to the brook. Nothing can exceed the effects produced below the Picked Stones Spring; and the growth of the succeeding grasses, from stage to stage, clearly demonstrate the cooling of the stream as it becomes assimilated to the air.'

Robert Smith points out that irrigation serves two purposes. Water from springs at temperatures above that of the soil-water stimulates an early growth of grass, before nature has started the herbage into life; storage water applied in the summer and autumn promotes a later growth of grass, when plant life is still active and requires only moisture to keep it productive.

While this ringing of the changes amongst his farm tenants was going on, Frederic Knight was making what use he could of the unreclaimed hill-land for summer grazing. The pony stud had been brought up to some 400 head, and until the plan of annual sales at Simonsbath gave place, owing to inaccessibility, to the practice of sending the annual draft to Bampton Fair, it was disposed of in the field where now stands the church. 'Squires and clergymen, horse-dealers and farmers, from Northamptonshire and Lincolnshire, as well as South Devon and the immediate neighbourhood' attended these sales. In spite of the trouble taken to improve the stud by the introduction of well-bred pony sires, the prices realised were poor in the main, and the returns from this branch of Exmoor farming were unremunerative. The letting of the best land drove the ponies more and more on to the hills, where the conditions of life in winter were too rigorous for any but those mainly pure Exmoor bred. Three cattle and pony herds were employed.

As to summer grazing with cattle, the hills would keep one full-sized beast to 3 acres from 1 May to 1 October. Any number of them was forthcoming from the neighbouring corn lands and dairy districts, the farmers of the latter placing out their yearling heifers, and those of the former their steers and in-calf heifers. Other farmers again, from places more remote, would consign

their better animals to these men who were sending their rougher
cattle up to the Forest, paying them a rate for 'best keep' about
double that which they, in their turn, were charged by Frederic
Knight. There was thus a double movement of cattle northwards,
during summer, from mid-Devon towards Exmoor.

The rates charged for depasturing upon the Forest during the
grazing season were as follows:

		£	s.	d.
Cattle:	Three years old and upwards . . .	1	0	0
	Two years old, and under three years . .		15	0
	Yearlings, and under two years . . .		12	0
Sheep:	Any age, including young lambs and shepherding		2	3
Horses:	Any age	1	5	0
	Ponies for the summer		15	0
	Ponies for twelve months	1	5	0

This business was very profitable, and this explains the resentment
of William Howchin at the competition he encountered from the
tenants of the new farms. But Robert Smith has recorded that
there was no difficulty in getting a sufficiency of stock,[3] and
Albert Pell, who visited Simonsbath about this time to attend one
of the pony sales, noted that 'on the moor itself, cattle were taken
in to joist, and the sums realized seemed to have been steadily
rising. Beginning at £400 a year, they had gone up to £500,
£1,000, and at last to £1,400. Ewes bought at 16s. produced lambs
which went off at 27s.'

Notwithstanding the scheme for the colonisation of Exmoor by
letting off land, intensive farming by the landlord continued, and
Frederic Knight has left full notes of his system of sheep-farming
which entitles him to be regarded as the pioneer of the method
known, in more recent times, as 'continuous cropping'. Writing
about the year 1851, his instructions were—'Plough 4 inches at
the end of September, press if possible, and sow winter vetches,
manured with guano, in two equal parts at a week's interval, in
the last week of September and the first week of October; a little
rye with the vetches of the first sowing. The first half to be fed off
about 1st April, and when the sheep are removed to the second
sown vetches, the land to be ploughed for swedes; when the sheep
are removed from the second sown vetches to the young grass,

the land to be prepared for yellow turnips. While the sheep are eating vetches, rape and seeds to be sown in two equal parts at 14 days' interval, commencing first week in April, upon land that was in yellow turnips, ploughed not more than 2 in. or 2½ in. deep. The rape will be fit to stock about the middle of July, and the most forward sheep come to it off the grass. The sheep to be sold fat off the rape, and lambs bought in. Begin to eat yellow turnips in October; then swedes till April.' In other words, Frederic Knight's practice at this time was to buy lambs in the autumn, and to fold them on yellow turnips till Christmas, and then on swedes till the end of March, when they started on the vetches. From these they went on to the young grass (last year's rape and grass) and next, about July, on to the new rape pastures, upon which they were finished. To what extent this time-table was possible in practice does not appear. Modern experience has proved that the vagaries of the seasons tend to defeat such accuracy in planning.

Steps were taken at this time to abolish the fallow deer, kept in the Deer Park, between Blue Gate and Prayway Head. In spite of the loss of fawns by stealing, of which John Knight complained, the deer had done well on Exmoor; but it was impossible to confine them, and as the cultivation extended so the damage done by them increased. All through this period, entries in the estate cash account of payments for 'deer damage' are common, and the allowances made to tenants recorded in the rental include considerable sums, deducted from rents due, in respect of the same. On the Forest the tenants of Warren and Horsen farms seem to have suffered most, but the fallow deer did not confine their attention to Frederic Knight's estate, for they wandered farther afield and caused much annoyance to neighbouring farmers by 'slithering' the ears of their corn crops and by other forms of damage. So their destruction was resolved upon, and none have survived. There were some good heads of Exmoor fallow deer at Wolverley, each with the bullet hole in the centre of the forehead.

As regards the indigenous wild red deer, their numbers had fallen to a very low figure on Exmoor at this time, and they were in danger of becoming extinct. It was a bad period in the history of stag hunting; from 1837 to 1855 there was a constant succession of masters—varied by short spells when the country was not hunted at all—and poachers and deer-stealers took a heavy toll. The Knight family were staunch supporters of the hounds; John Knight figures in a list of subscribers to the old pack, sold in 1825, and Frederic Knight had hunted with it when a boy. 'Miss Turner writes that the Duchess of Bedford saw 70 head of Red Deer one day at Brendon. What a fine sight! Can it be true?'—inquired Charles Knight, writing from Leghorn, in 1844, to his brother Frederic. Probably not; anyhow it was only nine years later that Samuel Sidney, staying at Simonsbath, saw 'a great red stag', with four hinds and a calf, and remarked that 'these were one of the few herds still remaining on the Forest. In a short time the wild deer of Exmoor will be a matter of tradition. The efforts made, at great cost, by Mr. Knight for the preservation of the deer, do not seem to have been supported or appreciated by the gentlemen of the district.

'We had hoped to have a day's wild stag hunting, but the Hunt Committee had had the incredible barbarity to catch a wild deer, put him in a cart, and carry him to the other side of the country.'

The Rev W. H. Thornton has recorded that, in 1848, the estimate of the number on all the Exmoor Commons was thirty head, with thirty more round Haddon, and a few on the Quantocks. Fortunately for the preservation of the largest and most beautiful of English indigenous wild creatures, stag hunting was on the eve of a new era in its history, and instead of becoming extinct as Samuel Sidney foretold, the red deer are more numerous today, probably, than at any period within the past century. But nothing other than regular hunting has preserved them from the fate which has overtaken them everywhere else in England.

It was during this period that most of the plantations were formed. The need for them was a subject for comment by Sir Thomas Acland, in 1850, and Samuel Sidney, writing a few years later, notes the presence, here and there, of young plantations 'but no trees of sufficient magnitude to deserve the name of a wood'. These, and the rapid extension of inclosures, with their high walls surmounted by beech hedges, soon added to the shelter of which the district was so much in need. Altogether, about 100 acres were planted up in various places.

The years 1851–61 mark the most active and important period in the story of Exmoor reclamation. Practically all the farms were made and occupied during this time; tenants came, and unfortunately went; the system of farming which was ultimately to succeed began to be evolved. The search for iron ore began; as will appear presently, mines were opened and the Forest had its first and only experience of industrialism, but, as with the farmers—though much less regrettably—the force of the invasion was soon spent. The growth of population due to all these activities led to the formation of the civil and ecclesiastical Parish of Exmoor out of the extraparochial district comprised in the ancient Royal Forest, to the erection of the present church of St Luke and the parsonage, in 1856, and to the nomination of the first perpetual curate. A school had already been built by Frederic Knight, and, with the appointment of overseers of the poor and the first assessment of the parishioners to poor-rate, Exmoor experienced, for the first time, all the advantages, both spiritual and temporal, of rural parochial society.

The work that devolved upon Frederic Knight during this time must have been immense. He was a Member of Parliament all the time, and for part of it Secretary to the Poor Law Board; he conducted lengthy and difficult negotiations with the South Wales ironmasters who became his mineral lessees, and the lawsuits in which, subsequently, he became involved with them must have caused him much trouble and anxiety; he was a director of a large life insurance company whose affairs became seriously involved. Over all, for the first ten years of the period under review, he was answerable for all his administration of the Forest to a receiver, appointed by the Court of Chancery, in connection with the family action which was entered over his executorship of his father's will, and he was liable to be called to account for everything that he did. Physical and mental vigour of an exceptional order would be needed in anyone to stand such a strain, and Frederic Knight was well endowed with both. He lived at Lynton while Simonsbath House was let, first to Charles Le Blanc, and then to the Rev J. Torr, who was curate to the first incumbent, the Rev W. H. Thornton. In addition to his clerical duties, Mr Torr farmed 128 acres of land included with his tenancy, but when he vacated, in 1860, Frederic Knight made the old house his Exmoor headquarters once more, and it was never let again in his lifetime.

In 1861 Robert Smith left the Exmoor agency. He had spent thirteen years in the post, going there when farming on the Forest, as implying tillage, was in practice only at Cornham, Simonsbath Barton, and Honeymead, and remaining to participate in the evolution of all the other holdings, the erection of the greater part of the village of Simonsbath, the mining adventure, and the creation of the civil and ecclesiastical parish of Exmoor.

The manner of his going is curious, for, as Hannam recorded, with obvious pleasure, 'Smith was turned out of the Stewardship at Lady Day 1861'. The week before, the *North Devon Journal* had reported his resignation with a glowing account of the improvements he had made on Exmoor, but this brought forth a sharp rejoinder.

Exmoor

Sir,—I observe an article in your last paper professing to give an account of my Exmoor property. The account contains many inaccuracies.

Among other things it states that Mr. Robert Smith has resigned my agency. I beg to assure you that, on the contrary, I felt it necessary to dismiss him from the agency.

If I did not trace the hand that penned your article, I should not have felt it necessary to make these remarks.

Your Obedient Servant,
F. W. KNIGHT

Simonsbath, March 25, 1861.

Robert Smith replied from Emmett's Grange on 2 April, disclaiming all knowledge of the article, which the editor confirmed. He then stated, 'As regards the agency: I stated to the Receiver in Chancery that I would rather resign the office than be held responsible for the changes of management. This led to some recrimination, and the issue was—my dismissal from an unthankful office.' Whether this was, in fact, the true reason will probably never be known. If Hannam's account of Robert Smith's finances is to be believed, these might have contributed to his dismissal, though he still continued as tenant of Emmett's Grange.

To compensate for the loss of the agency he set up in general practice—

Mr. Robert Smith . . . who has for many years had the management of nearly 20,000 acres in the North of Devon, having opened
his Office for General Surveying and Land Agency Business,
desires to make it known that he has arranged with the [Land Loan
and Enfranchisement Company] to represent them in this and the
adjoining Counties.

Emmett's Grange   South Molton
May 8th 1861

It is uncertain how successful this venture was, for though he
was advising the Dowlais Company on their South Wales farm
later that year, he is listed in an 1866 directory only as 'farmer', at
which time he was still at Emmett's Grange, which he did not
give up until Lady Day 1868. He then moved to Chew Magna,
near Bristol, where he announced himself as a 'Land and Com^n
Agent Late of Emmett's Grange'. That year Robert Smith also
left the Council of the Royal Agricultural Society, though his
membership did not terminate until 1875.

(See pp 295–9 for notes)

VI

1862-79 RAPE RECLAMATION AND SHEEP RANCHING

In the later years of Robert Smith's stewardship the system of husbandry appropriate to the district was becoming clearer. He had been an advocate of stock farming as the only objective possible at this elevation, and the real question was how to produce keep for sheep and cattle all the year round within the economic limit. His own practice was by the growth of turnips, followed by rape-pastures left down so long as they would endure; and he had witnessed the coming and going of other farmers who had sought in vain to establish the methods of other districts. These up-country tenants had been replaced, one by one, by men from the neighbourhood, some of whom had come to see the possibilities of farming on Exmoor at Frederic Knight's low rents, whilst others were men who had spent their lives on the Forest and had accumulated some capital in it. By 1866 the rent roll included names which were to appear for generations: Carter, Elworthy, Fry, Hayes, Kingdon, Richards, Steer and Thorne. Thus after two earlier tenants had failed, Crooked Post farm had been let by 1861 to William Carter, who had begun as an ox-boy on Honeymead, and later became a postillion in John Knight's stables at Simonsbath. He reclaimed much of the peat land at Crooked Post and became a noteworthy breeder of Devon cattle. His son, Henry, 'a most desirable tenant', bought the farm some sixty years later and was, in turn, succeeded by his son, William. William Hayes had been one of the cattle herds but by 1864 was renting 400 acres on Sparcombe (still known as Hayes allotment). He had Coombe Farm at Exford, and about 1870 took Warren also, which his son (also William) took over on his death in 1877.[1]

Francis Coomer, after working as a day-labourer for Frederic Knight, had saved money as a lime burner, before taking Picked Stones about 1860, and when he retired 'with a good competency' in 1874, was followed, as tenant, by William Fry, who had come to Exmoor twenty-five years before, to work in the nursery.

Frederic Knight later recorded, in a letter written to William Little in 1880, his own experience of the social advancement of the agricultural workers of the estate, and in the adjacent parishes:

'I know of no part of England in which so large a number of agricultural labourers have risen from the actual plough tail to the position of farmers and masters in the same County in which they worked as men, as in the north of Devon and the adjoining district of Somersetshire. I take from my own rent roll the names of Blackmore, Carter, Comer (2), Elworthy, Fry (2), Hayes, Steer, Crowcombe, Locke, Pile (2), Ball, Richards, etc. . . . I find that I have 16 tenants paying me respectively the rents of 27£, 100£, 180£, 40£, 50£, 111£, 110£, 100£, 13£, 59£, 60£, 200£, 95£, 80£, 26£, 17£. These 16 men paying me together the annual sum of 1,270£, were all of them within my recollection agricultural labourers, excepting two whose fathers rose from the ranks equally within my remembrance; and these rents are without any arrears and paid regularly to the last shilling. Several of these men who began life with little or no education, and with nothing but their heads and their hands to help them, occupy land to a considerable amount in adjoining parishes and under other landlords. There is no parish in the country that does not contain such self-made farmers—the country is full of them. . . .

'In my belief, there has been no part of the United Kingdom in which, during the last 50 years, the agricultural labourer has had a better opportunity of emerging from the ranks into a higher position, nor in which he has availed himself of it to a greater degree than in the north of Devon, and the closely connected parishes of West Somerset.'

There was never any period during which all, or even the majority, of the farms were in hand, as is so often asserted; tenants were always forthcoming for the more attractive holdings, and the gross rental at the end of Robert Smith's time was about £3,600 per annum. By the early 1860s, steady tenants were occu-

pying not only Crooked Post and Picked Stones, already referred
to, but also Driver, Emmett's Grange, Honeymead, Horsen, Red
Deer, Simonsbath Barton and Warren, all of which were to remain
continuously tenanted throughout Frederic Knight's lifetime.
Nevertheless, several farms had come back to the landlord, and
were apparently unlettable at the beginning of the period now to
be considered—Larkbarrow, Tom's Hill and Winstitchin, whilst
before long, Duredon, Pinkery, Cornham and Titchcombe, and,
later, Wintershead also fell vacant. In addition, there were still the
great tracts of open Forest land, extending to some 8,000 acres,
which were only utilised by the pony stud and for summer grazing
by stock at agist. The mining and the railway to Porlock, of which
so much had been hoped, had come to nothing; although the
gross return was considerable the net income from the estate was
practically nil; clearly something had to be done about it.

For a while the bailiff at Simonsbath, William Scott, apparently
acted as agent, but in 1866 Frederic Knight found a permanent
successor to Robert Smith in Frederick Loveband Smyth, the
tenant of Wistlandpound farm, in Kentisbury, under Earl Fortescue. When Challacombe Common had been inclosed, several
hundred acres of waste land, composed of peat, varying in depth
from 12–30in, and resting on the usual impervious clay-iron pan,
were added, thereby, to his farm.[2] He determined upon the cultivation of this land, and his experiment in its reclamation was
based on the substitution of rape for Robert Smith's more expensive turnip crop, with all the preliminary cultivations and after
care that it entailed. The practice Smyth developed, first at Challacombe and later on Exmoor, was to pare, burn and plough (once)
the wet peat-land, to lime at the rate of about 3 tons to an acre,
and then to sow rape-seed. The seed was sown in June, and it
produced a crop in six weeks, being the only crop that would
grow before the land was laid dry, whilst it was claimed that the
tap-roots penetrated to the pan and even pierced it. This crop was
eaten off by sheep, and the same practice, rape-sowing and sheep-
ing, was repeated during the next three or four years. By this
time, the combined effects of cultivation, liming, sheep-treading,
and penetration by tap-roots are described as having 'decomposed'
the peat right down to the pan, which was then broken up with

the subsoil plough. A sowing of rape and grass-seeds, mixed, followed, and the land was thus laid down to permanent pasture. The grasses recommended as being most suitable on this improved peat are 'Timothy grass, Yorkshire fog and Cock's foot, with rye-grass and perennial clovers'.

Rape-pastures were no new thing; the system of sowing rape-with grass-seeds had been practised with success by Robert Smith, and had been known in the district for many years. But the idea of reclaiming moorland by successive crops of rape, eaten down by sheep, was entirely that of Frederick Smyth. Many commons partly composed of peat-lands had been inclosed in North Devon and West Somerset during the first fifty years of the past century, and although much of the dry brown-peats had been broken up and cultivated, every attempt to reclaim the black-peat lands had failed to produce the immediate return needed to justify the farmer in this task, and most of them remained in their natural state until Smyth's introduction of these lime-grown rape crops. 'Nothing on these hills', wrote Samuel Sidney, who visited Exmoor ten years after Smyth had taken over the agency, 'feeds sheep so surely and so rapidly as this rape crop. Sheep turned on it have been known to increase in value from 3*s*. to 4*s*. a week, and on an average may be calculated to gain 2*s*. in that time.'

It must be remembered that in the earlier part of last century the principal object of the farmers of Exmoor and the surrounding country was the production of wool, and mutton was only a secondary consideration. This is not extraordinary, seeing that there were no markets other than the local ones, which might on any day be glutted by an extra consignment of fat sheep. So ewes and wethers alike were often kept on the commons until they died of old age, and it was the interest of every farmer to winter as many as possible, however thin they grew, so long as they remained alive to be turned on to the hills in spring, and give him another clip. The rape-reclamation came into practice at a time when the increasing demand for meat for the supply of distant markets, together with the improvements in transport, were encouraging the hill-farmers to think more of mutton, and it assisted to bring about something of a revolution in their methods of flock management.

Frederic Knight resolved upon the replacement of the pony stud by sheep. 'The attempts which he had made with great perseverance and more than ordinary knowledge of the principles and practice of breeding, to improve the size and quality by using stallions of a superior character, did not pay. So long as the ponies were treated as wild animals, finding their living on the open moor, helped with a little forest hay in the rare snowstorms, they cost next to nothing; but so soon as they were improved in breed it was found necessary to feed them well in winter on hay and roots, grown on reclaimed land, and even with corn, if they were to grow into animals of any value. If crops had to be grown for feed, it would evidently pay better to feed flocks, whose ewes would give a fleece and a lamb every year.'

Frederic Knight experimented, at first, with a flock of some 500 Exmoors on Winstitchin, but the local breed could not be wintered on the Forest, and once more he travelled to Scotland in search of a type more suited to his purpose. After many inquiries he decided to bring down a flock of Mountain Blackfaces, and to give another trial to the Cheviots—a breed with which his father had experimented some thirty years before; and, as related already, he had seen flocks of both kinds on Exmoor more recently, when one of his first tenants stocked a large allotment on the Forest with them, and brought down Scottish shepherds, with their dogs, to herd them. All the unlet portions of the Forest were to be stocked with these sheep, and again Scottish shepherds were to be engaged to tend them. The North Devon men of this day made indifferent hill-shepherds, possessing but little of the practical science which distinguished the Scottish hill flock-masters; and so shepherds from the Highlands and the Border—Davidsons, Johnsons, Grahams, McDougals, Littles, Murrays and Gourdies—found their way to Exmoor with the sheep amongst which they and their forebears had been raised.

The black-faced sheep were placed on Hoar Oak, and then Winstitchin, Duredon, the South Forest, Larkbarrow, and later, as they came in hand, Cornham (1873), Pinkery (1873) and Wintershead (1885), were stocked with Cheviots—each as a separate herding in charge of its own shepherd. These men were accommodated either in such of the farmhouses as were empty, or in cottages convenient to their work. Each was allowed a cow, and grazing ground, and they settled down, with their wives and families, under conditions not dissimilar from those of their native land. Most of the sheep came by boat to Lynmouth, but the last large purchase of Cheviot ewes, which arrived on the Forest in 1871, was trucked by rail as far as Williton, and then driven over the 30 miles of road to Simonsbath.[3]

Thus began the third and last experiment in Exmoor reclamation, the conversion of the Forest grass into permanent pasture for ranch-farming with hill-breeds of sheep.

Altogether, some 5,000 Blackface and Cheviot ewes were brought down to Exmoor. The permanent flock consisted entirely of ewes, and the practice was to keep them until five years old, when they were fatted, with their lambs, for the butcher. In the last year, the lambs were got by a Shropshire Down or a Leicester ram; for the rest of the flocks only pure-bred Cheviot rams were used, a number being purchased in Scotland every third year. The Blackfaces survived for a long time on Hoar Oak herding, but by degrees they were superseded everywhere by the Cheviots.

The Scottish sheep were much more hardy than the native breeds and found a living on the Forest in all weathers, except in snow-storms, which are rare in comparison with the North of England. Mowing and hay-making machines were introduced on to Exmoor now, for the first time, and proved of the greatest value in a district where the supply of grass is almost unlimited, where labour was scarce, and where the days on which hay-making is possible are few and uncertain. With the use of this machinery a large quantity of the natural Forest grass was turned into hay good enough to keep these mountain sheep in hard winters. All the grass not cut was burned periodically.

Frederic Knight's object, like that of his former tenant, Gerard Spooner, before him, was to get his annual draft, both ewes and lambs, fat for the butcher or as near to that condition as possible, on the rape and grass. The rape came into use by midsummer if sown early in May, but it was liable to be taken by fly when grown so early, and Frederick Smyth preferred sowings made from June to August. Ewes and lambs fattened on it without roots, corn, or cake, and went off to market, alive or dead, between August and

Page *121*   Warren: (*above*) the homestead; (*below*) an Exmoor fence at Dry Hill

WINTERSHEAD FARM NEAR SIMONSBATH.

VOWLES

Page 122   Wintershead: (above) house; (below) yard and buildings

November. By the latter month the whole of the draft was expected to be sold, as the rape could not be relied upon after that
date if the weather turned frosty. Frederic Knight experimented
at this time with thousand-headed kale, which was then just becoming known, with the object of filling the gap from November
onwards with another cheaply grown crop, but apparently without much success.

Some of the lambs were purchased on the spot, by butchers and
dealers who came to Simonsbath for that purpose. The rest were
driven to South Molton, where they were killed and dressed, and
the carcasses forwarded to the Metropolitan Meat Market hung in
meat-vans provided by the Great Western Railway. It is said that
the meat was in special demand by reason of its superior flavour.

Turning, now, to the fresh start in the reclamation of the Forest
by rape cultivation which marked the advent of Frederick Smyth,
the first work was carried out in 1868, on Duredon, where 140
acres were cultivated and sown. The crop was fed, and rape was
then sown again with grass seeds, which were fed for four years,
and then mown for three more, yielding in the seventh year 2 tons
per acre of excellent hay after a dressing of $1\frac{1}{2}$cwt of nitrate of soda
and salt. The great object of the reclamation was the production
of permanent pasture, and it was found that the rape pastures,
when established, could be maintained by occasional dressings of
lime. Couch-grass was unknown on Exmoor, 'and so grassy is the
soil that a well-limed fallow will find its way into good permanent
pasture without a grass-seed being sown on it'.

So far work had been confined to the dry land, and the areas
broken up and sown to permanent grass were selected so that they
could be added to existing holdings if desired. By 1874 the success
of the experiment 'had made urgent the necessity for breaking-up
and subsoiling extensive tracts of the wet peatland, for conversion
into permanent pasture.

'Already a great break had been made in North Devon agricultural customs by the introduction on the hills of such advanced
implements as iron wheeled ploughs, mowing machines, and hay-
making machines. The time seemed to have arrived for trying if
steam could not do quickly, effectively, and economically, what
ox-teams had done slowly and expensively in 1824.' Thus wrote

H

Samuel Sidney, who visited Exmoor in 1853, 1875, 1876 and 1877 as Frederic Knight's guest, to study his work. The account of the last phase of land reclamation on the Forest, the harnessing of steam-power, to the task, is best given in his own words:

Having decided on trying steam, Mr. Knight had the difficult task of selecting from the various rival makers and systems the best machinery for his purpose. He found that Fowler's double-engine set had the advantage of going at once to work without any preliminary fixing of machinery, as well as the immense power of a straight and single action, so necessary in carrying out the Duke of Sutherland's bold determination to manufacture arable land out of deep peats accumulated during centuries over the rough debris of perished forests. But in order to use double engines, nearly parallel roads or tracks, along which the engines can travel, are necessary, and such did not exist on Exmoor. To make such roads would have been very costly; and as Mr. Knight's object was to cultivate for permanent and improved pasture, and not to establish tracts of arable land, they would become useless in a few years when the final object of the reclamation had been achieved. On the other hand, the number of men required for working all the old round-about systems rendered their employment too costly.

So stood the matters until, at the Taunton Show of the Royal Agricultural Society in 1875, Messrs. Barford and Perkins exhibited a new system, invented by Mr. F. Savage, C.E., of King's Lynn.

After careful inspection of the ground to be ploughed, Mr. Barford undertook to construct a 10-horse engine and set of tackle to work Messrs. Fowler's Sutherland or Marshland plough on Exmoor. The trial took place, to Mr. Knight's complete satisfaction, in 1876. The principle of reducing the speed to meet an extra heavy strain makes this 10-horse engine master of all the power needed—and by passing the large subsoil-hook along the bottom of an empty furrow, instead of ploughing and subsoiling at one operation, the whole tackle is relieved from a strain that might be detrimental to it. In some wet places this hook has succeeded in grubbing the subsoil nearly three feet below the original surface.

The ploughs, both the marshland and four-furrow plough, used by Mr. Knight, were made by Messrs. Fowler of Leeds, and so good are they, that no stone has yet been met with in the process of steam-cultivation on Exmoor that has seriously damaged either of them.

Mr. Savage's system does away with the heavy detached drums which form an essential part of all the old single engine sets, and he has arranged the road driving-wheels so that they can be used, when ploughing, as most efficient winding-drums, the ropes working in boxes sunk in the wheels, and the end of the engine being blocked up as a platform while at work. By this arrangement the entire machine is simplified, the boiler is spared the strain it is subjected to when the winding-drum is attached to it, and the large driving-wheels do all the work, whether on the road or in the field. The road-wheels can be driven either together or one at a time, or one forward and the other backward, so that the engine can actually be turned by steam on the ground on which it stands. But the invention that makes this engine more particularly suited to Exmoor is, that it has a very low speed-gear attached to it, by which it can be lifted in a very few minutes out of any hole or bog into which it may have sunk. The ploughing-tackle is worked by Campain's anchors, moved by chains and balls, on Mr. Savage's latest plan. If, then, water can be led along a plough-track to the foot of the engine, which can frequently be done on Exmoor, the engine and rope take only one man to work it. The Campain's anchors are pushed forward by the balls at the discretion of the ploughman; and although a spare man usually attends the plough, to carry the signal flag, to manage the rope-porters where needed, or to turn a stone out of the way, the set can be worked under favourable circumstances for half-a-day with two men only—one with the engine and the other with the implement. The men who now work the apparatus successfully were agricultural labourers when Mr. Barford came to Exmoor. Compared with the six or seven hands usually employed with the old roundabout sets, the advantage is immense. The engine works with a very small quantity of coal.

Passing over the details of what might make a very interesting agricultural tale under the title of 'Adventures of a Steam-Cultivator on its Journey through Devonshire Lanes and over Somersetshire Moors', it will be enough to state that, in the autumn of 1877, the engine working a Sutherland plough by a roundabout apparatus, was in steady work in exterminating some 400 acres of natural forest grass growing on a skin of primeval peat, nearly all moist, and in some parts with the water standing for an acre or more ankle deep.

This Sutherland plough consisted of two huge shares, that is, one at each end of the implement, and also at either end a subsoiler in the form of a fluke of an anchor without palms, the whole resting on four barrel-like wooden rollers, which acted as wheels as well as rollers. The engine having been by signal set to work, the plough was slowly dragged forward between two automatic anchors, cutting a huge slice of peat, and making a furrow 12 inches deep and nearly 2 feet wide; the sod, as it was turned over by the plough, being rolled flat by the barrel wheels. When a double journey had been performed forwards and backwards, the machine was stopped, and one of the hooks let down; and this, in nine cases out of ten, reached, penetrated, and broke up the before-described *pan*, and, with one effort, thoroughly dried, and for ever, the peat which had already been destroyed by being torn from its roots.

The result was equally wonderful and capital. When the subsoiler was set in motion the water stood in pools several inches deep. The moment the iron had penetrated the pan the water passed away as through a cullender, and it remained perfectly dry after rain for some part of every day of the week. The work was done at the rate of nearly three acres a day, for it is one of the peculiarities of Exmoor that 'rain does not stop ploughing'.

In the opinion of one of the most experienced land-agents in North Devon, the one operation just described doubles the value of the land.

The next steps would be to cross it with a plough or cultivator, then to break it up roughly with a strong harrow, to lime it at the rate of 2½ to 3 tons an acre of lime drawn by Mr. Knight from the kilns at Combmartin or Lynmouth, with his own horses,[4] and finally to sow a crop of rape to be fed-off with sheep. After two or three crops of rape, paid for in fat lambs, the land will be ready to lay down for permanent pasture, requiring no further expense for drainage and no manure beyond lime, which is essential, because the natural soil, being almost devoid of the calcareous element, will not grow the most nutritious grasses until limed.

As to the proportionate extent of deep peat on the last reclaimed tract, Titchcombe—an enclosure of 400 acres broken up by steam power—there were about 50 acres which could only be broken up and drained by the Sutherland plough and hook. Six or seven acres are so deep that they will require tile or stone drains. About 150 acres have been cultivated and the land laid dry by a four-furrow plough, connected by a chain in hauling the last furrow with a light subsoiler, formerly worked by four horses. The rest of Titchcombe could have been broken up by horse or ox labour; but the steam-engine being at work, it saved time to use it.

The following is as nearly as possible the actual cost of ploughing and subsoiling 19 acres of the above-mentioned land on the west side of Titchcombe; this being part of 400 acres that were effectually reclaimed up to Christmas, 1876:

Cost

	£	s.	d.
2 Men, 20 days at 3s. 2d. each per day . . .	6	6	8
1 Youth, 20 days at 1s. 8d. per day . . .	1	13	4
2 Boys, 20 days at 1s. each per day . . .	2	0	0
8½ tons of coal at 20s.	8	10	0
4 gallons of best oil at 5s.	1	0	0
2 gallons of common oil at 3s. 3d.		7	8
Interest and Depreciation on tackle, 14 days at 15s. per day	10	10	0
Interest and Depreciation on tackle, 6 days, when worked for a few hours only each day at 5s. .	1	10	0
Total .	31	17	8[5]

The Sutherland plough, as briefly described above, was manufactured by Messrs John Fowler and Sons, Leeds, to participate in
the great scheme of land reclamation carried through, in Shinness,
in the seventies of last century, by the Duke of Sutherland. It
superseded the multiple furrow plough, which had proved quite
unsuited to the conditions. Charles Gay Roberts recorded the
following description of its use in 1879:

> The first step in adapting the steam-plough to work in a peat
> bog was the substitution of a single monster turn-furrow for the
> four or five usually carried. To prevent the implement burying
> itself in soft ground, the frame was next supported on very broad
> wheels or rollers. It was then found to work fairly where there
> were no obstructions, but whenever the share struck against a
> landfast rock or root it was liable to receive some serious injury.
> To meet this, the revolving coulter was invented by Mr. Wright,
> the Duke's secretary. It consists of a vertical disc of steel placed in
> front of the sock, and cutting the soil, as it revolves, to a depth of
> about two inches below the point of the sock. When this revolving
> coulter meets with a landfast stone, or with a root too large for it
> to cut through, it revolves over it, thus lifting the plough clearly
> over the obstruction. The cutting disc has proved to be better
> adapted for cutting through the tough mat of grass and heath
> roots often found on the surface than any fixed coulter of the
> ordinary form.
>
> The next improvement was suggested by the Duke. It consists
> of a huge iron hook, like the fluke of an anchor, trailing behind the
> plough, and pivoted on the back of the iron frame-work of the
> implement. This contrivance, commonly called 'the Duke's tooth-
> pick', acts as a subsoiler, stirring the soil to a depth, varying with
> its hardness, of from 8 to 18 inches. Every obstruction that the
> revolving coulter has been unable to cut through or to force aside
> is next attacked at a lower depth by the toothpick. In most cases
> the root or stone is at once turned over and brought to the surface;
> but as this cannot always be done, the hook is made of sufficient
> strength to withstand the full power of the engine. There is a dead
> pull for a minute, then the engines are reversed, the implement is
> backed, and a second attack is made. If this also fails, the toothpick
> is lifted over the obstacle, and a stake is driven in, to mark the spot
> till the offender can be blown up by dynamite. At first the stirrer
> was made to terminate in a steel point; in 1877 a small short
> turn-furrow was attached; and this was replaced in 1878 by a turn-
> furrow of an ordinary shape but of extraordinary size.
>
> The accompanying figure is drawn from a photograph showing
> the whole of the implement, standing upon a hard surface, but with
> its parts arranged for travelling towards the left. AA is an iron
> frame, about 10 feet long and 18 inches wide, carried upon six

rollers. The ploughman sits upon the seat B, facing his work, and steers by means of the handle at C. The head of the plough, D, is hung from the centre of the frame and is double-ended, having a lateral cutting-share of a triangular form, so as to cut either way. To the centre of his head the mould-board E is hinged; it is self-acting and turns either way to suit the direction of the plough. Of the six rollers, two [not visible] are for the land-side, two, G G, press on the top of the furrow, while the two, H H, in the centre, in connection with the revolving coulters, form the steerage. The revolving coulters, I I, are seen projecting beyond the middle rollers, which they bisect. They are flat iron discs, about 3 feet in diameter, rotating upon the same axes as these rollers, but can be made more or less eccentric with regard to them, so that they may be set to penetrate from 4 to 15 inches deep. The two land-side

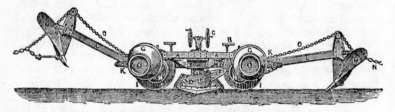

The Sutherland Plough

rollers give balance to the implement, and assist in carrying it through gullies or other inequalities of the surface. The two furrow-wheels assist in completing the turning of the furrow after it leaves the mould-board, and press it into its position; they also assist in balancing and guiding the implement. At each end of the frame, which is a strongly trussed structure of malleable iron, the lateral pieces are united together by a transverse iron bar, K, which passes through, and serves as a pivot for the end of the shaft, L, of the trailing subsoil plough, M. This second plough is kept down to its work by the tension of the tail rope, N, acting on the loop line of wire-rope, O, which passes over the plough and connects the tail of the pulling ropes. It will be seen that the pull for drawing the implement is taken through the plough beam; and when it is required to be reversed, the engine pulls the one plough out of work, while it presses the other, by means of the looped line, into its place for working. The effect of having the plough hung in the centre, K, and kept in its work by means of the pressure of the tail rope, is to give an elasticity to the working of the implement, and to allow it to override obstructions that cannot be pulled out. . . .

Gradually the sheep evicted the ponies which were reduced from 400 to about 40 brood mares, whose produce were sold annually as foals instead of being kept till three or four years old, and by 1879 the summer and winter pastures in hand, with the additional rape crops, were being consumed by some 9,000 ewes and lambs. Steam cultivation and subsoiling had broken up and reclaimed several hundred acres on Duredon, Titchcombe, Prayway and Ashcombe, and were rapidly preparing further wild land for crops which would have enabled the breeding flocks to be increased by at least one-half. 'These substantial improvements have not been executed without the "master's eye". For many years, Mr. F. W. Knight has spent the greater part of the Parliamentary recess on Exmoor, superintending the details of his pastoral and agricultural innovations in person.'

His agent during this period, Frederick Loveband Smyth, died in 1887. For several years prior to this date, he had been assisted in his work on Exmoor and elsewhere by his son, George Cobley Smyth, who later added the name of Richards, and he succeeded his father at this time.

(See pp 295–9 for notes)

VII

1880–97 CARRYING ON

Probably farming on the Forest in the period just closed had reached a high water mark not to be surpassed until World War II. Except for the farms already enumerated (page 117), all the agricultural holdings were let to native farmers who knew the district and its capabilities; there were tenants, also, in the cottage holdings at Simonsbath, and several of the large inclosures, such as Long Holcombe and Sparcombe, were let to men from neighbouring parishes, for the value to them of the summer grazing. The untenanted farms and the open lands upon the North and South Forests were employed in a profitable system of sheep-farming in the owner's hands. Further reclamation of these unimproved lands by steam cultivation was going forward. Exmoor had shared, at last, in the general prosperity of agriculture during two decades and more.

When John Knight bought the King's Allotment, in 1818, and other lands adjoining it, the gross income of the whole of the Royal Forest was about £350, and there were five people resident on it. Sixty years of reclamation and improvement had turned three-quarters of this wilderness—the 16,000 acres representing his acquisitions—into an estate with a gross rental of some £4,500 per annum (of which £2,500 was from lands let), which was providing both a living and a life for nearly three hundred souls.

When Earl Fortescue had spoken disparagingly about the Forest, in the House of Lords, Frederic Knight was able to write to him (from Wolverley on 7 August 1881), that:

The gross income, which when R. Smith was there only once reached £6,000, has been raised in the last 5 or 6 years from 9 to 11,000 £. I thought I was doing fairly well and am grieved to find that my *best* neighbour has published a contrary opinion.

This may have been a little optimistic for the actual known receipts from all sources (comparable to those for 1850–1 quoted on page 98) were £2,746 in 1848 rising to £4,017 in 1852 and reaching £6,099 in 1861 when Robert Smith left. Thereafter receipts grew to £6,934 in 1869 and to £8,492 in 1878, and though they may have improved still further by 1881, as it will be seen later, Frederic Knight had a good reason for wishing to impress his neighbour.

From this point onwards a general slowing down has to be recorded. In 1879 Frederic Knight had lost his only son, at the age of twenty-seven, and the blow was a very severe one. The rape-reclamation and the Scottish sheep had proved a success, and his object was to extend the system to its limits, so as to build up a property which he could hand on to his son as a profitable estate. The story current that he stopped the steam ploughs on the day of his son's death and never worked them again, is not literally true; on Honeymead Allotment and on Titchcombe further work was done, and the last land to be broken was about 60 acres on Parson's Allotment. Then, however, the steam tackle was laid up, and though it is said that, shortly before his death, he was having the plant overhauled with a view to bringing it into use again, no further cultivation was done. The Forest had settled down to a state more or less stabilised as regards its agriculture.

As regards the farms let, the same generalisation can be made. The years now passing under review were bad times for English farmers. Wheat, which in the years 1876–8 was selling at an average price of 49s 9d per quarter, made only an average of 24s 1d per quarter for the years 1893–5; mutton of first quality dropped in the same period from 6s 11d to 5s 9d per stone (or 20 per cent in first and second qualities and 30 per cent in inferior), whilst wool showed a decline of upwards of 50 per cent, taking average figures for the country. Exmoor farmers were not affected by the drop in corn prices, and in common with the stock-farmers of other districts they were better able to face the general decline in agricultural values than the arable farmers; moreover, they were 'family farmers' as a class, with little or no labour to pay, and if a fall in prices meant a tightening of the belt for them, they were able to escape the financial disaster which overtook so many of the

more highly developed farming enterprises of the valley country.
Evidence is on record in confirmation of this. It was in the year
1879 that the serious state of the British farming industry led to
the issue of a Royal Commission on Agriculture

> to inquire into the depressed condition of the Agricultural interest,
> and the causes to which it is owing; whether those causes are of a
> permanent character, and how far they have been created or can be
> remedied by legislation.

This Commission, known generally as the 'Richmond Commission' from the fact that the Duke of Richmond and Gordon
presided over it, presented its final Report in 1882, and appended
to it are the reports drawn up, county by county, of the various
assistant commissioners appointed to survey the country. Somerset was included in the district allotted to Mr William C. Little.

He spent some time as Frederic Knight's guest, at Simonsbath,
in 1880, and he has left a valuable record of the state of agriculture
on the Forest at this date.

> In the extreme West of this Hill country, and running over the
> boundary of the County into Devon, lies the Exmoor estate of
> 20,000 acres, formerly a Royal Forest; but within the present
> century purchased by J. Knight, Esq., and by him and his son
> F. Winn Knight, Esq., M.P., the present owner, inclosed and
> partially cultivated. If the bright hopes which were once cherished
> as to this estate have not been altogether fulfilled, so great an
> improvement has been accomplished, and so much still in progress,
> that I cannot pass over without notice the work that has been
> going on there.
> A considerable portion of what was once a rough moor main-
> taining a number of Exmoor ponies and Sheep has been cultivated.
> Farmhouses, Buildings, and Cottages have been erected, water-
> meadows have been laid out in suitable spots, and on the better
> soils the natural pasture has been replaced by a sward of greatly
> superior character.
> For some years, I believe, the late proprietor was convinced
> that the four-course system of farming, which he had seen so
> successfully practised elsewhere, might be made to succeed even
> on Exmoor, and too much attention was paid to the growth of
> Corn; the soil, climate, and elevation, however, renders the greater
> part of the estate quite unsuitable for the growth of grain. Of late
> years a different course has been pursued, and the main object kept
> in view has been to replace the natural growth of rough grass,
> bilberries, etc. by good pasture. Excluding occupations of less

than 20 acres each, there are at the present time in the hands of
tenants about 40 farms, ranging in size from 20 to more than 1,000
acres, the great majority of them being between 200 and 500 acres
each. About 10,000 acres are in the hands of the proprietor. In the
autumn of 1880 I had an opportunity of inspecting the Moor in the
company of Mr Knight, who entertained me most hospitably at
his cottage at Simonsbath.

As I have said previously the great object now pursued is to
make Pasture. On the hills there are two classes of soil, a yellow
loam of decomposed slate and a black peat. The former in an
uncultivated state is the sounder land, but the latter is found to be
most capable of improvement, and after good treatment the most
valuable land. The peat in its natural state retains the water on its
surface; but, as a rule, it has been found that if the retentive pan
which forms the subsoil is broken the water rapidly disappears,
finding its way into the slate rock. To break up this soil a steam
plough is employed, and at the time of my visit one of Savage's
engines, which coils the rope around the periphery of the travelling
wheels, was working a plough on the roundabout system, some
1,300 feet above the level of the sea.

In some places it has been found necessary to cut open surface
grips; but these are very quickly and cheaply made at a cost of
10s. 6d. per 25 chains. Where the moor is very thick the pan cannot
be broken by an ordinary plough, and here a Sutherland plough
has been used, and enormous furrows of 21 to 24 inches depth
have been turned over. A few main drains cut across these furrows
carry off the water, the peat rots and dries up, and the land is
brought into cultivation. The usual system of management after
breaking up the moor is to apply 100 bushels of lime to the acre,
and to sow the land for three years in succession with rape, which
is eaten off by sheep. By the time these crops have been grown and
consumed the turf has been well rotted, and grass seeds are sown.
I saw a good deal of land which had been treated thus, and raised
in letting value from 5s. an acre to 25s. or more, even in these
times.

Upon the home farm Mr Knight keeps a flock of 4,000 Cheviot
ewes, greatly preferring them to the horned sheep of the neighbourhood. These Sheep lie out on the moor all winter and lamb
there. About 4,000 lambs are raised. The younger ewes are put to
Cheviot tups, but the off-going ewes are crossed with a Shropshire
Down, and the lambs from these are fattened off, slaughtered at
South Molton station, and sent direct to the Metropolitan meat
market. The Cheviot wether lambs are sold in the autumn. Some
had been sold on the day before I was there (18 Oct.), and had
made 33s. each. They are not much in favour in the neighbourhood; but they are chiefly sent into Worcestershire, where they
have an established reputation. Mr Knight told me that his sales of
wool and mutton would in 1879–80 give him 20s. for every head
of Sheep he wintered.

Though water frequently stands on the moor, and there are many boggy spots not a single case of Sheep rot has been known, and the livers of great numbers slaughtered at South Molton have been carefully examined, and not a trace of 'fluke' has been discovered.

A number of Irish heifers are purchased and grazed, and Exmoor ponies are bred and sold as suckers at Bampton fair in the autumn.

I visited several of the tenants on this estate. I found that they grew more Corn than Mr Knight does, indeed some of them persist in attempting to grow enough Wheat for their own household consumption, there being evidently a strong feeling among the smaller men against *buying* anything. One of the larger farmers with 700 acres had about half the land under cultivation. His system is to break up about 40 acres of dry ground every year, and to sow it with Turnips after applying 100 bushels of lime and 4 cwt of bone superphosphate; after Turnips a crop of Oats is taken, and Rape follows with seeds sown among it. The farmyard manure is chiefly employed upon the permanent pasture. A herd of 13 Devon Cows is kept on this farm; the calves are reared and the steers are sold at 2 or 2½ years old.

I was informed that, though it was so evidently the wisest course to make grass and improve it, there were many tenants who, if they had their own way, would immediately break up all the best pasture for the sake of getting a single Corn crop.

The farms are let with liberal compensation for improvements of every kind. Rents range from 5s. an acre to 25s., tithe free. The water-meadows run up to 70s. an acre.

Mr Knight says, 'This is, I am quite sure, the most improvable part of England to make excellent and healthy breeding land for stock of all kinds.' I am told that the tenants have suffered little in these adverse times, and that the rents have been punctually paid. The low prices for stock in 1879 frightened men for a time, and the price of Wool has for some time been disheartening, but on the whole little depression is felt. Farms that were let in the spring of 1880 made somewhat less money, because so many farms in other districts were to be had; but in the autumn of 1880 there were several applications for the one farm which was about to be vacated, and it was let while I was there at the old rent.

I have given a rather full notice of this estate, not only because it is interesting as a record of agricultural progress, and progress still continued and maintained notwithstanding all discouragements, but also because it is a real relief to myself to write, and it may be the same to some to read, of a district where agricultural depression is a thing unknown.

In an Appendix to Mr Little's report are given the answers to a schedule of questions submitted to the principal landlords of the county, and it happens that particulars of Frederic Knight's moorland estate are followed immediately by those of Lord De Mauley's fertile property almost at the sea-level, at Pawlett, between Bridgwater and Highbridge.

The similarities and the contrasts in the condition of the two estates and of the tenants upon them are remarkable:

1880

Frederic Knight's Exmoor Estate.	Lord De Mauley's Pawlett Estate.
Soil: Light loam and peat. About one-tenth arable.	Soil: Heavy loam and clay. About one-eighth arable.
Cattle and sheep of various breeds bred and fattened.	Cattle and sheep of various breeds bred and fattened.
Rent from 5s. to 30s. an acre. Rents have increased of late from 10 to 25 per cent.	Rents about 42s. per acre. Rents have decreased in the last three years. From 10 to 30 per cent remissions have been made.
The present state of agriculture is good generally. On the whole, there has been an advance as compared with 15 years ago.	The present state of agriculture has retrograded the last three years.
There has been no unusual number of changes of tenancy. No bankruptcies nor distraints for rent.	There has been an unusual number of changes of tenancy of late. A great many farmers have recently become bankrupt.

Cornham had come permanently in hand in the year 1873, for the first time since it had been let in 1844, but all the rest of the tenanted holdings were carried on as such. With this, Frederic Knight's farming operations reached their maximum extent. The land he occupied was divided into eight 'herdings', as follows: Tom's Hill; Larkbarrow; Hoar Oak; Pinkery; Cornham; Duredon; Winstitchin; Wintershead. On Tom's Hill, Larkbarrow and Duredon, two shepherds each were employed, the rest had one each. The new land broken up and the old inclosures were tilled almost entirely for sheep-keep.

It was Frederic Knight's practice, at first, to grow a considerable breadth of oats on these lands, but, owing to the frequency of failures, the acreage was reduced to that which was needed for horse-keep. His final and best system of cropping was to farm for a ley: rape or turnips; rape and seeds; seeds-ley left down so long as it would stand. There was no hard-and-fast rule as to the duration of the ley, and when it had to be broken, oats were taken, and the rotation began again. But while he held that over-cultivation meant the ruin of the moor, and that without long leys 'they would plough all the soil away', the improved grass on the Forest cannot be maintained in what may be termed 'Knight order' unless broken and re-sown from time to time, though it will never revert completely to the forest grass condition. Lime was essential, and Frederic Knight used large quantities, not only on arable land but also on the grass. It is said that three carters and their teams were kept on no other task than that of bringing lime up to the Forest. The turnip acreage steadily declined as the value of the rape-crop was realised, for the aptitude of this plant for the Forest soils is remarkable. On the new ground a mere skim-ploughing of the peat, well worked *and limed*, would give fine crops for several years, and the penetrative power of the tap-roots was wonderful. On the reclaimed soils heavy dressings of lime, kainit and phosphates were used, and the rape crop came so tall and strong that 'you could catch a sheep against it'.

As regards the utilisation of the crops, the hoggs, draft ewes and lambs, the product of a Shropshire cross, were fattened on the rape. As much of the seeds-ley as possible was cut for hay, and the rest was made into huge silage stacks, the grass being compressed by the wire-rope system. The ewes were wintered on the inclosures, and a large number of the lambs were sent away into the low country, round Dunster, to be wintered. Although it is possible to farm profitably only on the Forest, the lack of land at a lower elevation for wintering young stock was a definite handicap to Frederic Knight's system.

Whilst the management of the cultivated land was directed entirely to the maintenance of the Scottish sheep, and these formed the principal object of the farming, the summer grazing of the unreclaimed tracts on the Forest by cattle was still an important feature. Stock from the lowland farms was taken in to keep, as in former periods, and Frederic Knight bought large numbers of shorthorn heifers at Bristol, and elsewhere, which were brought up to the Forest. He created a name for the quality of his down-calvers, which were disposed of at the Simonsbath autumn sale, at Bridgwater, and at other places. Some cattle were fattened in the

summer on the improved land, and in winter there was usually
sufficient hay and silage to keep a fair number in very good condition for finishing next summer. They were not often wintered
away. Frederic Knight and his father had tried many breeds before
coming back to Devons and Shorthorns, and the latter were the
final choice, as it was said that the Devons were liable to dysentery,
though, as a whole, Exmoor is extremely healthy for stock of all
kinds.

As regards the work-horses kept, Suffolk Punches were the
favourite breed. A number of these of excellent quality comprised
the stud, and a few stallions were kept.

Since the death of his son in 1879, Frederic Knight had been
considering how best to realise the assets he and his father had
created on Exmoor, and yet to ensure the continuity of the estate.
He decided to sell the reversion and, first, approached the widow
of his brother Charles, with the suggestion that she should buy it
for her son, Morley Knight, but, though she visited Exmoor,
nothing came of this. After abortive negotiations in 1881 with a
syndicate of private investors, the reversion was offered to Earl
Fortescue, and eventually an agreement was concluded on 10 April
1886, whereby the whole of the Exmoor and Brendon estates,
totalling some 21,893 acres, was sold to Earl Fortescue and his son
Viscount Ebrington for £193,060, subject to Frederic Knight's
life interest. The initial deposit was £12,000, with a further
£33,000 payable after six months, and the purchasers assumed
liability for a mortgage of £123,060 from the date of the agreement. The balance of £25,000 was not payable until one year
after the death of the widow of the second Earl (who lived
another ten years), but interest on this had to be paid from 1886.

The total purchase price originally paid for the estate, had been
just over £110,000, of which about £32,000 related to properties
in Brendon, whilst the sale price of £193,060 was subject to the
life interest, and it had been calculated that the value with possession was £246,060. The Brendon estate (much of it unimproved
common) was generally in the same condition as when bought,
and would not have so greatly increased in value. Thus, on the
Forest, effectively £200,000 at least had been obtained for that
which had cost only about £78,000.

For the typical 300 acre farm (referred to on page 97) the subsequent expenditure on improvements was not quite as great as the original cost of the land, so that, even allowing for the money expended on fruitless experiment, the sale must be reckoned a good bargain for Sir Frederic Knight (he had been made a KCB in 1886), who lived to enjoy the estate and its rents and profits for eleven years, with the added satisfaction of having convinced his 'best neighbour' of the worth of his lands.

So things continued, on a well-established routine, through the eighties and nineties of evil memory amongst agriculturists, and Exmoor farming held its own as well as any other system or district. Apart from the fact that Sir Frederic Knight had parted with the reversion to the property, and so might have felt little inducement to any further capital outlay on its development, these were not times for the intensification of farming, and the man who spent the least got the biggest return on his investment, here as everywhere else in England. Nevertheless, a certain amount of cottage building was done during this period, and minor works of improvement, but the building of the mansion which was to replace Simonsbath House which had been stopped was never renewed.

Sir Frederic Knight died on 3 May 1897. At this time he was farming about 9,000 acres, with a stock of some 9,000 ewes and lambs, fourteen farm horses, besides the cattle and few ponies. He maintained his interest in what had been the biggest task of a very busy life right up to the end, driving everywhere over the Forest in a four-wheeled dogcart when he could no longer ride. His disappointments had been many, his reverses severe, but it would be impossible to find an example, in the length and breadth of England, of courage, determination and resource greater than that which he had displayed in his effort to complete the stupendous task, conceived and started by his father, of the reclamation of Exmoor Forest.

Page 139 (*left*) The last of the Scottish shepherds. John Gourdie at Winters-head

(*right*) The second generation. James Little at Tom's Hill

Page 140 Traditional farming: (*above*) Devons at agist; (*below*) Sheep dipping at Wintershead, 1922

VIII

1898–1926 LANDLORD AND TENANT AGAIN

The sale by Sir Frederic Knight of the reversion to his Exmoor Forest estate, following the death of his son, has been recorded already. Earl Fortescue transferred his own rights to Viscount Ebrington (later fourth Earl) to whom the estate was conveyed on 12 January 1898. The Fortescue estate already included part of the Forest, allotments 257 to 268 north and south of the Challacombe road at Edgerley Stone, but this continued as part of the Challacombe estate and was not merged with the land now acquired. A valuation of Sir Frederic Knight's live and dead farming stock, cultivations, etc, made for the executors, reached the figure of £14,400. This included some 6,500 sheep (of which nearly 5,000 were ewes), 75 cattle, 30 ponies, 15 horses and 4 pigs, but it must be noted that about 1,200 of the sheep belonged to Badgworthy herding, in the parish of Brendon, which lies outside the boundary of the ancient Royal Forest, though forming part of the Knight estate and for many years run as part of the Exmoor farm.

There is no doubt that Sir Frederic Knight had retained so many of the farms in his occupation because they were necessary to his system of fatting out as many as possible of the produce of his flocks. This necessitated the growth of rape and turnips, and the periodical renewing of the pastures as already described. Only in this way could stock be got ready on Exmoor for the butcher.

Under the new ownership, much better facilities for finishing and for wintering stock were available through the proximity to the Forest of more fertile lands in Earl Fortescue's own occupation, in the more favourable climate of Castle Hill. Thus the Forest came to be used, and more profitably, as a breeding and lying-off ground for the better lands below it. So, in this phase, the policy was to let off all lands for which tenants could be found, and, except as regards the great sheep-ranching enterprise, to apply to Exmoor the traditional principles of English estate management. In succession Wintershead, the cottage adjoining Honeymead and a part of the farm (1898); Cornham, (1899); Duredon, (1901); Winstitchin, (1903); and Pinkery, (1912), were let off. Some of the herdings were given up, or curtailed, as a consequence, and Sir Frederic Knight's eight herdings with eleven shepherds were gradually reduced to seven herdings each with one shepherd, after 1912. Although sheep numbers fell from 6,500 to 5,400, the number of cattle rose from 75 to 200.

Apart from the sheep ranch, the Forest was a normal example of conventional estate management. The entries in the Estate Journal over the thirty years following the change of ownership, are a record of regular maintenance and steady improvement as opportunity offered. The road past the front of Simonsbath House was diverted to its present line for greater privacy, and the telegraph was extended from Exford—both in 1898. The hotel was improved, new cottages built and old ones reconditioned, new woodlands planted, and several of the old plantations enlarged. A sawmill was equipped, and a turbine installed, in the river to run it. In 1913 Pinkery Pond was emptied in the course of a search for a suspected suicide, 'and the herons for miles around had good sport in the mud'. It would have helped to drain the Chains if the pond had been left empty, but it was found to be dangerous for the stock on that part, so the vents were plugged again, and it was refilled.

The Forest shared the general experience of the tragedy and the comedy of the Great War. Of the former, nothing need be said here; of the latter, a hundred years' experience of arable farming at the 1,200ft level did not suffice to stay the issue of Cultivation Orders by the County Agricultural Committee, and some 80 acres were ploughed on Winstitchin and Titchcombe. Dyer's field, at Winstitchin, did not return so much as the weight of the seed sown, but it is of interest to note that tractor ploughs appeared now for the first time on the Forest, and did good work. Against this unnecessary waste of effort may be set the plantations, formed mostly by Frederic Knight, which were now valuable; and the Government felled most of the timber in Cornham Brake, Halscombe and Flexbarrow. Hoar Oak Tree, known to be over 200 years old and one of the boundary marks of the Forest, was blown down in December 1915. The following year the Brendon Estate, which had passed to the Fortescue family with the rest of Sir Frederic Knight's land in 1898, was sold to Sir Edward Mountain.

With the return of peace, agriculture was to suffer the lean years of the depression experienced by the country as a whole. The Forest was inevitably affected, but due partly to the background of the tenants, and partly to the system of farming they practised, there were no bankruptcies and no land went out of use. On the estate farm, Badgworthy had had to be given up in 1916, and with only six herdings and subsequent depressed conditions, the number of sheep fell to its lowest point, less than 4,200, in 1924. Three years later, however, Badgworthy was rented back and restocked so that sheep numbers rose to some 4,500 with a ewe flock of about 3,500 head, though rather fewer cattle were kept.

The remainder of this chapter is an account of the Forest and those who farmed it during the latter part of the 1920s, as recorded in 1929.

The social history of the tenants is interesting and peculiar, for farmers on Exmoor have become almost a hereditary class, and fully 75 per cent of them began at the bottom of the ladder, or at one generation from it. With hardly any exceptions, every farmer on Exmoor today was born on the Forest, or worked on it for many years in the landlord's employ before taking up his holding. Thus two of the shepherds (John Gourdie of Wintershead and Robert Cann of Honeymead) have left their herdings to become tenants; another man (Mr Hooper of Driver), who was carter both to Sir Frederic Knight and to Earl Fortescue, now occupies a considerable holding rented at £200 per annum; three brothers, now tenants of the present landlord (the Elworthy brothers), started life as labourers on the estate and are the sons of a man who helped to build and equip the farms they occupy. Other tenants represent the next generation, being the sons of men who started very much as those just cited have done. With one or two exceptions there has been a constant migration of tenants from the smaller farms to the larger ones. Men have made money and have retired, or have moved off the Forest to bigger or better farms; the two shepherds, mentioned above, were each of them able, after a few years, to purchase farms of their own; others move from the smaller or inferior ones into those that these men vacate; their sons, or some of the estate employees, follow these last into the occupation of the holdings they have left. Capital was naturally limited in several cases, but here the landlord has given to many a helping hand—not by lending money or stock, but by letting the house and a few acres at first, and adding field by field, as the tenant made good.

Details of one case may be given as an example, perhaps rather outstanding, of this process. A former tenant (Robert Cann of Honeymead), son of a small farmer in an adjoining parish, came to Exmoor to work as a labourer, when a young man. In 1892, some time after, he was made a shepherd in charge of a herding. In 1898, he became tenant of 132 acres, forming part of a farm in hand, at a rent of £95, living in the cottage attached to the farm. Three years later, 235 acres, mostly moorland, were added to his holding, at an additional rent of £53; and, in 1903, a further 20 acres of good land was included, for an increase of £17 per annum. In 1910, another allotment of 156 acres of Forest land was given to him, for which he paid an additional rent of £39; and so, in the course of twelve years, his holding had increased from one of 132 acres, held for a rent of £95, to one of 543 acres, for which he paid £204 per annum.

So things remained with him for the next ten years. In 1920, he agreed to an increase of 10 per cent in his rent, rejecting the landlord's offer of an arbitration in the alternative, and in the same year applied for, and obtained, the tenancy of another Exmoor farm of 250 acres, at a rent of £107, in which he settled his son (William Cann of Picked Stones). About the year 1925, he bought a farm in the valley country to the south of Exmoor, and, in 1927, he quitted the Forest to farm his own property. The farm he gave up was then re-let at a slightly higher rent.

As with the tenants so with the management of the Forest, for Mr F. G. Smyth-Richards, the present agent (he was appointed on the death of his father in 1929), represents the third generation of the family which has acted in this capacity, without intermission, since the year 1866.

The prosperity of the Forest farmers, continued over a number of years, is beyond question; there are no recorded cases of insolvency, and rarely even of difficulty. This position is the outcome of the type of farming and of the system of labour organisation. Exmoor farms are concerned, in the main, with stockraising. There are sundry sales of butter, cream and eggs in the summer, and of rabbits in the winter—in fact, these items are said to produce enough to pay for the housekeeping—but the main dependence of the farmer is on the autumn sales of store stock, both sheep and cattle, and for a long time past no branch of agriculture has been safer than this. The sheep kept are exclusively Exmoor Horn; lambing starts about Lady Day, and, after weaning, the ewes are turned on to the Forest allotment which forms a part of each holding. The ewe hoggs are wintered either on the farm or on land taken away. Wether lambs are nearly all of them sold at the Simonsbath autumn sale, or at Blackmoor Gate or other fairs held annually at various places round the Forest. None of the tenants have adopted the Cheviots: while some of them agree that they are better suited to the climatic conditions, the prejudice against 'foreigners' in the local markets is too strong.

As regards cattle, few but the Devons are seen. The cows are all spring-calvers; they run out till Christmas, when they are brought up at night, and they can run into the yard in bad weather, during the day, for hay. The bullocks are mostly out all the day-time, being taken in at night, though some of the young ones may be yarded in winter, to make dung. The quantity of feeding stuffs used is very small, and no cattle are finished. Calves are hand-reared, on skim-milk and meal, the cream being scalded or made into butter. A few of the tenants take stock at agist for the summer grazing, but the practice is by no means general.

Practically no stock is bought, neither cattle nor sheep. Contagious abortion is rare, and the sheep are exceptionally healthy. Most of the farms feed a pig or two for home consumption, but there is no production for sale.

As to cropping, the fundamental thing is still the ley, but the practice of breaking it, and re-sowing after a short rotation, seems to be dying out. Several of the tenants say it does not pay, though they admit that the improved grass cannot be maintained in the best condition without it. When tillage is still practised, the old rotation seems to hold good—that is, roots after the ley, then oats, and then rape and seeds, the seeds being left down for an indefinite period before being broken again. Basic slag works wonders on these leys, but the cost of getting it on to the Forest is almost prohibitive. Liming is still practised here and there; but to make a generalisation, there are definite indications of a slowing-down of the pace of the husbandry. Prices, though remunerative, are not of an order to encourage men to take risks; the easier system of leaving things more to Nature pays; why not leave well alone? But the experience and the skill is still to be found, and a more intensive practice may develop at any time if the prophets of better prices for English sheep and cattle should be justified of their optimism.

As to the other factor in the prosperity of the Forest farmers, the system of labour organisation, practically the whole of the work is done by the tenants and their families; hired labour is almost negligible. Thus there are no weekly wages cheques to be drawn, no overtime nor special rates of pay for Sunday labour, no half-holidays. Labour is working for itself all the time and trades-union conditions have no meaning. The womenfolk and the children all take their turn, in fact the women work as hard as the men; two of them remained tenants of their holdings for many years, following the loss of their husbands (Mrs Reed of Red Deer and Mrs Thorne of Emmett's Grange, whose late husband, William Thorne, had by coincidence taken over from the widow of the former tenant, John Tucker). Some of the tenants at one time employed lads sent out by a society, to whom they paid a few shillings a week and their board and lodging with the family. The lads earned a little extra by cutting turf for house fuel, but the urban demand created by the war has stopped this source of labour. The Forest farms are large, but in respect of labour organisation they compare with the holdings of 30–50 acres on the more intensively farmed lowlands of England.

Exmoor farmhouses are remarkable for their severity, both

outside and inside, but there is a great contentment with the life on the Forest, and the loneliness does not seem to be felt. The 'wireless' aerial has made its appearance, and, in summer, isolation is now a thing of the past, for visitors occupy all the available accommodation. The landlord has assisted in the cultivation of this new 'crop' by equipping many of the houses with that necessity of modern existence, the bathroom, and there is no doubt that this summer harvest plays an important part in the farming economy of the district.

Outside the tenant farmers, farming on the Forest today is restricted to Earl Fortescue's sheep ranching and the summering of cattle. The Cheviot sheep and their shepherds—the former entirely, and the latter mostly, the descendants of Frederic Knight's original stock imported sixty years ago—are distributed over seven herdings (Tom's Hill, Larkbarrow, Hoar Oak and the Chains, Badgworthy, Duredon, Titchcombe and Winstitchin), practically all of them on the unimproved land. A ewe flock of close on 3,500 head is maintained, and it is said that they have preserved all their original character and type unimpaired. 'You might take them to Hawick and no one could see any difference.' About 100 rams are used, and these are all bred on the South Forest herding. Every two or three years some tups are purchased at Hawick and brought down to this herding, and the other flocks are supplied from the best of the ram lambs they leave. Thus most of the tups in use may be described as being one year from Scotland.

Lambing starts about 1 April, and the long record kept at Castle Hill shows that this big flock, living under entirely natural conditions on unimproved land at an elevation of from 1,200 to 1,500ft, averages about 95 per cent. Ewes and lambs run together until the September sales, when the wethers are, for the most part, trucked to Bridgwater and sold to up-country farmers. The rest are taken to Castle Hill. Ewe lambs required for the flock are also wintered there, being returned to the Forest in the following spring, and the remainder are sold off. No lambs, either ewe or wether, are wintered on Exmoor. The ewe flock remains there throughout the year, and is never fed except in exceedingly heavy weather, when some hay is given. Cull ewes are mated with

Shropshire rams, and they and their produce are got fat for the butcher on the improved pastures and rape fields of Titchcombe, which affords the best keep of all the 8,000 acres of land in hand. The size of the flock is determined by the number of sheep that can be maintained in April—the month when keeping on Exmoor, as in most places, is at its lowest worth.

A good many cattle are summered on the Forest to utilise the excess of grazing. Some 150 heifers, mostly Shorthorns, are sent up annually from Castle Hill, many of which are sold as down-calvers at the Simonsbath autumn sale, thus following Sir Frederic Knight's practice. The rest are returned to Castle Hill at the end of the season. The Forest would carry a far larger head, and it is open to farmers to send up cattle to be agisted, and upwards of 100 are grazed in this way. But it is useless to press the business today, as the general decline in arable cultivation in the surrounding districts has led to a reduction in the number of beasts wintered in the straw-yards, and so to a falling off in the demand for summer keep.

Ponies, once the great feature of the Forest, apart from the sheep, are practically unknown here now. Mechanical haulage in the coal mines, and the runabout car on the roads, have killed the demand for these most attractive and only indigenous animals, and they are almost unsaleable. The Estate pony book records that suckers which had sold at Bampton Fair at about £5 each at the turn of the century and reached £15 in 1918, had fallen in price to less than 20s by 1925, and it is said that more than a hundred ponies, of all ages, were sold off Brendon Common, in 1928, at 16s per head all round, for conversion into sausage meat. Moreover, the reasons which, sixty or seventy years ago, led Sir Frederic Knight to reduce his stud and to increase his flocks, apply with even greater force today. A fleece and a lamb are worth far more than a pony sucker, and the Forest will produce far more of them.

IX

1927-45 DEPRESSION AND RE-AWAKENING

In 1927 there had taken place the first sale of any major part of the estate collected by John Knight upon the inclosure of the Forest in 1818, though the outlying Crooked Post Farm at Litton had earlier been sold to the tenant. Honeymead, Picked Stones, Winstitchin, part of Winstitchin Allotment, Red Deer and Exe Cleave, in all about 1,743 acres, were purchased by Sir Robert Waley Cohen, KBE, who had rented the house at Honeymead since 1924. Sir Robert, who wished to have a country estate to which he could retreat from the stress of an international business career, extended and improved the house, but as almost all the land was let, the landlord-and-tenant relationship continued unchanged, and the Fortescue Estate rented back from him some 243 acres which had been in hand.

There was now no thought of further reclamation, for although the tenants, by farming with the minimum of expenditure, remained reasonably prosperous, there was no spare capital to invest in improvements. The landowners were in no better position, and the sale price of Honeymead, at a little over £8 per acre, was appreciably less than it had cost forty-one years earlier subject to Sir Frederic Knight's life interest. Indeed, it realised only £3 10s per acre more than John Knight had paid on average for the unenclosed Forest over a century before.

The Fortescue Exmoor Farm was no exception to the general depression in agriculture. After paying rent to the Estates Company, the Badgworthy Land Company and Sir Robert Waley Cohen, the enterprise had made a modest profit in 1928-9, but by 1931-2 it was incurring a small loss, in spite of agricultural land having been de-rated in the meantime. Sheep were considered rather more profitable than cattle, and over a ten-year period the cattle stock had fallen from about 200 to 170, whereas the sheep had increased from some 4,250 to 4,700. In August 1932, barely two months before his death, Earl Fortescue had written to his Agent, 'While we can up to a certain point control expenditure there seems to be very little we can do to improve Receipts for the nature of the land and climate make any but small changes in Management or system impossible. But with prices so bad it does not seem worth while to spend money or labour in trying to get Exmoor to carry more stock than it will support in its natural state.' The Agent was still Mr F. G. Smyth-Richards, but the bailiff of the Exmoor farm, Mr George Molland, retired at Christmas 1936 after no less than forty-four years' service starting under Sir Frederic Knight.[1] He was succeeded by Mr John Purchase.

The practice of buying Irish shorthorn heifers at Bristol was dying, largely due to tuberculosis, though it did not end finally until 1939. They were put to the bull, wintered indoors at Cornham, and either sold, often as in-calf heifers, or the bullocks retained and summered for two seasons on the Forest, spending the intervening winter at Castle Hill. The greatest change in cattle breeding came in 1933–4 when, as a result of the success of Galloway cattle on the Duchy of Cornwall Estate on Dartmoor, ten heifers and a bull were bought in Scotland (apparently with the advice of Lord Allendale, brother-in-law of Earl Fortescue), to form a foundation herd. By 1937 the herd had grown to fifty-one and by 1939 to eighty-seven, the cows being crossed with a white Shorthorn bull to produce 'blue greys'. These were also spring calved, in-wintered the first year, but being sturdier than the pure shorthorns they could then spend the next eighteen months on the moor, when they were sold at two and a half years as stores.

For some years there had been no margin of profit to pay for the quantities of lime and basic slag the land needed, which, even with the advent of motor transport, was expensive on Exmoor. By 1935 prices had improved a little, and Mr John Thorne, the tenant of Driver, ploughed and re-seeded some of his pasture to good effect. This did not go unnoticed, and it was decided to improve some of the pasture at Cornham, which came in hand in 1937, though it took the whole of the first winter to plough 40 acres using a pair of horses.

The Agriculture Act of 1937 provided for Government subsidies both on lime and basic slag and, as most of the land needed from 2 to 4 tons of lime and some 10cwt of basic slag to the acre, this greatly encouraged reclamation. A steady programme of grassland improvement was initiated on the Exmoor Farm and tractors were reintroduced, the land being seeded directly to grass and rape. Turnips had been tried as a break crop, but it was found that this enabled weeds to gain a hold, with only twelve men to run the entire farm.

Though farming on Exmoor meant hard work for modest profit, it was no longer quite such an isolated existence. The first telephone was installed at Honeymead in 1924, when Sir Robert Waley Cohen had guaranteed the cost of a line from Exford and, once this was in existence, others soon linked to it. For some years tourists' motor-cars had been commonplace, but by the 1930s many of the tenants ran cars, albeit usually elderly and second hand. For the first time it was possible for a farmer and his wife to drive to Barnstaple or South Molton in an hour or so in comfort, instead of a visit taking all day by pony and trap, or even sometimes necessitating a stay overnight in winter.

As an unemployment relief measure, the road through Winsford to Exford was widened and improved in stages from 1926. By 1931 the work had reached Simonsbath, where land was bought from the Fortescue Estate to divert the road to its present line in a side sweep nearer the river, the workmen living in a hutted camp at Red Stone. At the same time the Lynton road was improved, the sharp bend below Simonsbath Barton being eased, and the road had been enclosed along its last open stretch from Blackpits Gate to the County Boundary at Brendon Two Gates in 1929, though it was not until 1952 that a cattle grid was installed here.

The South Molton road had been enclosed between Blue Gate and Kinsford Gate in the nineteenth century and, about 1927, this was extended across Deer Park (the original oak fencing posts still survive). On the Challacombe road, the section from Goat Hill to Driver remained unenclosed though Pinkery Gate had been removed when Goat Hill was fenced. Driver Gate, like Brendon Two Gates, provided a useful source of income to local children, who were often rewarded for opening and shutting it for passing traffic. A scheme to improve this narrow road was started in 1939, and had to be abandoned on the outbreak of war, but extensive widening and straightening took place between 1956–9, the notorious loop at Westgate being cut off in 1963.

The threat of war in 1939 quickened Government interest in farming, but though the Agricultural Development Act that July introduced ploughing grants, the subsidies on oats, barley and fat sheep mainly benefited lowland farmers. Indeed in 1939 the price of store sheep was the lowest for three years, and the ploughing up of lowland pasture further reduced the demand for stores. To counteract this and encourage stock rearing on the hills, a special subsidy was introduced for hill ewes in 1941, and one for hill cattle followed in 1943.

On Exmoor the greatest changes were at Honeymead, where Sir Robert Waley Cohen, whose immense driving power, coupled with his scientific training, had earlier taken him to the position of effective second-in-command to Henry Deterding, in the giant Shell group, determined to obtain the maximum possible food output from his land. In this he was aided by being entitled to set off losses on his farming operations against his considerable income, for tax purposes, which enabled him to afford the high capital investment and to ignore the need to make a short-term monetary profit; a procedure which is impossible today. With his business background, his passion for improving the land, and even with his more extravagant ventures, Sir Robert was not unlike John Knight both in character and motives.

Until now all the farms on the Honeymead Estate had been tenanted, but in 1939 the tenant of Honeymead farm retired, and the 550 acres were taken in hand. Though, in Sir Robert's biography, it has been stated that the estate 'was agriculturally a wilderness. No serious attempt had been made to farm it for at least sixty years', in fact it had been farmed quite well, but in the only way possible during the depression, with the minimum expenditure and a low rate of stocking. The farm was carrying 425 Exmoor Horn sheep and 34 Devon cattle, but only 40 acres were under the plough (30 for roots and 10 for corn), whilst no less than 294 acres could only be described as rough grazing. The following year Picked Stones became vacant and was also taken in hand, while Thorne Farm was bought in 1941. These additions, together with the land taken in hand or rented from the Fortescue Estate and others, brought the total holding worked by Sir Robert Waley Cohen to 1,175 acres, by 1943.

Sir Robert sent his gardener-handyman, Joe Perry, to a course at the Somerset Farm Institute at Cannington, and then appointed him Farm Manager. An ambitious scheme of reclamation was started, with the aim of improving as much of the rough grazing as possible, but though the acreages are described in the farm records as 'ley ploughed for first time', strictly this was for the first time in living memory, as broken ploughshares and other evidence of the Knights' reclamation were sometimes found. By 1939 the first 30 acres of rough grazing was ploughed, mainly by one pair of horses, but in 1940 no less than 230 acres came under the plough, the peak being 239 acres the following year, much of the work being carried out by the Somerset WAEC. By 1945 a further 349 acres had been ploughed and the proportion of rough grazing had dropped from a maximum of 409 acres in 1941 (out of a total of 916 acres) to only 164 acres out of the final total of 1,175 acres worked in 1945. By then most of the land capable of reclamation had been dealt with, and less than 100 acres were ploughed after the war, all in the period 1948–54.

Most of this work resulted in vastly improved pasture, capable of supporting far more stock, but there was the occasional, often inexplicable, failure, and one section of the road to Warren Farm across Honeymead Allotment, still forms a boundary between good pasture on the east side and rough reedy land on the west, though both were ploughed within a year of each other and appeared to have an equal chance of success. The eastern part of Honeymead Allotment is a good illustration of the effort involved, for the 25 acres were first burnt and ploughed in 1943 by the SWAEC, and the following year dressed with no less than 154 tons of stone dust lime and 65cwt of triple phosphate, before being sown with turnips and subsequently folded with sheep. In 1945 it was seeded to rape and grass and since then left as permanent pasture, though regularly dressed with lime and basic slag.

A break crop of roots, usually turnips, was invariably used at Honeymead, in contrast to the experience on the Fortescue lands, though some direct re-seeding to grass was carried out successfully in later reclamation. Apart from true root crops, such as turnips, swedes and mangolds, both potatoes and kale were grown as well as beans, peas and cabbage. Cereals were also sown both during and shortly after the war, oats, barley, winter wheat and dredge corn, but the high rainfall made harvesting hazardous. In 1951 Thorne Horses Field yielded over a ton of barley to the acre, but the previous year Middle Cleave had been sown with oats, and the field book records simply 'no harvest, extreme wet'. At times, such grain as could be salvaged had to be passed through the grass drier which Sir Robert had installed. Hay making could also be risky, as field book entries such as 'never mown, because of much rain', and 'baled but left in heaps owing to rain and never saved' show only too clearly.

By the end of the war, the improved pasture enabled 2,455 sheep and 158 cattle to be carried on the 1,175 acres in hand. Starting with a foundation flock of 400 Exmoor Horn breeding ewes, numbers were increased to nearly 700 ewes, with another registered flock of 300 Devon closewool ewes on the better land, and some 30 Devon cows and their followers were kept for beef. But Sir Robert's greatest interest was his pedigree herd of British Friesians, which he founded in 1939 'purely from a patriotic motive with the idea that milk could and should be produced under conditions that were normally considered to be most unsuitable', to quote the auctioneers' catalogue when they were ultimately sold. The foundation stock was purchased mainly at Reading market, often from hardy Wiltshire and Hampshire herds, and mated to outstanding bulls such as Terling Formidable, Terling Laureate (bought at Reading in 1944 for the then record price of 1,400 guineas) and Elmwood Lion. The resulting herd was a magnificent gesture of defiance to farming conditions 1,250ft above sea level and, though it could never be an economic success, over 21,500 gallons of milk were being produced annually by 1945, from fewer than thirty cows.

To cope with the increased stock, existing buildings had been modernised and new buildings added at Honeymead, and a 'power station' installed to provide electricity, not only there, but to other parts of the estate, while the staff had increased from two men to over twenty men and women.

At Honeymead extensive improvements had been made in a short time by substantial capital investment, often without regard to the short-term commercial effect. The Fortescue Estate was run as an investment and expenditure of that order could not be economically justified, but the grassland improvement, started before the war, was continued both on the Exmoor farm and the tenanted farms, including a substantial acreage of rough grazing, untouched since the nineteenth century, and the rate of stocking rose accordingly. Some cereals were also grown, but with an annual rainfall of over 70in, results were no happier than at Honeymead. Two factors limited the reclamation possible on the Fortescue part of the Forest; the amount of truly waste land, such as the Chains, and the fact that Larkbarrow and Tom's Hill were requisitioned for use as an artillery range by guns stationed on Fyldon Ridge. Both farmsteads were damaged and wind and weather continued the process until they have both become mere ruins today, while hidden, unexploded shells still prevent the land being ploughed.

Apart from the requisitioned land, the neglect of the lean years had been made good, and by 1945 the Forest was in better heart and producing more than ever before, thus finally vindicating the reclamation commenced by John and Frederic Knight.

(See pp 295-9 for notes)

X

1946–69 RECLAMATION OR CONSERVATION?

The advent of peace did not, this time, result in the neglect of agriculture and the government, acutely aware of the shortage of foreign currency, determined that a high level of home food production must be maintained. The Agriculture Act of 1947 formed the basis of a general system of 'Guaranteed Prices and Assured Markets' whereby subsidies were payable if the prices of produce fell below levels fixed at an annual price review, and hill farming received additional help by the Hill Farming Act of 1946 and successive legislation. The wartime hill sheep and hill cattle subsidies were to continue and grants were to be payable of half the cost of approved schemes for the improvement of land 'suitable for sheep of a hardy kind but not of other kinds'; an ingenious definition of hill farms. The schemes covered, not only work on the land itself, but on farmhouses and buildings, roads, water and electricity supplies, and the planting of shelter belts. They were to prove of great benefit to farming on the Forest, though their first use was to mitigate the heavy sheep losses in the disastrous winter of 1946–7 by providing an incentive to rebuild flocks.[1]

In the meantime Exmoor was to become known throughout the world as the source of the Lynmouth flood disaster. There had been heavy rainfall during the first fortnight of August 1952 and this culminated in a torrential downpour on the 15th, when during twenty-four hours 7·35in of rain were recorded at Honeymead and no less than 9in at Longstone Barrow. The fields around Pinkery were flooded 6–8in deep and, by evening, large areas of the moor were awash to a depth of several inches, with every stream a torrent and every river a raging flood. Much of the north-western

Page 157   Frederic Winn Knight 1884. *Cartoon by Leslie Ward*

Page 158 (*above*) Simonsbath showing the shell of John Knights mansion behind the house about 1890; (*below*) Simonsbath House

part of the moor drains into the confined valleys of the East and
West Lyn and, where these met at Lynmouth, a mass of water,
boulders and debris tore the heart out of the village, and killed
over thirty people. Every valley leading from the moor became a
scene of devastation and other lives were lost at Parracombe and
Filleigh. The Forest itself was sufficiently open, not to pen up the
water and it escaped the worst of the damage. Even so, a flood
over 10ft high deluged the hotel and cottages at Simonsbath, and
the bridge was so badly damaged that a temporary Bailey bridge
had to be laid across it, until permanent repairs could be made. At
Honeymead, a sheet of water 18in deep came down the drive and
through the house and many other farms were similarly flooded.
Great gulleys were scoured in the beds of streams, farm roads
were washed out and topsoil carried away, but surprisingly little
stock was drowned.

It was more than a week before the main roads on the Forest
could be reopened, but a national relief fund was started and
gradually the work of restoration completed, though the scouring
is still apparent in the combes.

At this time the Fortescue Exmoor Estate consisted, not only of
the remaining 14,000 acres purchased from Sir Frederic Knight,
but also included a further 1,130 acres of rented rough grazing,
much of it originally belonging to the Brendon Estate and now
owned by the Badgworthy Land Company. Some 5,000 acres were
tenanted, the greater part in seven farms, Pinkery, Driver,
Emmett's Grange, Wintershead, Horsen, Duredon and Simonsbath Barton, the rents ranging from 10s per acre at Driver and 15s
at Emmett's Grange to 20s per acre at Simonsbath for the best
land. There were also six blocks of bare moorland let at between
2s 6d and 10s per acre. By 1954 all these seven farms had been
improved with the help of government grants, the work being
supervised by Mr F. G. Smyth-Richards, and later by the resident
agent, Mr J. M. B. Mackie, who succeeded him that year.

The estate farm now covered 10,700 acres, including the homesteads at Cornham (from 1937) and Warren (from 1943), together
with Larkbarrow, Tom's Hill, the Chains and Hoar Oak, and was
divided into seven herdings. John Purchase had retired as farm
manager at Christmas 1953, and Mr John Hayes, who took over,

K

ran the farm with a staff of eighteen men. Cattle were now more profitable than sheep and the ewe flock, at 3,400, was marginally smaller than in 1928, all Cheviots, save for 440 Scotch Blackfaces on the Chains. With 160 rams, lambing averaged almost 95 per cent and the ewes were hardy enough to fend for themselves throughout the year except for a little hay during snow. When the Cheviots had dropped four lambs, the best were drafted to Castle Hill to form a flock of some 200 which were crossed with a Border Leicester and sold, with their lambs, in the autumn. Lambs on the Forest which could not be sold off by autumn, were also brought down to Castle Hill and sold off fat, after a second summer on Exmoor.

No cattle were taken for summer keep after 1954, but substantial numbers of Galloways and Galloway crosses were kept on the Forest throughout the year, numbers being limited only by the amount of fodder which could be produced for winter feed. Bulls were purchased at Castle Douglas from time to time, but, apart from a small herd acquired from Lord Poltimore in the early 1940s, no additional cows have ever been bought, the Galloway stock being maintained by a herd of forty purebred cows. After the White Shorthorn, a Devon bull was tried, but since the war, the Hereford has been found the most successful. Using pedigree bulls and culling poorer cows, the quality has been much improved while by 1960, in addition to the breeding herd, there were 140 Galloway cows and heifers for crossing with Hereford bulls, and 118 yearlings.

The basis of feeding was silage, with as much hay as the weather would permit, and 120–50 tons were made each year, but apart from concentrates for the calves, feeding straw and a little hay, the Exmoor Farm was self-supporting. Most stock was still being sold as stores at two and a half years and, though for a time some crosses were finished with an extra year at Castle Hill, a trend had started of selling off at eighteen months, enabling more cows to be kept and overcoming the drawback of slow growth in hard winters.

Reclamation was continuing steadily as well as the improvement of existing grassland, and by 1954 some 1,500 acres had been re-seeded.[2] Thus, for example, that year 30 acres were reclaimed and another 90 acres ploughed and re-seeded under turnips and rape. The leys were usually left down for three to five years (sometimes longer if the sward was good) and were limed the first year and dressed with basic slag the second, but spraying was needed to keep down thistles and rushes; a perennial problem on all reclaimed land on the Forest.

Grants, from the Hill Farm Improvement Scheme, enabled new shepherds' bungalows to be built at Blackpits (replacing a former army hut put up in the 1920s), and at Titchcombe by Bale Water, and two were built at Winstitchin Lane above Simonsbath. Improvements had also been made to the farmsteads, including a new water supply, and 10 acres of shelter belts were proposed. In all, there were about 100 acres of woodlands, including the 26 acres of beech at Birch Cleave, but mainly conifers in plantations at Simonsbath, Limecombe, and below Little Cornham.

At Honeymead, Mr Bernard Waley-Cohen had taken over the running of the estate in March 1951 and, when his father died in November 1952, it was evident that changes would have to be made. Joe Perry retired and his successor, Mr E. R. Lloyd, was to implement the new policy. Now that wartime conditions were over, the cost of the Friesians could not be justified and in the autumn of 1954 they were sold. For the last four years the herd, now forty cows, had produced over 32,000 gallons of milk annually, an indication of their quality being the average sale price of £177 for the cows, over £100 greater than the average price paid.

Since 1945 Sir Robert had been up-grading his Devon cattle, and their numbers were now increased until, ultimately, Honeymead could boast the largest herd of pedigree Devons in the country, with six bulls and some 140 cows, plus heifers and followers. The stock was exceptionally hardy and, like the Fortescue Galloways, they spent only their first winter indoors, though Honeymead had the advantage of more sheltered pastures than the Fortescue Farm could provide. Usually they were sold as stores at two and a half years, but latterly it was found more profitable to sell the steer calves on weaning, in October, saving vital winter keep for the cows. An interesting development was the breeding of polled Devon stock from a Red Galloway bull and a pedigree polled Devon bull obtained from the United States. Sir Bernard Waley-Cohen (as he became in 1957) was subsequently President of the Devon Cattle Breeders Society in 1963.

The number of sheep increased to over 1,500 ewes by 1961, but the Devon Closewools were sold and a ewe flock of 300 Scotch Blackface replaced them, being less demanding of winter keep. Red Deer Farm came into possession in 1959 and, though the farmhouse and 12 acres were sold the following year, with the inclusion of grazing formerly rented to the Fortescue Estate, the land in hand rose to its maximum of 1,846 acres in 1960. Woodland accounted for 45 acres, with a mixed plantation dating from 1949 below Picked Stones, well-established Norway Spruce at Cloven Rocks, and some useful shelter belts of Sitka on Honeymead Allotment, Reacombe, and at Slate Quarry, all planted in 1953.

One setback had occurred in April 1954, when Honeymead House was burnt out, though fortunately the office and farm records were saved. It was rebuilt and a new house constructed for the farm manager, while, with seven other houses and cottages, Honeymead had now grown to a hamlet.

Exmoor had been proposed as a National Park by both the Dower Report in 1945 and the Hobhouse Report two years later, but, though the National Parks Act became law in 1949, it was not until 1954 that it was formally designated. The term is a misnomer (for in this country 'National Parks' are neither nationally owned nor parks open to the public) which has led to much misunderstanding between farmer and visitor. Three years after its formation, the National Park Committee became involved in a national controversy concerning the future of the Chains.

The Fortescue Estate had agreed to lease to the Forestry Commission the Chains and Hoar Oak herding, in all about 1,200 acres. Viewed solely as a matter of estate management, this found a use for the wildest and least productive part of the Fortescue lands, but whether it would have been a wise acquisition for the Forestry Commission is another matter. Apart from the difficulties of afforestation at over 1,500ft, large areas would have had to be drained before planting could take place, and even if feasible the cost would have been considerable and the whole character of the area changed. An amenity group, the Exmoor Society, was formed to fight the proposals, the National Parks Commission were also opposed, and afforestation would have interfered with hunting. The Forestry Commission withdrew and the Chains remain inviolate.

Earl Fortescue died in June 1958 and his executors decided to sell both the Challacombe Estate and parts of the Exmoor Estate. Despite intense activity by many of the tenants and by preservationists, who wanted the National Park Committee to buy the Chains, it was decided not to sell piecemeal but as one lot, and the whole 9,721 acres was bought at auction on 18 September 1959 for £163,100 by a Crewkerne investment company, which outbid a consortium of tenants. A private re-sale followed three days later, and the Challacombe tenants were able to buy their holdings from the new owner, who sold the land on the Forest to Mr Darby Haddon from Gloucestershire. A further change on the Fortescue Estate occurred just over twelve months later, when Mr I. M. Lang succeeded Mr Mackie as agent at Christmas 1960.

The Forest, once owned by the Knights, was now divided into three main parts: the remaining Fortescue land, Honeymead and, what was to be known as, the Emmett's Grange estate. This was 4,643 acres in extent, and as well as Emmett's Grange it included Wintershead, Horsen, Pinkery, Driver, the Chains and Hoar Oak Herding, and the Exmoor Forest Hotel at Simonsbath. Mr Haddon obtained possession of the farms, modernised the house at Emmett's Grange, and built new cottages and farm buildings there, but, though various fences were bulldozed, no further reclamation took place. The holding was stocked with Exmoor, Cheviot and Scotch Blackface sheep and a number of Galloway cattle, and run with herdings at Emmett's Grange, Wintershead, Horsen, and Driver with Pinkery, but after eight years it was sold again.

Winter on the Forest must always be treated with respect and, in the years following the inclosure, the winters of 1895 and 1947 were memorably bad, but 1962–3 was to outdo them both. The cold weather started on 23 December and for the next seventy-one days until 3 March the mean temperature was below freezing point, whereas in 1947 the bitter weather did not start until 19 January and lasted only fifty days.

Conditions at Warren were typical of farms on the Forest and, at the first sign of snow on Christmas Eve, the sheep were turned off the high ground at Larkbarrow and Trout Hill, down into the Kittuck valley and the bottom of Manor Allotment, where they were less likely to bury. It started to snow on Boxing Day and soon the farm was cut off, but about seventy hoggs near the homestead were safely dug out and the ewes fed with hay dropped by RAF helicopter. On 9 January the helicopter took the shepherds and their dogs to Kittuck, and, with great difficulty, the ewes there were brought home by dusk.

The Galloway breeding herd was safe at Warren, but, to save fodder, they were driven to Simonsbath next day, while hay was taken regularly by hand or helicopter to the ewes still stranded on Manor Allotment, until 477 of them could be brought back on 4 February. Most of that night was spent preventing the worst snowfall of the winter from drifting and burying the sheep in the yard, and, for about a week, bales of hay had to be carried by hand across the Exe valley until a tractor could get through. It was 7 March before normal traffic could reach Warren and there was still snow on Manor Allotment at the beginning of May. With devoted work and the help of the helicopters, losses on the Fortescue Estate and at Honeymead were surprisingly low, but a prosecution was subsequently brought by the RSPCA, against the owner of Emmett's Grange, for causing unnecessary suffering to sheep at Pinkery farm, by failing to provide reasonable care and attention, and he was fined £20 and costs.

In recent years, several Exmoor controversies have attracted national attention, and afforestation of the Chains, the ploughing of moorland and hunting have all been under fire. Despite this, hunting has become such a part of the Forest scene that followers in cars create traffic problems, while there is now the best herd of deer since before the war and indiscriminate shooting is controlled by the Deer Act of 1963. Should hunting ever cease, other means would have to be found of controlling the deer and compensation paid for their depredations to fodder crops in winter, or they will face extinction, since this damage is now accepted by local landowners as the price of their sport.

Though the Forest did not escape the ploughing controversy,

this was brought to a head by the inclosure of land at Countisbury, Porlock Hill and Fyldon Ridge. The Exmoor Society bitterly opposed, what they considered to be, the destruction of natural Exmoor, claiming that this was accomplished with the aid of government subsidy and that some of the reclamation was of dubious agricultural value. Supporters of the hunt were also un-happy about the new fences. The farming community reacted strongly and a bitter and often personal acrimony developed, with accusation and counter accusation, pamphlet and counter pam-phlet. Ultimately, legislation to control the ploughing of open moorland in National Parks was included in the Countryside Act 1968, and by definition this includes rough grazing if it has not been used as 'agricultural land' for more than twenty years. Had such legislation existed in 1818, the Forest as we know it could never have been created. It would be without farms, village, or inhabitants, but, the reclamation having taken place, the effect of the Act is less here than on the adjoining commons, particularly as nearly all the land which reverted to moor in the past has now been ploughed again and re-seeded. It is to be hoped that the new powers of control will not be invoked to prevent limited useful reclamation (as has been carried out at Prayway, for example), nor the improvement of such small areas of reverted moorland as remain, where in any case the original vegetation has been changed. The recent formation of a working party (including representatives of the National Park, the NFU and the CLA) should help to maintain a fair balance between reclamation and conservation.

The ownership of the estate, originally created by John Knight, became further fragmented in 1967, exactly thirty years after the first major sale, and part of the same land was again involved. Sir Bernard Waley-Cohen decided to curtail his farming activities and that year disposed of Picked Stones and Thorne farms, with some 397 acres, to Mr Graham Leeves of Exford. Mr Tom Gage of Gallon House bought about 459 acres at Red Deer, extending over Exe Cleave, while a further 60 acres, just outside the Forest, opposite Red Deer, were sold to Mrs Gundry of Exford. It is some indication both of the improvement in the land and in agricultural fortunes generally, that the prices obtained ranged from £45 per acre for the poorest to £110 per acre for the best land, whereas the average price paid for the estate thirty years earlier (albeit subject to tenancies but including the house) had been little over £8 per acre.

That autumn Sir Bernard sold all his Devon cattle and his Scotch Blackface sheep. Now only Exmoor horns are kept, with a breeding flock of 850 ewes, but, in addition, some 230 cattle from lower lying farms are taken in each summer for the grazing; a reversion to ancient practice. Rather over 800 acres remain in hand, together with Winstitchin, which has always been tenanted.

Another sale in 1967 was the Emmett's Grange estate, which, with the exception of the hotel, was purchased that year by Mr J. Bradley. He ran Galloway cows crossed with a Hereford or Shorthorn bull, and Exmoor Horn, Scotch Blackface and Cheviot sheep, but the estate was again placed on the market after two years and is now divided into four ownerships. The northern portion, comprising Pinkery, Driver, the Chains and Hoar Oak, in all some 1,990 acres, was sold in 1969 to Somerset County Council on behalf of the National Park; the first land on the Forest to be publicly owned since it was sold by the Crown.

Whereas thirty years ago only the Exmoor Farm was in hand, now apart from Winstitchin, the only tenanted farms are Simons-bath Barton and Duredon, with some blocks of land without buildings, all on the Fortescue estate, and the tenants regret the passing of the social life they enjoyed before the war. Even the Barton is being given up and will be taken into the Exmoor Farm, though Pinkery and Driver are, once again, being let. The tenants farm in the traditional way with Exmoor Horn sheep and Devon cattle, but their farming policy differs. Mr Watts at Duredon stocks only as many animals as he can feed in winter, but Mr Thorne at Simonsbath Barton, whose Exmoor Horns have brought him many prizes, winters his ewes away enabling greater numbers to be kept. Butter, cream and eggs are now produced only for home consumption and myxomatosis has killed most rabbits.

The Fortescue Exmoor Farm is the direct descendant of the Knights' ranching on the Forest, though both the fertility of the land and the stocking rate have been improved to an extent unimaginable forty years ago. There is a strong resemblance to farming north of the border, for Scottish breeds and methods have been successfully adapted to suit Exmoor conditions. Since the sale of the Chains and Hoar Oak in 1959 the farm covers some 8,500 acres, including about 1,100 acres of rented rough grazing, but only 3,000 or so is enclosed pasture, of which about half is of good quality with the best at Titchcombe, Cornham, Limecombe and Ashcombe.

The breeding herd, now fifty Galloway cows, is kept at Warren, but the rest of the cattle are centred on Cornham Farm, where there are two Galloway and nine Hereford bulls and 300 Galloway Hereford cross cows and heifers, though the aim is to increase the number to 400. The Galloway heifers are put to a Galloway for their first calf and subsequently crossed with a Hereford, but though breeding from first cross heifers has been very successful, beyond this they lose the hardiness and foraging ability of the Galloway. Calving starts in mid April, the cows being brought to the better pastures where they stay until the calves are strong enough to be sent to rough grazing in the summer. When weaning takes place in November, pure and some first cross heifers are kept for breeding and brought into the yards, but other calves are sold. This enables more cows to be kept through the lean winter months than was possible when cattle were sold as stores at two and a half years. New buildings were erected at Cornham in 1961 and 1966 to in-winter the calves retained for breeding, and permanent feed areas have been constructed to simplify feeding of the out-wintered cows.

When the Chains and Hoar Oak were sold the Scotch Blackface sheep were dispersed and thereafter only pure Cheviot ewes have been kept. The farm is divided into six herdings at Badgworthy, Titchcombe, Limecombe, Ashcombe and Mines (Winstitchin), each with a shepherd and 565 ewes, while Warren, which includes Larkbarrow and Tom's Hill, has two shepherds and 1,130 ewes. Each year four or five rams are brought from Scotland and mated with the Mines ewes, and the tups then go to the other flocks. The better pastures at Titchcombe enable cull ewes, from other flocks, to be brought in and crossed with a Down ram, both ewe and lamb being sold in the autumn. With the improvement in grazing, the stock is healthier, lambing is over 100 per cent and, considering numbers, losses are few, even though no lambs are wintered off the moor. The only feeding is in winter, when a little hay or silage is provided with some concentrates for the ewes and a field of turnips for the rams, but the high rate of stocking has meant that precautions now have to be taken against such troubles as copper deficiency, previously unknown on the Forest. Shearing starts about 8 or 10 June and in a fortnight between 5,000 and 6,000 ewes, rams and hoggs are shorn at Simonsbath, Warren and Cornham. The wool, originally famed for its robust characteristics, is now softer with a lustre more often associated with lowland flocks, this being the result of the much improved grazing.

The farm staff consists of the manager, Mr Hayes, eight general farmworkers, a carpenter, a mason, a herdsman and his assistant, and seven shepherds. Housing is provided free, at Simonsbath, except for the herdsman at Cornham and shepherds at Warren, Titchcombe and Badgworthy (Blackpits), while shepherds own their dogs and ponies and can keep two house cows. Equipment is simple: a land rover, six tractors, and a ditcher, which is most effective in reopening ditches first dug in the time of the Knights.

Compared with forty years ago, the farm is larger and better situated, for while it has lost the Chains, Hoar Oak and Duredon, it has gained Cornham and Warren farms. But whereas then its only permanent stock was a ewe flock of about 3,500, with about 250 cattle summered, it now permanently supports, not only 4,000 ewes, plus shearlings and lambs, but nearly 400 cows and their followers. Equally important, the stock is healthy, of excellent quality, with a low mortality rate, and is almost wholly fed from the Forest itself.

Life on the Forest can never be soft at that altitude, but amenities are now available which were undreamt of before the war. Most families run a car, and although there is now no regular bus service to Simonsbath, a bus takes the older children to school (the younger ones still attend Simonsbath school until it closes in 1970). Mains electricity came in December 1962, bringing television for the winter evenings, though some of the more remote houses such as Warren and Blackpits still have their own generators, and a new estate water supply from Limecombe came into use in 1963. Simonsbath even has two council houses, though as everyone on the Forest has a house provided with his job these are now occupied by families from Exford.

Prophesies are apt to be confounded, and nowhere more so than on Exmoor, but most of the Knights' land worth putting under the plough has already been improved and effectively the restrictions in the Countryside Act of 1968 may be said to mark the end of the reclamation of Exmoor Forest. Existing grassland will continue to be maintained so long as financial support is forthcoming, but hill farming is even more at the mercy of government policy than agriculture as a whole. The trend to intensive dairying or continuous cereal growing by lowland farms is affecting the price of stores, and man-made fibres are competing with wool. The future may lie in reducing numbers and finishing more stock, but hill sheep and cattle subsidies would have to be altered to compensate for the loss in calf subsidy and the reduction in numbers of cows and ewes eligible for payment. The Agriculture Act 1967 continues these subsidies and grants for improvements benefiting hill land, but if these were ever abandoned there would undoubtedly be a reversion to subsistence farming and low stocking rates. The Forest provides a good example of this assistance wisely used, for in 1969 most of it is in better heart than ever before. One regrettable consequence of recent changes, however, is the loss of almost all the tenant farmers and, with them much of the community life previously enjoyed.

When John Knight purchased the King's Allotment both Exmoor and Dartmoor were thought of as barren wastes awaiting reclamation and colonisation. A century and a half later they are regarded as lungs for the suffocating townsman, but whilst sport, natural history and recreation all have their place, without a healthy agriculture Exmoor could become a near derelict land, with few people save the summer visitor. One can but hope that the work of John and Frederic Knight and their successors will not be sacrificed, but maintained, to continue to play its part in feeding this country.

(See pp 295–9 for notes)

XI

MINING

One of the shortest but not the least interesting chapters in the story of Exmoor reclamation relates to the few years during which attempts were made by Frederic Knight to exploit the deposits of iron ore which occur here and there upon the Forest. It was an enterprise based on high hopes, and conducted for a time with almost feverish activity. Had it succeeded, Exmoor might have become an important mineral district, owing to the nearness of the South Wales iron industry, but it came to a speedy and complete collapse.

Throughout the hill-country of North Devon and West Somerset, which forms a belt about 5 miles wide and 30 miles long extending from Hangman Hill, near Combe Martin, and the North Molton ridge, on the west, to the neighbourhood of Wiveliscombe, and the Stogumber and Crowcombe valley, on the east, veins (so-called) of iron ore are to be met with. The strata of this district belong exclusively to the Devonian system, and they comprise alternations of sandstones, arenaceous and argillaceous shales, calcareous beds, etc, interstratified in endless variety and exhibiting numerous changes of character over the extensive area which they occupy. Though the strata have suffered much disturbance, their contortions take a direction almost exclusively at right angles to the line of bearing, so that they preserve a remarkable degree of parallelism, and may be followed, from east to west, over an extensive range of country.

Between the divisions in these strata, casual deposits of metallic minerals, particularly of iron ore, frequently occur, especially at or near the intersection of the strata by slides or cross-joints. These deposits cannot properly be termed veins or lodes, which are faults, or fissures in the rocks, running across the line of the strata—usually at a considerable angle to the line of strike—and filled with minerals of various kinds. Veins should continue at depth, whereas the deposits found in formations such as those of the Exmoor district are almost always shallow, and tend to pinch out or die away as they are explored in depth.

On Exmoor, and in the adjacent Brendon Hills, these deposits of iron ore were known in ancient times, and they exhibit signs of extensive working, here and there, where they happen to lie at or near the surface. The name 'Roman' applied to these old workings, however, is to be taken rather as indication of their antiquity than in the literal sense. In 1550 Edward VI granted a license to Michael Wynston to work 'iron and steel ore' and 'moor coal' on Exmoor and Dartmoor, and the recital claimed that he had 'found divers mines of iron and steel within the King's Forests of Exmore and Dartemore'. Another possibility is that the mines may date back to the time when Elizabeth invited German miners to England, and the idea may derive support from the names Ison Hill, Ison Common, etc, which occur in the vicinity of the old workings south of Wheddon Cross, whence considerable quantities of iron ore have been extracted in recent times. The most extensive of the Roman mines, so-called, on Exmoor are to be seen on Burcombe, adjoining the road from Cornham Ford towards Blue Gate; they extend for some distance, and give evidence of considerable production by means of 'patching', or surface working.[1] Other old workings occur throughout this country, as at Blackland, Mole's Chamber and Whitfield Down.

That the possibility of mining on Exmoor had occurred to John Knight is clear from his payment of £762, being 3s per acre, for the mineral rights reserved to the Crown under Sir Thomas Acland's and Sir Charles Bampfylde's allotments, in the year following his acquisition of the property. As an ironmaster himself, the question would be, naturally, in his mind, and he would have been familiar with the old surface workings in various places on the Forest. 'It does not appear from the inquiries which we have made', say the Commissioners of Woods and Forests in their Third Report to Parliament, dated 18 June 1819, 'that there is any reason to suppose that there are mines or minerals of any value under the property in question; considering the rights of the Crown therefore in the present instance to be merely nominal, we have offered them to Mr. Knight for one year's rent of the land, which has been reported to us to be about 3s. per acre.'

John Knight made no attempt to exploit this acquisition, nor were the Crown rights ever conveyed to him. Mining on Exmoor during his lifetime was confined to a single venture, the object of which was to develop supposititious, but really non-existent copper ore.

THE WHEAL ELIZA COPPER MINE

The first mine to be opened in the district in modern times was the Wheal Eliza mine, on the Barle, between Flexbarrow and Cow Castle. On 1 March 1846, John Knight executed, at Rome, a lease of all silver, copper, lead, tin, iron, and all other ores on Honeymead Farm, then occupied by Henry Matthews, to Russell Martyn Riccard, of South Molton, gentleman, at that time his solicitor, John Cock, of South Molton, builder, Richard Sleeman, of Tavistock, surgeon, and Oliver Matthews, of Molland, mining agent, for twenty-one years from the twenty-fifth day of the same month. The lease recited that these gentlemen were 'about to form a company of adventurers for working a mine intended to be called by the name of the Wheal Eliza Mine'. The negotiations for the lease had been conducted by Frederic Knight, on behalf of his father, and there is reason to believe that the mine had been worked before. 'I am much pleased with your account of the Copper Mine'—John Knight had written to his son, in December 1845—'and if it is what I used to consider an Iron Mine no doubt it will prove of great value. I was told 10 years ago that it was a copper mine, at bottom, but as my informer was a great Rogue, tho' a clever miner, I did not believe him.'

No dead rent was provided, but the lessees covenanted to keep not fewer than six miners at work, and to pay the lessor one-fifteenth part of the value received (ie 1s 4d in the pound) by the sale of the ore raised, the only deduction allowed before arriving at the figure to be the cost of carriage of the ore to the place of delivery. Alternatively, the lessor reserved the right to take one-fifteenth part of all the ore brought to bank.

The lease is very brief; there is no plan of Honeymead, nor are its boundaries identified in any other way, but the extent of the farm included, at this date, those known today as Cloven Rocks, Picked Stones and Winstitchin farms. Covenants by either party are few. The lessees were to build six cottages, of a size specified, so soon as they had raised 200 tons of ore, and they covenanted not to 'kill or molest the Red Deer on the Forest' under penalty of £25 in each case, as liquidated damages. The lease could be determined by the lessees at any time, by giving two months' notice to the lessor, and at its expiration, or whenever otherwise determined, all works, buildings, etc, above and below ground, were to pass to the lessor, without compensation to the lessees except as regards any waterwheels, which the lessor could take at a valuation, and as regards any other machinery, which the lessees could remove.

As a result of exploratory work, which had been going on since August 1845, a prospectus was issued that December, offering 256 shares in the proposed mine, which was to be named Wheal Maria.[2] It was this prospectus which induced Richard Sleeman to take the majority holding, and at his request, the name was changed to Eliza. Unlike some of the investors, he realised the risk he was running—'Exmoor Eliza, although esteemed so highly by judges, is, like other untried mines, a speculation'. This did not deter others, and soon 'shares on which £2 has been paid up are eagerly sought for £16 each', while Frederic Knight was hopeful that 'The Exmoor Hills may contain the wealth of the Paris [Parys] Mountain'.

Oliver Matthews did not execute the lease, but was appointed Captain, and by May 1846 the supposed lode had been uncovered at the surface for a length of between 300yd and 400yd; an adit driven at its commencement from the river bank, and a shaft sunk about 100yd to the east, from which a cross cut was driven at a depth of 17ft, to act as a drainage level. 'In driving this cross cut, several branches produced good stones of copper', and although there was a general letting to the adventurers of all metalliferous minerals, it was copper ore that they were seeking.

At the first recorded meeting of the company, held at South Molton on 11 August 1846, Richard Sleeman took the chair and

Captain Matthews reported that the shaft was down 24ft and recommended building a smith's shop and material house and erecting a waterwheel. His services were, however, 'discontinued' at the end of September, when Captain Joseph Pryor took over, at a salary of 7gns a month. To reach the mine, a road had been made along the Barle from Simonsbath, and by December the wheel pit had been sunk, the leat commenced, part of the machinery delivered, and a smith's shop, a carpenter's shop and an account house constructed. The 25ft diameter wheel was completed during the spring of 1847, and on 17 May work was restarted on sinking the shaft, which, by October, had reached a depth of 72ft below adit level. Here it was hoped that copper ore would be found and a cross cut was driven southwards.

Five months later, only a few lumps of ore had been uncovered; Captain Pryor had his pay reduced by a guinea a month, and Captain W. M. Whitford was appointed visiting agent. By September 1848 Pryor had gone and Captain Whitford was recommending sinking deeper, but before this could be done more money was needed and, the next month, the purser was 'requested to write the shareholders in arrear, urging immediate payment'. The pumping engine was improved to give the extra lift needed and, by January 1849, the shaft was down a further 36ft. Sinking continued, but was hampered, first by the wheel being frozen, then by floods caused by melting snow, and always by shortage of funds, so that it was not until May that it had reached 144ft, where the 'caunter lode' was '3 ft. wide—beautiful gossan spotted with rich copper ore'. Though improved, the engine could not cope with water from this depth, and work ceased for a month, while it was strengthened, but the spots of ore never materialised into a workable lode and, though it was claimed that 'with a little more outlay the mine will stand conspicuous with those whose shares are sought after', the purser could no longer get in calls and work was suspended in October 1849.

Following a meeting at Plymouth in February 1850, however, further shares to a total of 1,024 were issued; the engine further strengthened; and, by May, Captain Richard Moore, with nine men, was sinking the engine shaft. Encouraged by optimistic reports and threatened by a resolution that 'All shares on which

Page 175   The Post on Exmoor: (*above*) Red Deer c 1929;
(*below*) Simonsbath Post Office c 1910

Page 176 Long service on t
Forest

(*left*) G. C. Smyth-Richar
Agent 1887–1929

(*right*) George Molland. Bailiff
1892–1936

calls are unpaid to be forfeit', the shareholders found enough
money to continue sinking the shaft throughout 1851 and 1852,
using a gang of eleven men, working on contract at £20 per
fathom. By January 1853 the 300ft level had been reached and
cross cuts were driven east and west, but there was still no workable copper and, by June, yet another Captain, William Dunstan,
had been appointed. Troubled by floods in winter, which over-
powered the engine, drought in April 1854, when the wheel could
only pump down to the 216ft level, and a shortage of miners, who
were ill housed and ill paid, Dunstan lasted a year, and W. Williams
took over.

No workable copper ore was ever found, for the reason that
there was none; an analysis of the ore made at a subsequent period
in the history of the mine indicated the presence in it of less than
1 per cent of copper.

The mine contained good iron ore, however, analysing up to
60 per cent of metallic iron, and in 1855 Frederic Knight was
anxious to get possession of it, in connection with a scheme which
he was then maturing for the development of iron mining on
Exmoor, on a large scale. He arranged, accordingly, that a
nominee, a Mr William Thomas Whyte, should approach the
lessees with a view to obtaining an assignment to himself of their
lease, which, by this time, they must have realised to be worthless.
Whyte was an Irishman who had had considerable experience in
the north of Ireland in executing contracts under the Board of
Works; at this time he was acting as agent for the Ruabon Coal
Company and the North Wales Coke Company, but he was employed also, from time to time, in various matters by Frederic
Knight. On 5 June 1855 he obtained an assignment of the lease,
from the three parties to it, in return for a payment of £300, which
included the whole of the equipment of the mine, from the 25ft
waterwheel and the pumping plant, down to the bedsteads,
blankets, knives and forks, and other furnishings of the counting-
house and bothy. Frederic Knight's cheque 'for the purchase of
Wheal Eliza mineral lease, with plant and machinery', was drawn
for £328 17s 6d, the oddment representing, presumably, the
expenses of the transaction.

As an iron mine, the Wheal Eliza proved no more successful

L

than when it was first operated for copper, for though it contained
good ore it was not present in workable quantities. In April 1856
the mine was included in the tract leased by Frederic Knight to
Schneider and Hannay, who de-watered it and prospected for iron
ore for a while, but all operations ceased early in 1857. It was
derelict when, in July 1858, Wheal Eliza was selected by the only
Exmoor murderer, William Burgess, as the hiding-place for the
body of his little victim, an unwanted daughter. The story of the
detection of the crime and the recovery of the body from the
bottom of the shaft after months of search has been told by Mr
Thornton. A mining engineer, Thomas Scuse, contracted to pump
the shaft dry for £250 and started work on 16 October. According
to Thornton, when it was partially cleared, the dilapidated machinery broke down and the water rose again, and certainly it was not
until 2 December 1858 that the mine was finally de-watered for
the last time, and the body found.

THE BURCOMBE, DEER PARK, AND PICKED STONES
IRON MINES

Frederic Knight's attention had been attracted to the possibility
of discovering iron ore on Exmoor by events on the adjacent
Brendon Hills.[1] To quote his own record—'The first iron ore
found in our district was about the year 1847 or '48, when Mr.
Smith Tibbets drove a level under the Roman workings at Goosemoor, on Sir John Lethbridge's property, to look for copper.
When the level arrived under the vein, it cut through a compact
mass of spathic or sparry iron ore, which is a variety of iron ore
that had never previously been used in England. Mr. Smith
Tibbets sent several cargoes of this ore to the iron-masters in
South Wales, who, finding after trial that it did not assimilate with
their ordinary processes of iron making, and that it was not very
rich in metallic iron (containing 33 to 35 per cent.), declined to
purchase it at a remunerative price. Mr. Smith Tibbets, having
spent more than £2,000 in driving the level, ceased his operations,
but not before he had made his discovery known in scientific
circles. On the establishment of the Great Exhibition in Hyde
Park, in 1851, iron and iron ore were brought from all parts of the

Continent, and some of it of a very superior nature. The spathic iron ore, named above, was shown as the ore from which the best qualities of iron and steel were made, and the foreign iron-masters gave it as their opinion that iron and steel of quite first-rate quality could never be made in England for want of such ore.

'Mr. Samuel Blackwell of Dudley, one of the most scientific persons in the iron trade, undertook to arrange the iron depart-ment of the Exhibition, and knowing that considerable quantities of this spathic iron had been found in the Brendon Hills as before stated, examined the mine, and in conjunction with his brother-in-law, Mr. Ebenezer Rogers, of Abercairn, in South Wales, bought the sixty years' lease of the iron ore under Sir John Trevelyan's [? Lethbridge's] Brendon Hill property, which had been granted to Mr. Smith Tibbets.

'This lease was soon afterwards transferred to the Ebbw Vale Iron Co., at a premium of £1,000 per annum during its con-tinuance, and that Company soon afterwards took leases of the adjoining portions of the Brendon Hills belonging to Lord Carnarvon and Sir Walter Trevelyan.

'In 1853, when I first discovered iron ore on Exmoor, the first persons whom I invited to look at it were Messrs. Blackwell and Rogers.

'These gentlemen opened, in a short time, the vein called Rogers' Vein, which they pronounced of very great value, and they told me that they thought they could make a Company to work my iron mines. Their plans were broken through by a period of severe distress in the iron trade which prevented the persons they had applied to from joining in the speculation.'

The shaft on Rogers' vein was sunk in 1854 to a depth of 45ft before work stopped, William Dunstan, who had been Captain at Wheal Eliza, being in charge of the mining. Sixty-two tons of ore were raised, and sent to Mr Blackwell's works, at Dudley, for trial. Frederic Knight and his agent, Robert Smith, continued their search for minerals, working on the assumption that the ore deposits formed veins following the line of the strata right through the district, and thus they claimed to have identified the Brendon Hill and Combe Martin veins in their passage through Exmoor. Such identification is open to very serious question, though deposits of ore were discovered and proved, in many places, by trial workings on the surface.

By 1854, Frederic Knight had satisfied himself of the potential value of the minerals underlying his property. By means of trenches and holes and by making a few cuts into the side of the hill, the existence of deposits of ore was proved—for the most part on either side of the South Molton road, in the Deer Park and Hangley Cleeve to the south, and on Burcombe to the north. Other deposits were identified in the regions of Picked Stones and Hoar Oak Hill.

In January 1855 he journeyed to South Wales with the object of interesting the Welsh iron-masters in his discoveries. He was recommended to get the advice of a mining engineer, and, on the introduction of the manager of the Dowlais Iron Works, the property of the Guest trustees, the services of William Llewellyn, of Glanwern, Pontypool, a man of considerable local reputation and experience, were secured. Llewellyn arrived on Exmoor in May, and spent a week examining the various deposits and forming a judgement upon the property generally, regarded as a mining proposition.

The result was very favourable. In the month of July he embodied the conclusions to which he had come, following his examination of the ground and the analyses he had caused to be made of the ore samples, in a report to Frederic Knight, from which the following passages are extracted:

> The indications I observed in my examination of the district afford satisfactory evidences of the existence of iron ores throughout the property; but I am disposed to think they will be found to be chiefly red hematites in the North Forest and Brendon Commons. At all events, almost everything remains to be proved in those quarters, and the workable character of the veins, already discovered, has yet to be established. Not so, however, on the South Forest; for here every lode found to occur in the workings of the Brendon Hill Company seems to me to have been satisfactorily proved to be workable both as regards quality and thickness. . . .
>
> The inspection I have been enabled to make, and the information I have acquired during the week I spent at Exmoor, has been highly satisfactory to me, and such as to give rise to the strongest conviction of the great value and importance of the iron ores contained in the property.

The proofs and indications that I observed, and verified, as far as was practicable, were very numerous, amounting to not less than twenty-six veins. Of these, a great many had been opened out so far as to afford conclusive evidence of their value; and I am fully satisfied that the trials you have now in progress will show most of those I saw to be workable, and important veins. . . .

HANGLEY CLEEVE VEINS. Commencing at the southern extremity of the property, on the South Forest, the first veins that have yet been proved are those to which the name of the Hangley Cleeve Lodes has been assigned. There are three veins here, associated together at a distance of not many yards apart; but the only one completely proved is that which may apparently be termed the master-lode, inasmuch as, at its outcrop, it is considerably larger than the others. . . . I carefully measured the thickness of the great vein, and found the dimensions, from wall to wall, fully 15 feet, the lode being composed of a remarkably rich brown hematite, having, however, the distinct spathic structure, and being unquestionably the upper extremity of a vein of that character. . . . The sample assayed of this vein gave 60·63 per cent. of metallic iron, which exceeds the usual produce of the brown ore worked at the Brendon Hills; the specimen I have had tried from thence yielding only 52 per cent. . . .

The rest of Mr Llewellyn's report, dealing with at least a dozen other veins, is equally enthusiastic, and he concluded it as follows:

The veins I have enumerated, in the foregoing observations, are all included within the limits of the South Forest. It will be observed that they are unusually numerous, and several of those that have been proved are of remarkably good quality, and of such a thickness as to admit of their being very economically worked. If the resources of the South Forest were limited to the Hangley Cleeve Lode, the Double Lode, Rogers' Lode, the Roman Lode, and the two Cornham Ford veins, ranging as these do over an average distance of about four miles, there would, in my judgement, be an ample field for mining enterprise, and the tract would be sufficiently extensive, both as regards area and productive capabilities, to justify very extensive operations, and, after a fair trial of the veins, the construction of a railway, or tramway, for the conveyance of the ore to the Bristol Channel.

With a report such as this from an experienced mineral agent, who, as receiver in Chancery for the Lethbridge estates, had been responsible for the valuation and leasing of the iron mines on the neighbouring Brendon Hills, can it be wondered if Frederic Knight concluded that he had a valuable mineral property in Exmoor, and laid his plans accordingly? On the advice of Mr Llewellyn operations were to be restricted, in the first place, to the

South Forest, or rather to that portion of Exmoor lying south of the Challacombe–Exford road. Large deposits of iron were said to exist on the North Forest and on Brendon Common, but of a lower grade than the rest and not immediately attractive. On the South Forest and the land up to the Challacombe road there was a mineral-bearing area estimated at 6,250 acres, and with Llewellyn's report in his hands Frederic Knight again visited South Wales. At this time the trustees of the Guest estate, who carried on the great Dowlais Iron Works, the largest in Britain, were George Thomas Clark and Henry Austen Bruce. Mr Clark was a railway engineer by profession, and a director of the Ottoman Bank. He had worked under Brunel, and had had much experience of railway construction in India. Mr Bruce was Member of Parliament for Merthyr. They had only taken control as trustees and managers at Dowlais a few months before this time, on the re-marriage of Lady Charlotte Guest, the widow of Sir John Guest, Bt, who had left his wife sole trustee during her widowhood.

In October of this year (1855) Mr Clark visited Exmoor in the company of his own mining managers, and it is clear that they formed an opinion of the mining possibilities at least as favourable as that of Llewellyn. A memorandum to Frederic Knight, written by Mr Clark immediately after his visit, contains the following passages:

> The Dowlais agents report that the lodes of iron ore upon Mr. Knight's Exmoor estate are of quality at least equal to the best ones now in use, and in quantity sufficient for the supply of all the iron works in the kingdom for a long period. The lodes are intersected and laid open by deep valleys, and admit of being worked for many years to come without the aid of pumps, in this respect having a great advantage over the lodes on the Brendon Hills, and most of those at present worked in Ulverston and elsewhere.
>
> Mr. Knight, therefore, possesses an ore which he could supply in sufficient quantities at the mine mouth, of at least as good quality, and at a much cheaper rate than any ore at this time used by the Dowlais Iron Company.

'My hopes and expectations of enormous quantities of iron ore being found on my estate were not excited to the utmost pitch until after the visit of Mr. Clark and his agents, to Exmoor, to inspect the mines', wrote Frederic Knight, when, at a later date, trouble had arisen.—'If ever I formed an exaggerated opinion of the iron lodes, it was after perusing their document.' Negotiations proceed rapidly, and after meetings between the parties at Bristol and at Dowlais, agreement as to the terms of a lease was reached.

It had been recognised from the first that one of the most important problems in the exploitation of minerals on Exmoor was the provision of transport to the coast. Llewellyn dealt with it at length in his report, discussing the alternative advantages of Lynmouth and Porlock as places for shipment, and Mr Clark, on the occasion of his visit to Exmoor, accompanied Frederic Knight over the Commons to both these harbours, in order to form an opinion, as an experienced railway engineer, of the feasibility of making a railway from Simonsbath to one of them. At Porlock they met Colonel Blathwayt, and with him they visited the new dock which he was then constructing at Porlock Weir. It was impossible for the Guest trustees to involve the Dowlais Iron Works in the construction of a railway, but they were anxious to do all that was possible, within the terms of their trust, to facilitate the enterprise. Frederic Knight had explained his inability to finance the scheme himself, owing to the Chancery suit in which he was then involved with his brothers and sisters, and thus a compromise was agreed upon whereby the Dowlais Iron Company was to supply the rails and ironwork.

The agreement for the lease was signed by Llewellyn, on behalf of the Dowlais Iron Company, on 15 December 1855. The lands included in the agreement were Great and Little Cornham, Horcombe, Burcombe, Wester Emmetts and Hangley Cleeve. The term was to be forty-two years from 1 January 1856, determinable after three years by twelve months' notice. A royalty of 1s per ton on all iron ore raised was payable, subject to a minimum dead rent of £500 in 1857 and £1,000 per annum thereafter. By an 'independent agreement' the Dowlais Company covenanted to supply Frederic Knight, in the event of a railway being constructed from Simonsbath, either to Lynmouth, or to Porlock Weir, 'with all rails, machinery for inclined planes, and other ironwork as can be and is customarily manufactured at the Dowlais Works, and that may be required in the construction of the said line of railway . . . at the lowest trade prices existing at the port of Cardiff at the time of supplying . . . payment for the same to be received by the

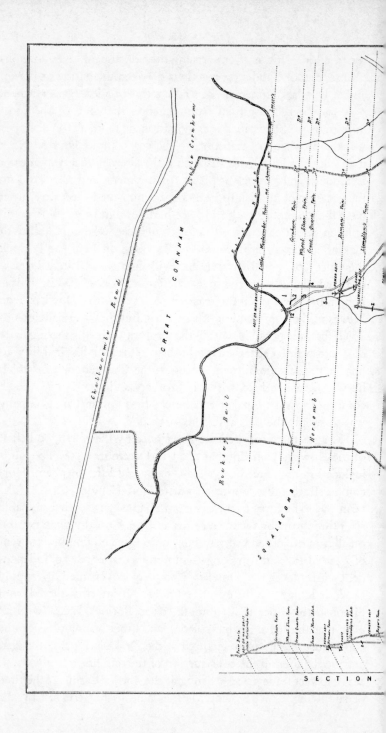

SECTION.

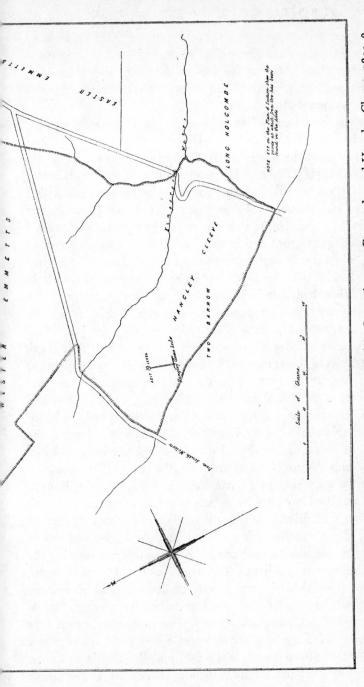

Plan and Section of the Dowlais Iron Company's Mining Operations on Burcombe and Hangley Cleeve, 1855–8

lessees out of the galeages on the ores raised from the demised tract as they arise and become due'. In return, Frederic Knight was to charge a higher royalty for ores on the South Forest leased to anyone else, or alternatively, to reduce the Dowlais Company's royalty by one-sixth.

Mining operations had already been begun, for on 30 November 1855 the first sod was cut by the Dowlais Iron Company at their lowest level on the Barle, by Cornham Ford. Here the 'Cornham Vein' outcropped and could be worked by 'patching', and George Martin, the Dowlais Company's mining agent, arranged with a gang of six miners, of whom Robert Comer, of Exmoor, was captain, to bring the ore to bank, at 3s 6d per ton. One hundred and seventy-five tons had been raised at this point, at a cost of £250, when the deposit began to peter out, and the working had to be abandoned in the following June. To aid the work, a black-smith's shop had been built early in 1856.

At the same time, arrangements were made to drive an adit, or level, afterwards called the Main Drift, from a point just below Cornham Ford, southward through the property. This work formed part of the agreement between the parties, and a glance at the accompanying plan will make the purpose clear. The land rises very steeply from the Barle southward over Burcombe Hill to the Simonsbath–South Molton road, which formed the boundary of this section of the Dowlais Company's lease, and all the veins, or lodes, of ore alleged to exist in this section, the Little Woolcombe Vein, the Cornham Vein, the Wheal Eliza Vein, the Great Quartz Vein, the Roman Vein, Llewellyn's Vein, Rogers' Vein, and the Deer Park Vein, pass through it from east to west. Thus an adit driven southward on the level, from the lowest point, would cut through the strata at right angles and would reach the boundary at a depth of some 400ft, after proving the veins, one by one, at depth. The work was let to John Hopkins, a miner from Dowlais, and a party of five other Welsh miners, four of whom soon left and were replaced by Devon men. Operations started on Christmas Eve 1855; three turns of men were kept at work, day and night, for two and a half years, except for a stoppage of fifteen weeks in 1857–8, and the level was driven 413yd. The total distance from the line of the Barle to the line of the supposed Deer Park Lode is 1,100yd and the work of driving the level had been estimated to take three years, but the ground proved very unfavourable, and the average progress made was only 2½yd per week. Although it never reached the boundary, and so cannot be said to have proved the property, the Main Drift passed through the ground in which the Little Woolcombe, the Cornham, the Wheal Eliza and the Great Quartz Veins ought to have been found, without disclosing the presence of any ore of the least value.

After the work had proceeded for some eighteen months, it was decided, partly to expedite matters and partly for the ventilation of the level, to sink a shaft on the Roman Lode, on the line of the Main Drift and down to the same depth. On the completion of this shaft it was intended to work north and south from it, so that operations on the Main Drift would be proceeding from three faces at the same time. The sinking occupied nearly two years; pumping was necessary to keep it clear of water until the Main Drift should be joined, when this would drain it, and a 20ft waterwheel was erected at Cornham Ford (by the existing foot-bridge) to provide the power for an 8in pump. The whole of the works involved represented an expenditure of nearly £1,000, and virtually no ore was met with. The shaft had reached the intended line of the Main Drift, at a depth of about 150ft, by the end of May 1858, and driving commenced on the north and south levels, but all operations were abandoned on 8 June when the north level, which was to have joined the Main Drift (then 176yd away), was only 8yd long.

The advice of the agents of the Dowlais Company, Messrs Evans & Martin, was to restrict operations to the Main Drift until the property had been proved. This was unsatisfactory to Frederic Knight, who thought that the position justified a less cautious policy. In January 1856 he wrote to Mr Clark, from Wolverley:

> *In my opinion* you are doing nothing on Exmoor. I will endeavour to explain to you what *I think* ought to be done, but Evans seems to me to be determined to stick to his old plan of driving one level at the lowest point, and leaving the rest alone, or at best patching a little on the surface. . . . Now, if you only continue your present plan you will not touch any of those which we suppose to be the larger veins for two years.

Now I believe that obstinacy is an indispensable ingredient in the character of a great man, and I believe John Evans to enjoy a full share of it, combined with many other good and great qualities. Now, John Evans has unfortunately decided from the first that Level BC [the Main Drift] shall be driven, and no other one. In short, he has decided to put off any inspection of the large lodes for 2 or perhaps 3 years. When it is considered that the celebrated *Goosemoor Lode*, in the Brendon Hills, was cut by a level only 90 feet below the surface, and proved to be 20 feet wide, which lode we believe to be identical with *Lode AC*, it does not seem reasonable to let it lie for years . . .

How to endeavour to overthrow the decision of the great man (for whom, and for whose opinions in all other respects, I entertain a high esteem) I know not.

I know that I dare not say another word to him on the subject. If you and Bruce were to go to Exmoor with Martin and inspect the ground personally, much might be hoped for and perhaps effected.

A fortnight later Mr Clark replied from Dowlais:

I have run down here for a day or two, determined to do something to restore our waning character in your eyes, and to relieve us from that laudable conjugal indignation which I am perfectly sure Mrs. Knight must by this time begin to feel towards Bruce and myself.

Bruce and I yesterday saw Martin and Evans, and having made our suggestions, and insisted on certain points, we met again this morning and sanctioned certain steps.

Martin leaves for Exmoor in a few days, and he takes with him our agent from the Forest of Dean, whom we propose to fix permanently at Exmoor, in consideration of the large expenditure we are about to make there; a large cargoe of trams, plates, barrows, and tools will be sent over at once.

Martin will consult with Smith, whose conduct seems to have been very judicious, and will take steps, by patching and opening lodes at the ends, to bring upon the banks as quickly as possible a large quantity of ore, say 10 or 12,000 tons.

Meanwhile we are refusing new and reduced offers of ores from Whitehaven, in the hope and expectation that the next three months' operations would justify us in looking to Exmoor for our sole supply. We have now either here or contracted for about 37,000 tons, so we shall long before the close of the year want more, and this, by some means or other, we propose to get from Exmoor.

All this ought to, and I have no doubt will, satisfy you that we are in earnest. . . . Martin will arrange to employ a large force, I hope at least 100 men; and I have undertaken to suggest to you the wisdom of letting Smith assist in lodging them as near as possible to the workings.

When the new agent is installed, Bruce and I propose to take advantage of the first fine week to go with you to Exmoor to meet a contractor, and to go into the question of the railway in good earnest. I am very anxious that Bruce should see with his own eyes the two ports, and that our collective wisdom, advised by the practical experience of a contractor, should be brought to bear upon the whole question.

From this letter it is evident that the Dowlais Iron Company had expectations of an almost immediate supply of very large quantities of iron ore from Exmoor, and that the construction of the railway either to Lynmouth or to Porlock was a pressing matter.

Following on the decisions taken as indicated in this letter, an active development programme was initiated. John White, the Dowlais Company's agent from the Forest of Dean, arrived on Exmoor on 2 February 1856, and immediately a drift called Comer's Level was commenced, at the point numbered 9 on the plan, with a view to striking Rogers' Vein. This level was driven about 150yd, passing through the ground which should have held the vein without any indication of ore. The expenditure on these works amounted to £230, and they were abandoned as useless in the month of December following.

In March of the same year two other operations were begun. At the point numbered 8 on the plan a drift was begun for the purpose of cutting Llewellyn's Lode, and at a point 83yd from the mouth a vein, from 3ft to 4ft in thickness, was encountered. Forty tons of ore were obtained, but it was too much mixed with quartz to be of any value, and workings on the vein, east and west, showed no improvement. The drift was continued to a total distance of 212yd, when, after an expenditure of £450 and no other vein found, it was abandoned. Simultaneously with this work, steps were taken for getting ore from the Hangley Cleeve Vein. This was one of the places where old workings were evident. Operations were begun by patching, or open work, and to drain the vein a drift from the point numbered 10 on the plan was begun. The vein was followed westward, where it proved to be 6ft thick, but eastward it quickly nipped out. The surface indications on this lode were of a very favourable character, but when the drift struck the vein at a depth of 40ft the indications were so much less favourable as to satisfy the Dowlais agents that it was only superficial, and so irregular as not to be worth working. Operations were abandoned in August 1857 when the drift had been driven 194yd, the total quantity of ore brought to bank having been about 1,200 tons and the total expenditure about £700.

Following the commencement of work at Hangley Cleeve, a fourth drift was begun, at the point numbered 7 on the plan, for the purpose of proving the Roman Vein. Upon this vein there was evidence of extensive old workings, and the indications promised a considerable yield of ore. The vein was struck by the drift at a distance of 86yd and was followed, east and west, for a considerable distance, until the ore became so thin that further work had to be abandoned. This was in May 1858, by which time about 640 tons of ore had been brought to bank from these works, at a cost of about £800, and the drift extended to a total length of 174yd through barren ground.

Nor did this exhaust the steps taken by the Company to explore their property. In December 1856, twelve months after the first beginning of mining operations by Cornham Ford, another level was begun, called the Platform Level, at the point numbered 5 on the plan. In the previous month of June, John White had been succeeded by Henry Scale as local superintendent on Exmoor, and it was at his instance that this level was driven, to get ore from a vein, not previously mentioned, of which he thought there were sufficient surface indications. A sum of £30 was spent on this level, but no ore was disclosed.

At various other times small openings were made, here and there, on the line of supposed veins, without disclosing any ore worth working. Nor were conditions easy at the mines. John White had written, in February 1856, 'You ask me how I like this place, not at all it's one of the most miserable places', and a year later after White's return to the Forest of Dean, his successor, Henry Scale, was lamenting, 'We have had a series of storms, snow drifting 10 feet deep—floods—and winds such as have carried men off their feet! now intense frost.'

At the end of two and a half years' active exploration, then, the position was that after driving a deep level through nearly one-

half of the property, and several shallower levels to prove particular veins; after patching, here and there, where the surface
indications seemed favourable; after sinking a shaft 150ft deep, no
considerable body of iron ore had been encountered at any point.
In the meantime, however, the hopes of the parties, as indicated
in the letter of January 1856 from Mr Clark quoted above, continued to run high, and the most cordial relations were maintained. In July 1856, Mr Clark wrote: 'We are in the heart of
Llewellyn's Lode and Scale is in raptures at the general progress.
Why, when you make your transit from Worcestershire to Linton,
cannot you pause here?'

In August 1856, 400 tons of ore were transported to Merthyr
Tydfil for trial in a blast furnace. Henry Scale reported to Dowlais
on 15 August that '400 tons of iron ore will be sent to Lynmouth
for shipment to Cardiff. 175 to 200 tons of "Cornham Ford" ore
and 200 to 225 tons of "Hangley Cleave" ore. The former is a rich
Hamatite small in character Dark red Colour. The latter Black in
larger masses. The ore will arrive at Lynmouth at the rate of 12
to 15 tons per day beginning on Monday.' 'We shall get it here for
about £1 per ton', wrote Mr Clark. 'Are you not coming here to
see your ore smelted and will you persuade your fairer moiety and
Master Fred into these dusty regions? We will find some Welsh
attornies to meet her, and you shall recite to them Templer's
epigram.'[4]

And in the following month he wrote again—'We are doing
better than ever at Exmoor . . . We are dabbling in Bessemer's
process, and have rolled two 19 foot rails. I want to try it with
your ore. Bessemer comes here this week; Exmoor ore and
Bessemer's process . . . My wife joins in kind regards to Mrs.
Knight.'

In November of the same year Mr Clark wrote concerning the
railway, that they would be ready for it in the following spring.
'Patience', he added, 'is my Goddess, to whom I am all the more
zealously obedient, as I am often an unfaithful worshipper.' On
the same point he wrote again a month later. 'My reports from
Exmoor are excellent. The time is fast approaching when it will be
prudent to commence the railway.'

In January 1857, the Dowlais Company was requiring upwards

of 1,500 tons of iron ore weekly. Messrs Bruce and Clark visited
Exmoor in May 1857, and the latter wrote to Mr Knight that 'all
looks as well as we could fairly expect'.

As may be supposed, one of the most pressing needs in connection with the development of the iron mines was the provision
of housing for the miners. At first they had to lodge at a distance,
and every cottage in Simonsbath had its quota of lodgers, while
miners lived 'at North Molton—5 Miles off, at Combe Martin 12
to 13 Miles off, at Lynmouth—at Challacombe.' Overcrowding
was common, and William Burgess, who was a surface worker at
the mines, shared a bed with his six-year-old daughter and another
miner, in their lodgings at Gallon House Cottage. The agreement
was that Frederic Knight should build the houses, and that the
Dowlais Company should rent them. 'Let me have a rough plan',
he wrote, 'of what you consider a proper and sufficient cottage for
miners. I do not wish to allow any nasty holes to be built.' And
Mr Clark replied that in Aberdare a good cottage, one in a row,
should not cost more than £70. He offered to pay a rent of £6 per
annum on each cottage erected, for five years, with the stipulation
that the cottages must be placed upon the company's land and
built according to their design.

Frederic Knight was unable to find a builder to erect cottages
on Exmoor at Aberdare prices, and, in spite of his objection to
housing people in 'nasty holes', he proposed a cheaper plan, to
which Mr Clark most reluctantly agreed on the score of economy.
'The design', he wrote, 'offends morally and physically against the
fundamental rules of cottage building. The two house doors are
under one shed—*ergo*, the women will quarrel. The lodgers go
through the two rooms, sitting and kitchen, and possibly through
a bedroom to reach their own, thus destroying all privacy, and a
miner's lodger is a rough fellow. There is a gutter along the main
wall, which, do what you will, will leak.'

How many cottages were built is not certain. The ruins of a row
of six at Cornham Ford still remain, and if they enjoyed the
advantage of being close to the scene of operations they were
certainly devoid of every other amenity of life. By mid December
1856, Scale reported 'the contractor is getting on with the houses
as fast as the weather will admit. We have got the roofs on two

Page 193 Before and after World War II. Devastation at Larkbarrow: (*above*) 1929; (*below*) 1954

Page *194* Before and after World War II. Improvement at Picked Stones: (*above*) 1ç
(*below*) 1967

of them', and at least one was occupied by March 1857. Robert Smith has described one pair of cottages and a mine-office which were erected for the Dowlais Company at this time, in an article contributed to the *Journal* of the Bath and West of England Society.[5]

The housing question was still acute in the latter part of 1857. 'Scale writes to me in the strongest terms about houses. Now, all hangs upon this, for if we do not push on faster and open more ground, we shall not have data to start the railway; and if we suffer our agreement with Blathwayt to lapse we shall be in a pickle.

'I assure you the settlement of this question is one of days. It presses hard upon us all, and upon no one heavier than upon you, which is right, since you will derive considerable profit from it, both in direct rent and far more in the sale of produce.

'I think when Scale pours a broadside into me, as he does pretty often about cottages, I shall step aside and direct it against you.' Thus wrote Mr Clark in October 1857, and this is the last reference in the still existing correspondence to the question of house accommodation, so far as concerns the Dowlais Iron Company. Some cottages were erected, and probably the doubts which shortly afterwards assailed the minds of the Guest Trustees about the possibility of getting ore in payable quantities from Exmoor disposed of the question as a matter of urgency.

It is now necessary to see what developments had been taking place with regard to mining on other parts of the Forest. Convinced of the value of the ore deposits, Frederic Knight had bought up, some time before, the remainder of the lease of the Wheal Eliza mine and the minerals under Honeymead Farm (see page 177), and in August 1855 he had paid the Office of Woods and Forests for a conveyance of the minerals which his father had bought from the Crown in 1819. Other people besides the Guest trustees had been interested in the prospect of discoveries of iron ore in quantity on Exmoor, granted that the transport problem could be solved. At this time the Merthyr Tydfil iron-masters drew their supplies from many places, most of them situated at much greater distances than the West Somerset coast. One district from which large supplies were drawn was that of Ulverston, in

M

Lancashire, where mines were operated by the firm of Messrs Schneider & Hannay.[6] They were already contractors for large deliveries of Ulverston ore to the Dowlais Iron Company, and if the Exmoor proposition was likely to materialise they were anxious to be concerned in it, not only as a potential source of cheap ore, but also so that they might control the competition which would arise.

On 3 April 1856, after due investigation, Messrs Schneider & Hannay entered into an agreement for a lease of a large part of the area not already included in the Dowlais Company's sett. The area included the whole of the tract north of the Dowlais Company's boundary, where the Hoar Oak Veins were supposed to run, and the whole of the Deer Park portion of the South Forest, extending from Wintershead to Winstitchin. Most of the lodes in the southern portion of Burcombe continued eastward under the Simonsbath–South Molton road into the Deer Park, and at the eastern extremity of the sett there was the Wheal Eliza mine, already equipped, which gave evidence of producing considerable quantities of iron ore.

Frederic Knight was fully alive to the danger of letting so large a part of his supposed mineral wealth to a company already actively engaged in the development of properties less favourably placed for the supply of ore to South Wales. By the payment of a comparatively small sum by way of dead, or sleeping, rent, it might be possible for them to hang up the property indefinitely, and greatly to his prejudice, while they continued to exploit their other mines. He took steps, accordingly, to secure that the area leased to them should be fairly worked, and there seems no reason to doubt that Messrs Schneider & Hannay entered into possession with the full intention of proving the property and of extracting any ore that might exist in payable quantities. As proof of this, it is recorded that they had offered to find £7,000 towards the cost of the projected railway to the coast, though there was no agreement with them upon the subject. Further, they contracted to pay a dead rent of no less than £2,000 per annum, the basic royalty being 1s 3d per ton for iron ore and 8d for clay ironstone.

They, too, were under contract to prove the property by driving an adit through it from the lowest level, and by sinking shafts upon the lodes at the top of the Deer Park, within a year. They decided to make a start with the shaft sinking; a pumping engine was installed near Blue Gate, and shafts were sunk upon the Top Deer Park Lode and the Double Lode; the shaft begun in 1854 by Mr Ebenezer Rogers on Rogers' Lode was reopened, at the same time, and deepened. (See plan.) Shortly after, an adit was begun in the valley, with the object of proving these veins at depth, and the old Wheal Eliza mine on the Barle, below Winstitchin, was re-fitted. 'The Druid', who visited Exmoor in 1860, notes that in riding from the South Forest to Honeymead he crossed the brook (the Barle) 'in the neighbourhood of an iron mine, whose water-wheel was lazily resting till the railway era sets in'. Rogers' Lode seems to have been the most promising, and Henry Scale reported, in August 1856, that 'Messrs. Schneider's Shafts upon the Deer Park are looking well—they have *all ore* in Roger's Shaft, full 4½ feet in the clear'; the shaft sunk upon it was continued to a depth of 96ft, and about 800 tons of ore were raised.

About the time of the lease to Messrs Schneider & Hannay, Frederic Knight completed his scheme for the development of the Exmoor minerals by letting the remainder of the property which he had prospected, and upon which William Llewellyn had re-ported so favourably, comprising mainly the region round Picked Stones, to the east of the Ulverston Company's boundary, and Exe Cleave, to Anthony Hill, of the Plymouth Iron Company, Merthyr Tydfil, Glamorgan. The agreement was dated 14 January 1857, and was for the same term and at the same royalties as the Schneider and Hannay lease, with a dead rent of £500 per annum, the lessee covenanting to drive adits or sink shafts on the lodes to a depth of at least 100ft below the surface. Work was begun forthwith, a shaft was sunk upon the Picked Stones lode to a depth of 65ft, and a level was driven westward upon the lode. East of the shaft an adit level was also begun, and a further shaft and an adit were driven in Exe Cleave between Red Deer and the river. Mr Hill spent less money than either of the other lessees, and it is doubtful if he entertained a high-opinion of the property. He had other interests in iron mining, in the north of England; in a letter to Mr Clark, Frederic Knight makes the imputation that both Hill and Schneider were more concerned to stop mining on

Exmoor than to develop it. And Mr Clark wrote that 'Scale has little faith in Schneider and thinks him trifling; certainly he and Hill take it very easy', though it is only fair to say that he added— 'Hill, however, speaks highly of the taking'. In March 1858, when the Dowlais Company discharged Henry Scale, their Exmoor superintendent, Mr Hill engaged him, although he must have been aware of the reasons for his dismissal. Scale lived at Honeymead. He seems to have been a man of enthusiastic temperament who at first impressed but soon disappointed his employers. 'Scale is active and popular', wrote Frederic Knight at one time; and later —'He is the greatest *liar* I ever met with'. And thus Mr Clark: 'He has conducted himself with great energy and great prudence, and I am thoroughly satisfied with him', and within two months—'his reports are so variable, and his opinions so fluctuating, that I have little confidence in what he reports'. Three months later he was dismissed and joined Mr Hill.

Scale had previously approached Mr Schneider, unsuccessfully, with a view to getting the management of his mines. Amongst other enterprises, he built a shop at Simonsbath, which was kept by Gifford, the innkeeper there (see page 233). He was a deeply religious man: 'he evinces strong signs of going to church after the approaching consecration' (1856) wrote Frederic Knight; and the Rev W. H. Thornton describes a strange scene at the deathbed of one of Scale's daughters, when he anointed the girl with oil and called upon her to rise up and walk. Mr Thornton says that he represented the Crawshays, of Merthyr Tydfil; but though Frederic Knight had tried to interest Robert Crawshay in the Exmoor minerals, his firm had not responded, unless, in some way, it was standing in with Anthony Hill.

Scale had always been pressing for more housing on Exmoor for the Dowlais miners. On joining Mr Hill, the first question was that of accommodation for the men, and some cowsheds at Winstitchin and Picked Stones were converted into cottages from his plans. They contained a living-room and two bedrooms—one lighted only from the roof—all on the ground floor, and they reverted to their original purpose when the mining operations were abandoned.

Thus, within a few months of the turning of the first sod, by Cornham Ford, in November 1855, the whole of the area upon which Mr Knight and his agent, Robert Smith, had prospected so successfully, as it appeared, was in the course of active development—the Dowlais Iron Company on Burcombe and Hangley Cleeve, the Ulverston Company in the Deer Park and at Wheal Eliza, and later the Plymouth Iron Company at Picked Stones and Exe Cleave—but before the first year was three parts spent there were indications of the disappointment and failure in which the enterprise was so soon to end. The trouble began with Mr Schneider's operations. In August 1856, Frederic Knight wrote to Mr Clark: 'Schneider has been at Exmoor and discharged his two agents; the principal one, finding that there were many reasons for not living on Exmoor, established himself, with a brace of doxies, at South Molton, and drove them all over the country in flies—always on business.

'Many men have been employed digging holes and puddling about, but next to nothing has been done, although they have more men at work than you, and have, I hear, spent nearly the same amount of money. The agents have been abusing the place and us all; indeed, before Schneider came down and discharged them, my wise men had strong suspicion that there was no wish to find the iron at all.'

Mr Schneider's agreement was for forty-three years, but he could withdraw at the end of twelve months if certain conditions had been fulfilled. By November 1856, he had formed a bad opinion of the value of the enterprise, and as most of the veins of ore in the Deer Park traversed the Dowlais Company's taking also, his attitude seems to have been to employ the minimum of staff possible under his agreement (twenty men) and to let the Dowlais people prove the property. Mining difficulties, too, were greater than had been anticipated, and the depth to which the shafts on the Deer Park had to be sunk before a level could be driven to the Barle (400ft) had not been calculated, and was twice as much as that which he had estimated. Certainly he told Frederic Knight that he did not intend to work on the Hoar Oak veins for fear that this should lead other people to seek for and find them on other properties nearer to the coast, and very soon he and his partner came to the conclusion that there was no ore on Exmoor capable of being worked with profit. In December he gave notice of his intention to withdraw at the end of his first year, and work on his holding was abandoned early in 1857.

Frederic Knight felt there had been no serious attempt by Messrs Schneider & Hannay to carry out the terms of their agreement, and after correspondence upon the point he commenced a Chancery suit against them in May 1857. Thereupon, Mr Schneider approached the Dowlais Iron Company, who were old customers of his for his Ulverston ore, with a view to inducing them to throw up their tenancy also. They, however, had just had a fresh report upon Exmoor from their agent, William Menelaus, which was hopeful to their enterprise, and no concerted action resulted. The case came on at the end of the year, judgement being given for Frederic Knight for specific performance of the agreement. Messrs Schneider & Hannay, however, were so convinced, 'as well by our own experience and observation, and those of our own agents, as also by the opinion of mining engineers and surveyors of high science and great experience, whom we consulted in consequence of the litigation, that to proceed with mining operations on Exmoor would only involve a waste of time and money, that we determined upon a compromise with the Plaintiff, and we agreed to pay him a very considerable sum to be relieved from our engagement'. The amount received by Frederic Knight as consideration for the surrender of their lease was £10,000.

As mentioned above, the Dowlais people were not discouraged by Mr Schneider's adverse opinion of the possibilities of Exmoor as a mining proposition; in fact, when it was apparent that his firm did not intend to proceed with the development of the property, and long before the hearing of the action against him, they made tentative proposals for taking over his tract, but these came to nothing. The long period of prosperity in South Wales was about to come to a sudden end, and the autumn and winter of 1857–8 was a difficult time for English iron-masters. Much of their market was provided by the great industrial development in America during the previous decade, and the over-speculation and unsound and even dishonest finance which accompanied it brought about a crisis which reacted severely upon the English manufacturers concerned. 'The year 1857', Woodrow Wilson has recorded of America,

> was a year of very serious commercial depression, paying the penalty for years of confident and adventurous speculation. For ten years, since 1846, the country had felt the exhilaration and excitement of a rapid business expansion, which the discovery of gold in California had greatly quickened. . . . Money was quickly enough invested, but was very slow to yield an increase. Enterprise after enterprise proved a dead loss. . . . Railways were built where there were neither towns nor farms to support them, sometimes on open reaches of the country, which the plough had never touched. . . . The bubbles of fatuous enterprise were pricked and a crisis of wholesale loss, panic, and depression occurred in spite of every token of trade and profit to come.

The Dowlais Iron Company suffered, in common with others, from the loss of their markets and difficulty in collecting payments due. 'You will not be surprised', wrote Mr Clark in November 1857, 'to learn that the pressure from America has affected the iron trade, both in Staffordshire and here, very seriously, and, indeed, so much so, that some works are closed, others doing very little indeed, and we ourselves entering upon half work, and in every way cutting down our expenditure even in very minute matters. I mention this that you may know to what cause to attribute the directions which I am about to send to Mr. Scale, to stop our works for the present.' There was a further letter from him, in the month following, which may be quoted as throwing additional light upon the industrial situation in South Wales, precipitated by the financial collapse in the United States.

> We, and indeed all our brethren, are much in the condition of sailors in a gale who are throwing overboard everything, to weather out the danger. We have reduced wages 20 to 25 per cent., dismissed many more, and are working more upon half time. The only symptom of a better state of things is that we have got a rail order by which we shall only lose something under £1 per ton! However, if we are to lose it is better to do so by means which will enable us to employ our men. Still we ought not to complain—bad debts we have none, our losses by the failure of other houses are very trifling and we have no very great quantity of iron locked up. Rumour says that the Baileys have lost £400,000 by American dealings, that the Ebbw Vale have been driven to get a credit for £200,000 at the Bank, and that Crawshay has lost—for the present

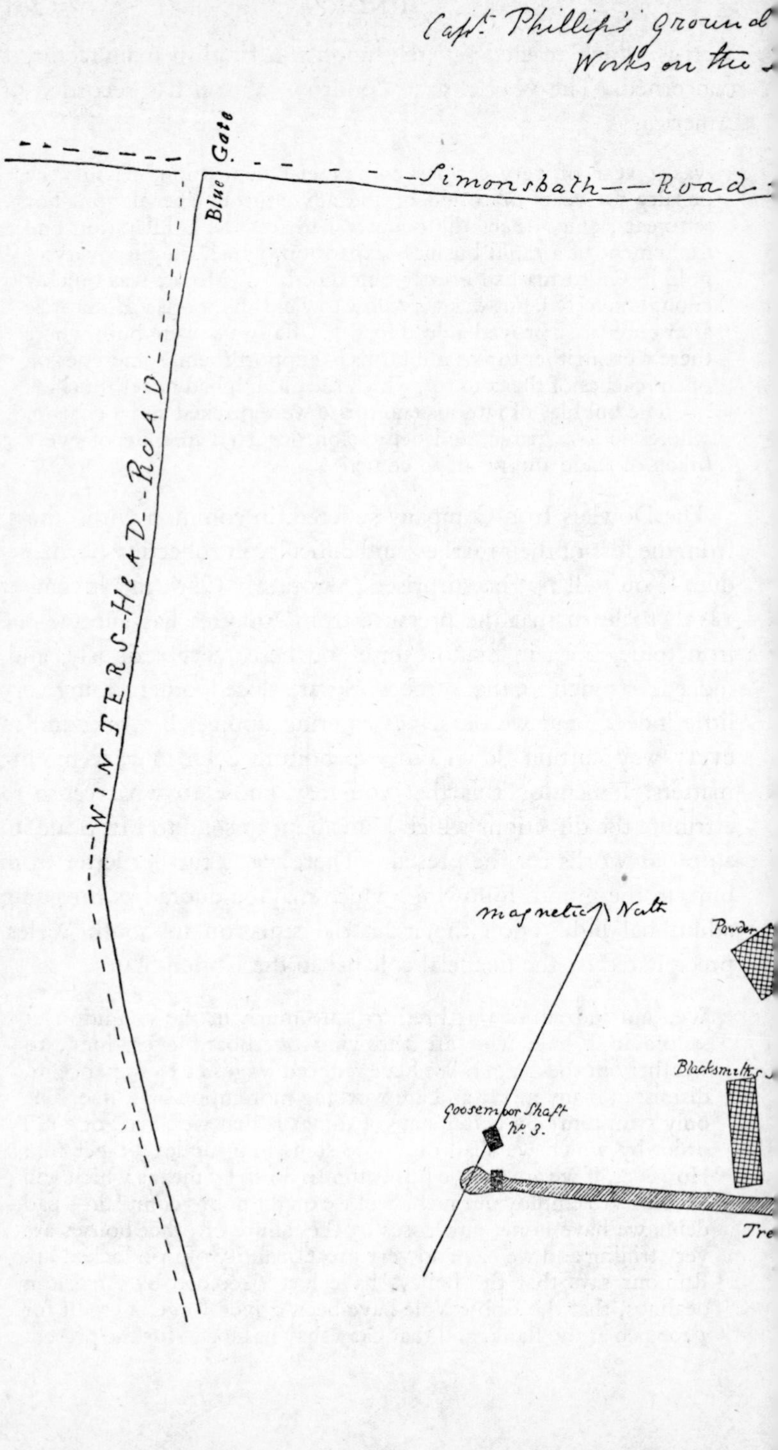

Capt. Phillip's Ground
Works on the
Blue Gate
Simonsbath --- Road
WINTERS-HEAD-ROAD
Magnetic North
Powder
Blacksmiths
Goosemoor Shaft
No. 3.
Tre

of Messr. Schneider & Co.
k

New Shaft by
onsbath Road.

Trench near Simonsbath Road.

This is the Bearing of the Double Lode.

This is the Bearing of Rogers' Lode.

Double Lode Shaft Nº 2

Double Lode Trench

Double Lode Trench

Rogers' Lode

North 69 degrees West

Engine House & Boiler

Double
Lode

Rogers'
Shaft - Nº 1

by Frederick Knight Esqʳᵉ

Trench cut by Schneider Hannay & Co

at least—£150,000 in Saunderson's house, besides what he may have locked up in America. In Aberdare and the adjacent valleys the colliers are out and the military, I hear, called in. Our men, however, shew the best spirit. They read the better class of newspapers, *Times*, etc., in the reading room and they see that the masters are also suffering; poor fellows, should cold weather come or prices of provisions rise I fear the pressure will be too great. However, it is a great comfort that they have no single political grievance. Further representative reform and ballot are not at present very much cared about, and our Chartists at Merthyr have behaved extremely well at the recent meetings.

Work on Exmoor was stopped in December 1857 for fifteen weeks, and though Scale offered to tender for the continuation of the Main Drift, this was declined. The period coincided with the hearing of the action against Mr Schneider, who did not fail to attempt to make capital for his case out of the circumstance, and Frederic Knight records that the stoppage at this particular moment was a heavy blow to him. As a precautionary measure, too, though only as such, the Dowlais trustees gave him twelve months' notice, from 1 January 1858, to terminate their agreement for a lease of the mines on Exmoor.

Work on the mines began again in March 1858, Henry Scale having been replaced in the meantime by William Dunstan as the Dowlais Company's agent. He was a Cornish mine-captain who had been in charge, at one time, of the Wheal Eliza mine, and who had sunk the first shaft on the Deer Park, in 1854, for Mr Ebenezer Rogers. Later, he was employed by him in getting iron ore from the North Devon Iron Mines, at Combe Martin, which petered out about this time. That the trustees, however, were now beginning to have serious misgivings about their mining prospects is evident from their correspondence at this time. In March 1858, Frederic Knight had written from Wolverley to Mr Bruce: 'If the proceedings in Schneider's case lead to his giving up the property, I shall be only too glad to increase the Dowlais Company's taking on the most favourable terms to them. Mr. Hill is also asking for an extension.' And two days later Mr Bruce replied: 'I do most earnestly hope (both for our own sakes and for yours) that the prospects of the Exmoor mines will justify us in extending our takings. We have spent the sum of £6,000 (I think),[7] and are, as you may suppose, much perplexed between our desire, on the one hand, to justify the prudence of the outlay, and our fear, on the other, of increasing it without an adequate return. I hope that Clark will now resume operations vigorously. I keep my expectations in suspense; but I confess that hope of such large discoveries as will justify the expense of a railway is not so strong as it was.

'Most sorry am I to say anything discouraging to you, but it is better on all accounts that you should understand our view of the case. You may still be right, and next to yourself, none are so interested as we are in hoping so.'

The work which proceeded throughout the spring and summer of 1858 was productive of no better results than that which had gone before. In May, the Dowlais trustees caused an independent report upon the property to be made by Stephen Eddy and John Taylor, as a result of which all work was stopped on 8 June, and although, as things turned out, this date was to mark the termination of the company's operations on Exmoor, the trustees were still willing, at that time, to go forward if they could obtain certain modifications of the terms of their agreement. They stated their position and proposals in a letter to Frederic Knight which follows here in full, as it seems to be a fair and complete summary both of their actions and of their point of view:

> Dowlais House, Merthyr Tydvil,
> 26th June 1858.
>
> My dear Mr. Knight,—I write to bring formally under your attention a matter which has already been the subject of conversation between us, and which, from the magnitude of the interest involved, deserves your serious, and for other reasons I think, your favourable consideration.
>
> When, above two years ago, we entered into the agreement with you under which we have worked at Exmoor, we covenanted, among other things, to drive a certain drift a specified distance, to pay a certain sleeping rent, and in the event of a railway being made, to supply, under certain conditions, the rails.
>
> These covenants were entered into by Mr. Bruce and myself with the firm belief, as stated by you and your advisers, and confirmed by our advisers, that the ore was present in large quantities, and that we should speedily find ourselves in a position to need a railway, and to find the making one a profitable investment. You pressed the matter strongly upon us, and we entered at once and cordially into the undertaking, and by our example led, as is well known, others to make similar ventures.
>
> In proof of the good faith with which we entered upon our

engagements, I may remind you that we did not confine ourselves to the letter of our agreement, but we opened the ground in various places, and in most respects in accordance with your opinion and advice, and, indeed, took every step that we could take to prove the ground rapidly and effectually; in fact, we have spent upwards of £6,000 in the works, and have only removed about £950 worth of ore.

We have built cottages, and we joined with you in applications to landowners for the construction of a railway.

For some months past we have been arriving at the conclusion that the prospect of ore held out to us is not justified by the facts; the lodes opened by us on the surface have altogether failed to produce any considerable supply of ore, as have those connected with the drifts which we have driven parallel to, though at a higher level than, our Deep Drift; and the lode which was always expected to prove highly productive, and which we hoped on the Deep Drift to reach, has turned out a complete failure.

We think, therefore, that it is useless expenditure to make us pursue the Deep Drift further into ground which we have in great measure proved by our parallel workings at a higher level.

We have thus, after considerable outlay and great experience, arrived at the belief that the ore is not in the ground in quantities to be worked to a profit, and certainly we have failed, notwithstanding our exertions to realize the expectations held out to us when we entered upon our agreement.

Having thus done our utmost to prove the Moor, we think we have a strong claim upon your forbearance; under such circumstances, it is usual with coalowners to waive their claims for dead rent until the tenant has had a reasonable time to prove the ground.

This, therefore, we request at your hands; and we wish also, before converting the agreement into a lease, to modify it in various respects, many of which will be advantageous to both parties.

With respect to the mode of proceeding, we have also a proposal to make to you: we wish to be permitted to leave the Deep Drift at once, or at the utmost when it shall have reached the Roman Lode, and in substitution for this to lay open the Roman and other lodes by working along their course, so as to obtain at once, if possible, a supply of ore.

By this means (always supposing the ore to be present) the character of the Moor will be raised considerably, and you will probably obtain tenants for the portion now unlet; whereas, if we are forced by you to proceed with the Deep Drift, through ground which we think likely to be very unproductive, our position will assuredly deter any other person from entering upon a speculation which we shall have found so utterly unproductive.

I feel sure, that if you look back at the liberal manner in which Mr. Bruce and I have entered into and forwarded your views, and have endeavoured to lay open the property, you will come to the conclusion that we may fairly expect at your hands, at the least, the measure of liberality usually accorded, under such circumstances, to mineral tenants. Requesting your early attention to this letter,

I remain, yours sincerely,

'Geo. T. Clark.'

An interview between the parties was arranged, at which Frederic Knight pointed out his inability to vary the terms of the agreement, without the consent of the Court of Chancery, on account of the litigation then proceeding between himself and his family as to the administration of the property. A desultory correspondence continued throughout the year, directed on Frederic Knight's part towards securing the execution of the lease in the terms of the original agreement, and on the part of the trustees towards securing a modification of those terms.

Early in 1859, further negotiations were abandoned, and proceedings for specific performance were instituted by Frederic Knight.

THE EXMOOR AND PORLOCK RAILWAY

By this time the real point at issue was the interpretation of the clause in the agreement under which the Dowlais Iron Company covenanted to provide the ironwork for a railway to the coast, to which reference has been made already. There was nothing to stop the company from giving notice to determine their agreement to mine, but the question was whether they were bound by the agreement to supply rails and other ironwork for the railway. The company was to have been paid by setting off the cost, estimated at over £12,000, against the royalties due from ore they might raise; thus if there was no ore there would be no payment. From the first discovery of ore, Frederic Knight had realised that the construction of a railway to Lynmouth or Porlock formed a vital part of any mining scheme on Exmoor. Before the agreement with the Guest trustees, and all through his relations with them, the question of the railway had been under discussion. Surveys of alternative routes had been made between Simonsbath and Lynmouth, on the one hand, and Simonsbath and Porlock Weir on the other, by Edward Brigden and William Evans, engineers employed by the Dowlais Company, the respective estimates being

£35,000 and £38,000 excluding land; and negotiations had been carried on with Mr J. Colwell Roe, of Lynton, the owner of the land outside the Forest boundary on that side, and with Col G. W. Blathwayt, the owner of Porlock Weir and of the land between it and Larkbarrow, on the other side. Finally, it was decided to try and reach agreement with Col Blathwayt, for whilst the Porlock route was the longer, the accommodation at the Weir was thought to be more commodious. All through these negotiations Mr Bruce and Mr Clark were interested parties; the question of routes and the problems of construction, finance, railway rates and other matters were constantly under discussion between them and Frederic Knight.

He was quite unconvinced by the failure, first, of Messrs Schneider & Hannay and, later, of the Dowlais Iron Company, to find payable ore. His own conviction was (and in this view he was confirmed by that of his advisers) not only that the property had not been fully developed, but also that such development as had been effected showed indications far more promising than his mineral tenants were prepared to admit. He thought he could re-let the ground surrendered by Messrs Schneider & Hannay, and he expected that Mr Hill would be willing to extend his tract, and to prosecute his search for minerals with renewed vigour, if only the obstacle of transport to the coast could be overcome. There was also the subsidiary purpose which the railway would serve in facilitating the removal of building materials, lime, and agricultural requisites and produce to and from Exmoor. The financial position in which he found himself made it impossible for him to equip the line unaided, and, believing as he did in the potential mineral and agricultural wealth of his property, he was determined to leave no stone unturned in his efforts to provide the one thing essential, in his opinion, to the realisation of his hopes.

Frederic Knight therefore made a formal application to the Dowlais Company for the delivery of rails, dated 4 January 1859, and, shortly after this, the breach between the parties widened to the point at which the question of the company's liability became a matter for the decision of the Courts.

Frederic Knight's contention was that he had never disguised his own inability, on financial grounds, to construct the railway at his own charges, and the agreement with the Dowlais Company for the supply by them of rails, etc, formed, and was always intended to be, an integral part of their contract of tenancy. The company, on their part, contended that the railway was useless to them unless there were payable ore on Exmoor to be transported, and they claimed to establish that their liability to equip the line was contingent on this eventuality, which, of course, they sought to prove had not arisen. Much evidence was taken, on either side, from the principals themselves, from their servants, and from independent mining experts, and, on the question of the existence of workable iron ore, it is remarkable to note how completely opposed were the opinions of witnesses of every class, expert mining engineers, mineral agents, and working miners testifying in support of either side.

As in the Schneider case, the decision of the Court was entirely favourable to Frederic Knight, and judgement was pronounced for him, with costs, on 10 November 1859. Frederic Knight continued pushing on with the project in every possible way. In July 1860 an agreement for a lease of the land, etc, required for the railway on Col Blathwayt's estate was executed by the parties. The term was for 100 years from 25 March of that year, and Frederic Knight was to complete a single line within five years of that date. The land to be leased included a piece for the erection and operation of limekilns, a provision made, no doubt, in view of the essential importance of lime in the husbandry of Exmoor and the difficulty of getting it on the estate. If the line were not made within the time stipulated, the agreement, or the lease if it had already been granted, was to determine automatically, unless the lessee should apply for an extension of time, which would be granted annually up to 1869, on payment of £100 to Col Blathwayt for each year.

The consideration for the lease was a covenant by Frederic Knight to pay a royalty of 2d per ton for iron ore and 3d per ton for other goods, with a minimum of £5 per annum for the first eight years, and £200 per annum thereafter. Power to assign the lease was reserved to him, and it could be determined by him at any time by his giving two years' notice of his intention.

The Guest trustees, however, were satisfied that no good would come to them by any further serious operations on Exmoor, and considered appealing against the decision of the Court. So far no work had been undertaken on the construction of the railway, and fearing that this might prejudice him, Frederic Knight decided to make a start. A Dowlais Company employee, Howell Jones, was present when the contracts were let.

I attended the letting of this Railway which took place at Warren Gate on Exmoor on the 4th. day of December 1860 at 11 o Clock in the forenoon.

On reaching the ground I had some specification handed to me, and I asked Mr. Smith if the Plans and Sections were not to be seen. Mr. Smith answered they were not, and that they were only going to take the turf off as the Engineer Mr. Cullen could not level the line properly without getting the turf off.

There was a length of formation to be done at the Porlock end which the Engineer said would be short. This was the only portion of the line to be formed at present.

There were six miles three furlongs of the line to be cleared of turf marked out in lots of one furlong or ten chains each. These lots were put up for public competition and given out at so much per chain, the lowest bidder being the contractor for each lot.

After going over some half a mile of the line I happened to be walking near Mr. Smith and he called attention to a piece where the soil had been taken off and pointed out some white gravel, and said what a capital thing, we will not require any ballast in this ground.

In continuing the conversation with Mr. Smith he informed me that the iron work of the line was not to be put up to competition as the Dowlais Iron Co. had to find it. He said you see we have been very lucky, the Dowlais Iron Co. must find all the rails, not only that, they must find all the iron work, even to a nail.

The letting was attended by labouring men from the neighbourhood who took the work in small lots between 4/– and 7/– per chain or £16 and £28 per Mile.

The Contractors were to meet at Mr. Cullen's Office at Larkborough at 9o'Clock A.M. on Wednesday the 6th. day of December 1860 to sign the Contracts.

My impression from what I saw was, that it was only intended to make a show and not actually to construct a Railway.

The whole of the work let will be done for a few hundred pounds.

William Dunstan, the former mine captain, subsequently visited the line on behalf of the Dowlais Company in October 1861, and reported as follows:

During the week I have gone completely over the proposed

Farming for beef: (*above*) Mr John Hayes, farm manager, and Mr Santa Lafuenti, head cattleman, with Galloway Hereford cross cattle; (*below*) Galloways at Warren

Page 212 Sheep farming: (*above*) Cheviot tups from Scotland; (*below*) sheep pens at Limecombe

Railway and beg to hand you the following as my remarks thereon.

On the proposed Incline from Porlock wharf to the top of the hill—a distance of one mile and seventy four chains—nothing whatever has been done since my visit in July last. All that ever was done here on the enclosed land was simply the cutting of a line through the copse wood for the purpose of taking sights or to mark the direction the line would take. No part of the wood is cleared for forming the Road. The only bit of work done on the proposed Incline is on the unenclosed or common land.

On the Porlock common the proposed line intersects Bogs and Roads. Nothing whatever has been done to cross these. The line only having been formed where the surface is even so that the depth of cutting is almost uniform, and very shallow.

The formation of so much of proposed Railroad as extends from Boundary Fence of Exmoor to Warren Farm has been completed so far as the removal of the sod or turf and the levelling of the loose earth and stones beneath are concerned but no low places are filled up nor Fences crossed.

The proposed part of line to extend from Warren Farm to a point near Simonsbath has not been touched except to mark it out.

No ballast has been put on the 'formed' parts of the line.

No Timber of any kind is seen on or near the line nor do I find that any is purchased for the Railway.

No Building Stones or other materials for Building purposes are found on or near the line at any of the respective places where required. No preparations made for building any House or masonry of any kind.

No men employed on or in any way connected with the line— even the Surveyor has left—nor can I find that any one has been employed on the line for the past two months.

I saw some of the Farmers and workmen of Exmoor and talked with them on the subject of making the Railway. Some of them perhaps expressed themselves rather unguardedly on the matter yet the general impression seems to be that the line will never be made. I did not closely press them for reasons why they formed this opinion they nevertheless hesitated not to say they doubted whether the Railway would ever be laid down or whether it ever was the original intention to make a Railway of it.

Rightly or wrongly both Jones and Dunstan concluded that there was no real intention of completing the railway, and the inference was that the work had been carried out solely to force the Dowlais Company to pay damages to escape its liability to supply rails and ironwork. The object was undoubtedly to force the company's hand, but to judge from Frederic Knight's subsequent actions, it may nevertheless have been a genuine endeavour to obtain the railway materials. Whatever the reason, the Dowlais

N

Company decided against further legal action, and finally, by an agreement dated 12 June 1862, the matter was settled by their undertaking to pay Mr Knight the sum of £7,000, of which £3,000 was paid on that date and the balance by four equal annual instalments commencing on 1 January following. In addition, they handed over to him all their mining works, buildings, machinery, plant, etc, upon the premises at that time.

The termination of the occupation of Burcombe and Hangley Cleeve by the Dowlais Iron Company marks the end of the attempt to work the mineral deposits on Exmoor, except for a tentative effort some fifty years later, which will be described presently, for Mr Anthony Hill seems to have faded away about the same time. Frederic Knight was still a believer, however, in the mining possibilities of his property, and he set to work at once to organise a new venture. His idea, this time, was to form a company for the comprehensive purpose of building and operating the railway from Simonsbath to Porlock Weir, and for raising and selling iron ore. The heads of the proposed agreement with the projected company included a payment of a royalty to him of 1s per ton of ore, with an annual minimum of £1,500; the construction by the company of the Exmoor and Porlock Railway and all works incidental thereto; the payment to Col G. W. Blathwayt of the rent of the land to be leased by him to Frederic Knight for that portion of the line, incline, etc, which lay on his estate; and the right reserved to Frederic Knight to transport the produce and merchandise of and for the service of his estate over the line, at certain maximum rates. For his part, he undertook to hand over to the company, free of charge, the works already executed on the line.

No complete plan of the direction to be taken by the railway has been found, but from the engineers' reports upon the project, and from references to it in deeds and correspondence, its proposed course may be identified fairly well. Starting at the Weir, the line was to proceed towards Worthy, whence the hill was to be surmounted by two inclines, the first carrying it up the western slope of Worthy Knap. From here an intermediate level section was to go along the 700ft contour to Yearnor Mill Bridge, where a second incline would ascend Porlock to Lynton public road at a point

some quarter mile west of the Whitstones, and a short length of
this was excavated between Westcott and the toll road and may
still be seen. A 'Plan of Inclines at Porlock' prepared by Edward
Brigden in December 1855, also shows two alternative routes via
Eastcott both terminating at the junction of the public and toll
roads, but these were discarded in favour of the Westcott line, and
it was to connect with this that Frederic Knight's excavations for
the upper section were laid out. Mr Thomas Marsh, an engineer
at Bath, who reported upon the scheme in May 1863, proposed to
work trucks up and down these inclines by self-action, no power
being required if the weight of the descending trucks loaded with
minerals were utilised to raise the returning ones, which, for the
most part, would be empty. From the top of the inclines, 2 miles
from the harbour, haulage would again be necessary, and after
crossing the main road, which was to be diverted a little at this
point, the line was to skirt the northern side of Whitstones Hill,
where its bed, as dug out by Mr Knight, is clearly visible. It can
be traced from this point along the Exford road to the Exmoor
Forest boundary wall, at Larkbarrow, across that farm and Tom's
Hill to Warren, where its line of continuation becomes doubtful.
At a later date, however, when the question of the construction of
the railway had been raised again (see page 219), the intention was
to carry it above Prayway Meads and across the Brendon road
towards Exe Head. It was then to turn south, crossing the river
valley by a bridge, and circling back to Prayway Head, whence it
was to proceed, 'by sweeping curves', over Duredon and so down
into the valley of the Barle. This would have enabled the line to
descend to Cornham Ford at a uniform gradient of 1 in 40 without
the need for a third inclined plane, and though Marsh intended
locomotives to work only as far as Prayway Head, his route continued for nearly 3 miles more, and he refers only to inclines at
Porlock. Although there is a reference to 'the Railway Terminus
at Simonsbath' on one of Messrs Schneider & Hannay's mining
plans, it seems probable that a direct incline from Prayway Head
had been discarded in favour of a longer, but less steeply graded,
route to Cornham Ford.

The line was to be nearly 14 miles long, of standard gauge, and
the locomotive line, between the Lynton road and Prayway Head,

was to be limited to 12–15mph. Though sufficient land was included in the Blathwayt lease for a double track throughout, Frederic Knight only covenanted to construct a single line and the excavation carried out was only wide enough for this. Mr Marsh estimated the total cost of the inclines and permanent way at £40,000, but suggested that a further sum of £10,000 should be provided for tramways and extensions in the Barle valley to connect the mines with the railway.

As regards the port of Porlock, a very comprehensive schedule of dues for goods, imported and exported, was drawn up—so detailed, in fact, as to suggest the probability of its having been copied, *in extenso*, from the schedule of some operating port, for only the amounts of the charges seem to have particular reference to traffic for or by the projected Exmoor and Porlock Railway. Thus, there were dues scheduled for the shipment or unloading of cannon, cannon balls and gunstocks; for masts and anchors; for macaroni, salad oil and anchovies; for hellebore, indigo and iodine; for whalebone, canary seed and ink, as well as for almost every conceivable article in ordinary requisition or production in the domestic and industrial life of a rural community.

The plans for the formation of the company had not matured by 1865, and Frederic Knight's solicitors applied to Col Blathwayt's agents, Messrs Bailey and Norman, for a remission of the payment of £100 required for an extension of time, and for certain alterations in the plans for the railway. The reply was as follows:

Proposed line of Railway to Porlock Harbour.

It is with much regret that we are obliged very sweepingly to decline the proposal made on Mr. Knight's behalf in your letter received by us this morning. The fact is that altho' suiting Mr. Knight no doubt uncommonly well they would be by no means satisfactory to Colonel Blathwayt. . . .

We may perhaps be pardoned for expressing some surprise that Mr. Knight should demur to pay such, after all, trifling premiums to retain possession of the key to the Casket in which he is sanguine that he has immense Wealth locked up. Whilst desiring much to facilitate Mr. Knight in his enterprise we are bound to say that neither our client nor ourselves are equally sanguine with him.

This was, virtually, the end of Frederic Knight's attempt to work his deposits of iron ore. The company was never incorporated, nor was the railway built. Whether he retained his belief in the project in the face of all the adverse experience gained and opinions expressed is uncertain, but he made no further effort to continue. Although the venture had not resulted in producing for him the very considerable income, as a royalty owner, for which he had hoped, it certainly did not end without profit to him. His own expenditure in prospecting, in trial workings, in levelling the track of the railway, in expert advice, law charges, and so forth, must have been considerable, and his conduct of the whole enterprise in the face of his many other preoccupations is evidence of the capacity for work and determination of character which undoubtedly he possessed. But it must be remembered that, in addition to the dead rents which he drew at the rate of £1,000 per annum from the Dowlais Iron Works, together with other payments under this head from Messrs Schneider & Hannay and Mr Anthony Hill, he had drawn £7,000 from that concern for permission to escape from their obligations, and £10,000 for the same consideration from Mr Schneider. Tradition says that he derived some £20,000 from these various sources, and the actual amount cannot have fallen far short of this figure.

Whatever opinion may be formed as to the sincerity of the efforts of Mr Schneider's firm to discover payable ore, there can be no question that Messrs Clark & Bruce made an honest attempt to exploit the property. It is equally clear that Frederic Knight believed unquestionably in the commercial value of the minerals known to exist on his property, and, unable as he was to prove it himself, he was convinced that his lessees had been, in the one case inefficient, and in the other case deliberately unsuccessful, in their search. Thus he felt compelled to take such action as was legally available to him to secure the performance of the agreements with them, and the Courts upheld him in his view of the position.

THE EXMOOR MINING SYNDICATE

In August 1874 the *Mining Journal* reported that it was a 'matter of current report that a strong and powerful company of adventurers contemplated taking for a long term the Exmoor property of Mr. F. W. Knight M.P.' and transport was to be by a projected railway either from Castle Hill (on the newly opened Devon and Somerset Railway) to Combe Martin, or from South Molton (on the same line) via Brendon to Lynton. Needless to say, nothing came of this, though a tramway was constructed from South Molton to serve the Florence and Bampfylde mines at North Molton.

When the estate passed to Viscount Ebrington, efforts were again made to find whether the property contained minerals of value. Iron ore samples were sent to the Dowlais Iron Company, to Barrow Hematite Iron Company and to the Consett Iron Works, but perhaps not unexpectedly, in view of the earlier experiences of the first, none was interested, though a local man, William Shaw of Brendon, did suggest forming a syndicate to work iron and possibly copper! A geologist, Mr Godfrey of Swansea, made a fresh examination of the property, and picked samples of ore from the Deer Park were found to analyse up to 70 per cent of iron, but no well-defined lodes of this quality could be traced.

The prospect of mining lapsed until 1908, when Henry Roberts of West Bromwich (who was also interested in Blackland mine at Withypool) obtained an option for the mineral rights over 5,300 acres of the South Forest, including Burcombe, Deer Park and part of Picked Stones, but not Wheal Eliza, and by October he was seeking a buyer for 400 tons of ore, lying at Rogers' lode. William Dixon, a Whitehaven mining engineer, was engaged to report on the mines and, when visiting Exmoor that September, he found that limited trials had been made at Rogers' shaft and the adit below it, and also at Bluegate.

In February 1910, Roberts assigned his interest to a small syndicate formed for the purpose of clearing the old workings and carrying out a further trial upon them, and he was employed as manager. The members of the syndicate were: Sir George Hingley, Bt, of the Dudley Iron Works; Joseph Ellis, of Workington; and E. P. Davis, of Bennerley Furnaces, Ilkeston. The shaft sunk by Mr Ebenezer Rogers, and deepened by Mr Schneider on Rogers' lode, was pumped out and refitted, and the Dowlais Company's Main Drift was opened out afresh.

Transport was an immediate problem, and detailed plans were

prepared for a tramway from Cornham Ford to the Challacombe road at Driver. The earlier scheme for a railway to Porlock Weir was taken out and dusted, though no full survey seems to have been made, and the suggestion was to follow Frederic Knight's route to Warren and thence to Exe Head, where the line would either reach the Barle valley by way of Duredon, or would descend Limecombe to Simonsbath, parallel to and on the west side of the Brendon road (presumably by inclined plane), terminating at Westgate. From here a tramway was proposed to run alongside the Barle to Cornham Ford, and thence over Wester Emmetts to Hangley Cleave. A line was even considered to Glenthorne via Badgworthy Water, and another idea was to build a 4½ mile branch to a tramway to the coast, which was being considered by a syndicate proposing to work peat on the Chains. The peat syndicate came to nothing, and there is no indication that work was ever carried out on any of these schemes, though estimates were obtained for aerial ropeways to Porlock Weir (£18,800) and to Combe Martin via Blackmoor Gate (£23,300). In fact, such output as was produced was taken by traction engine, and latterly by lorry, to South Molton station or Lynmouth.

In January 1911, it was decided to suspend work on the Main Drift, which had been extended to a length of 431yd, and to concentrate on Rogers' shaft, together with Llewellyn's and Roman lodes at Cornham Ford, and the Picked Stones adit, first started by Mr Anthony Hill, all of which the syndicate was now working. Llewellyn's level was driven to a length of 310yd, Picked Stones to 76yd, and a shaft sunk 70ft at Roman lode, but the enterprise was attended with no marked success.

In 1912, Sir George Hingley and Mr Ellis left the syndicate, which had expended some £4,000 in an effort to get ore, but work was continued by Mr Davis, who was joined by Earl Fortescue. On 16 December 1912, they formed the Exmoor Mining Syndicate Ltd, with registered offices in Wolverhampton, and Roberts continued as their manager. Several hundred tons of good ore were raised from Rogers' lode, where a tramway had been built, from the mine to the road. The total output from the mines, however, was not great; 250 tons in 1910, 200 tons in 1911, 400 tons in 1912 and 850 tons in 1913. By January 1913, the shaft was 102ft deep and a west level had been driven from it, for 256ft. A headframe had been erected and there was a portable boiler to work the steam winch and an oil engine for the compressors. Difficulties were encountered arising from the influx of water in great quantities during the winter and control by pumping cost more than the value received for the ore. The adit, which Mr Schneider should have driven through the Deer Park, at the level of the Barle, had never been completed, and would, in any case, have been too deep to drain the present workings, so an adit from Drybridge Combe, at a higher level, was proposed but never started, and after October 1913 Rogers' shaft was abandoned at a depth of 140ft. At the end of November, mining also ceased at Roman lode and work was confined to the Picked Stones mine, which was linked to the company's depot in Gipsy Lane, by a lengthy horse-worked tramway. A lode measuring 8–10ft in width was developed, and a considerable quantity of ore was brought to bank, but the want of Sir Frederic Knight's projected railway was badly felt, and road carriage swallowed up all the profit. All work was stopped in July 1914, by which time a further £5,000 had been spent by the company.

On the outbreak of war, the syndicate's lorries were commandeered, but Roberts stayed on as caretaker. After various efforts to sell their undertaking for £15,000, the company, in 1917, obtained yet another report on its mineral property, which recommended de-watering their principal mines, and also Wheal Eliza, in order to investigate the veins of ore. Doubtless considering that more than enough money had already been spent on investigation, the syndicate went into voluntary liquidation in April 1918, and an auction of its property was held at Bluegate that July. A Mr Llewellyn Davies, of Clydach, Glamorgan, then obtained a three months' license to investigate the minerals, but came to the conclusion that there was no hope of success without adequate transport.

Since that date there has been no resumption of mining on Exmoor, though some exploration took place at Bluegate in 1934, and further attempts at a commercial exploitation of the minerals seem unlikely. It is commonly stated that the failure of the original venture, in the fifties, was occasioned by the competition of higher-grade haematite ore imported cheaply from Spain, but there is no truth in this. The Exmoor iron ore analyses very well, some of it showing so much as 70 per cent of iron, but it is not present in sufficient quantity to constitute a workable mining proposition. The veins or lodes, so-called, are not continuous, nor have they much depth. They are casual deposits of ore, more in the nature of pockets; and even granted cheap transport to a port it is improbable that the quantity available would suffice to warrant the expenditure of capital on its development.

(See pp 295–9 for notes)

XII

THE PARISH OF EXMOOR

The formation of new ecclesiastical parishes has been a regular feature of the growth of industrial England for the last hundred years; the expansion of the towns creates a need for an increase in the number of clergy to serve them, and brings about a sub-division of many old parochial districts into two or more parishes for ecclesiastical purposes. In rural areas, too, from one cause or another, the rearrangement of benefices is not without example, but as a case in which an extraparochial district of more than 20,000 acres has first come into being as a unit both of Church and State, Exmoor must be unique in the social history of England since the mid nineteenth century.

In 1818, when the ancient Royal Forest ceased to exist, Exmoor enjoyed no social institutions of any kind. There was one house, and one only, upon the Forest, that named by John Knight 'Simonsbath House', which was built about 1654 by James Boevey, and occupied at the time of the sale of the King's Allot-ment, and for a long time previously, by the deputy-forester. It was licensed as an inn, and sheltered a family of five. That the settlement of the Forest would follow its inclosure was the general expectation of the countryside, and, in contemplation of this con-tingency, provision was made, under the Inclosure Act, for the reservation of lands for the erection of a church, etc, the endow-ment of a parson, and the formation of a civil parish out of what was then an extraparochial district.

It has been shown that, under John Knight's administration, settlement was a slow business. Most of the big constructional works—the boundary wall, the roads, the dam containing Pinkery Pond—were carried out by labour from the surrounding villages, or by gangs of imported labour, such as the Irishmen whom he recruited from the neighbourhood of his brother-in-law's home in County Kerry. His farming, too, is said to have been carried on by single men, in the main, accommodated in bothies. Writing in 1856, Henry Scale, the Dowlais Company's superintendent, remarked that 'the present houses in Simonsbath were then barracks, with regular hammocks slung up—and fuel and food were found by Mr. Knight'. However, some cottage-building went on at Simonsbath; but it seems, no new inn replaced the one which had been annexed by the new owner for his own accommodation, and there were farm labour staffs, single or married is of little moment, accommodated at Cornham and at Honeymead. John Knight's establishment at Simonsbath House, too, in connection with the stables, hunter stud, etc, must have been considerable.

By 1842, a start had been made in permanent settlement, when farming by the landlord began to give place to the letting of farms, and early in 1845 the first move was made to secure the fulfilment of the undertaking for parochialisation given by the Inclosure Act. John Knight had already retired from Exmoor, Frederic Knight was abroad at the time, and the initiative was taken by Harry (otherwise Henry) Matthews, the tenant of Honeymead Farm. He caused a memorial to be drawn up, in the following terms, to the Commissioners of the Treasury:

TO THE LORDS COMMISSIONERS OF
HER MAJESTY'S TREASURY
THE MEMORIAL OF THE UNDERSIGNED INHABITANTS
OF THE FOREST OF EXMOOR IN THE COUNTY OF
SOMERSET AND DIOCESE OF BATH AND WELLS

HUMBLY SHEWETH

That by an Act of Parliament made and passed in the Session held in the fifty fifth year of the Reign of His late Majesty King George the third intituled 'An Act for vesting in His Majesty certain parts of the Forest of Exmoor otherwise Exmore in the Counties of Somerset and Devon and for inclosing the said Forest' it is amongst other things recited and enacted as follows, that is to say

AND WHEREAS it may happen that some part of the said forest may hereafter become inhabited, in which case the inhabitants thereof, by reason of its remote distance from any Parish Church, and of its being locally situate out of the limits or boundaries of any Parish will have no place of Public Worship to resort to, and it is therefore expedient that as well for the convenience of such inhabitants as for extending the benefit and influence of religious worship and instruction that such provisions should be made in that respect as are hereinafter contained, be it therefore further enacted, that such a quantity of land as shall be necessary for the Site of a Church and for a Churchyard or Cemetery and for the Site of a proper Parsonage House and Offices to be erected and built, and for a Garden and Yard or Homestead to be attached thereto to the extent in the whole of Ten Acres at the least, shall be reserved by the Crown out of the Lands so to be allotted to His Majesty as aforesaid, and shall not be sold, and that in case at any time hereafter the number of persons who shall be resident and inhabiting upon the said Forest shall in the judgment and opinion of the Lords Commissioners of His Majesty's Treasury and the Bishop of Bath and Wells for the time being be such as shall render it expedient that a Church shall be erected upon the said Allotment for the performance of Divine Worship therein and for the affording religious instruction to the inhabitants thereof, then and in such case the said Commissioners of His Majesty's Treasury shall by and out of the Land revenues of the Crown cause a New Church and a fit and convenient Parsonage House and Offices to be erected and built upon part of the lands so to be reserved as aforesaid and shall appropriate other part thereof near to the said Church for a Church yard or Burial Ground and the residue thereof as a Garden, Yard or Homestead to the said Parsonage House and shall inclose the same accordingly, in such manner as the said last mentioned Commissioners shall think proper for such purposes, and shall cause the said Church when so erected, and the Church yard so to be attached thereto, to be duly consecrated according to the usage of the Church of England and the same Church shall be for ever thereafter set apart and dedicated as and for a place of Divine Worship according to the Rites and Ceremonies of the Church of England for the use of all the inhabitants who shall so reside within the bounds or precincts of the said Forest, and shall be named and called The Parish Church of Exmoor and that the said Forest shall for ever thereafter form and be a distinct Parish of itself, and be called by the name of The Parish of Exmoor. Provided always that there shall be set apart and appropriated in the Church to be erected and built by virtue of this Act, such a number of Seats for the gratuitous accommodation of the Poor of the said Parish as the Lord Bishop of the Diocese shall think necessary, proper and convenient.

That the said Forest of Exmoor has since been inclosed in pursuance of the above recited Act.

That part of the said Forest of Exmoor is now inhabited by your Memorialists and others to the number of about two hundred persons, which number in consequence of the erection of several houses, which will be compleated in a short space of time, is expected to be soon increased to Three hundred at least, and will in all probability continue to increase.

That the quantity of land of the said Forest, in a state of Cultivation, now occupied by your Memorialists and others, is at least Ten thousand and nine hundred acres, and such Cultivation is daily extending.

That the distance from the central part of the tract of land under cultivation, to the nearest Church, namely the Parish Church of Exford, in the said County of Somerset, is Five Miles and half, and the other surrounding Churches are situate at a much greater distance.

That in consequence of the general elevation of the Forest being about One thousand one hundred feet above the level of the Sea, and the greater part of the Roads being in a very bad condition, your Memorialists are prevented without great labor and trouble from attending at any Parish Church.

That your Memorialists and other inhabitants of the said Forest amongst whom are a large number of laborers and their families are therefore, for all practical purposes, almost destitute of the means of public religious worship and instruction.

That your Memorialists are earnestly desirous that a Church should be built and endowed and that a Parsonage house and Offices be erected and built for the use of the Minister of such Church in pursuance of the provisions of the said recited Act.

WHEREFORE your Memorialists humbly pray that your Lordships will cause such Church to be built and endowed and such Parsonage House and Offices to be erected and built under the provisions of the said recited act And your Memorialists as in duty bound will ever pray &c.

Harry Matthews[1]	Thomas Burfitt	John Stone
Edward Godwin[2]	James Lisbeck	William King
George Cox	James Hunt	Robert Coward
Charles Andrews	John Criddle	John Matthews[3]
Harry Cox	James Long	Edward Hunt
Daniel King	John Hale	William Hassell

Frederic Knight heard news of this memorial on his return to England, and the Lords Commissioners applied to him for his observations upon it. His reply, dated 4 July 1845, shows that he was very much upset that any such action should have been taken 'secretly during my absence from England by a Tenant who is in every way endeavouring to oppose and annoy me, as a sufficient reason for throwing difficulties in the way of the exertions and expenses I am undergoing to improve Exmoor Forest'. From it may be learnt that the population of the Forest had risen from 5 in 1818 to 51 in 1831, and to 160 at the date of the memorial, of whom 91 only, 49 adults and 42 children, would be gainers in distance from a place of worship, if a church were erected at Simonsbath. Referring to the signatories, his opinion of Harry Matthews is made quite definite by the quotation from the letter given above, but it should be stated that the reason for his dislike has not transpired, and Matthews was the only one of Frederic Knight's original tenants who can be said to have made good on Exmoor; going to Honeymead in 1842, he remained there for twenty years. The second of the signatories, Edward Godwin, is described by Frederic Knight as being 'a tenant not likely to remain', in which opinion he proved correct, and he points out that John Matthews, a brother to Harry, was not resident on Exmoor at all, being the tenant of a farm adjoining Brendon Church, where it may be presumed that his spiritual necessities were adequately provided for. For the rest, he remarks that nearly all the signatories were labourers employed either by Harry Matthews or by Godwin.

As to the statements in the memorial, Frederic Knight controverted them all. So far from there being 10,000 acres under cultivation, he says that the amount at this date was less than 2,500 acres, and that so far from the population being on the increase, it had been stationary for the previous fifteen years. 'Making a Parish of the Forest will be at this moment a great bar to my letting the new farm house I am building, [? at Driver or Duredon, which were the next farms to be let off, in 1847] and a great injury to me at this moment. If I succeed in the system of colonisation I am pursuing, a few years will probably increase the population so as to make a church desirable, and in that case I shall certainly apply for one to be erected. Under the present circumstances, however, I sincerely hope that you will not consider a *greatly exaggerated statement* . . . I am sincerely attached to the Church of England and pledge myself to apply for a church when it may be necessary.'

Probably the key to Frederic Knight's objections to the parochialising of the Forest is contained in his statement to the effect that it would interfere with his plans for letting the new farm and colonising Exmoor. A few years later, the fact that the Forest was extraparochial was advertised as an attraction of the new farms then awaiting tenants, and no doubt farmers would welcome the escape from parochial rates which this condition represented. The maintenance of the poor, the repair of the highways, the upkeep of the church, these were then, as now, liabilities which many would like to escape, and a landlord who could offer farms to let in a district exempted from them, was in a very exceptional position.

In their Report to the Treasury upon the memorial and the objections to it, the Commissioners of Woods and Forests remarked that 'it was not considered that the wants of the district were sufficient to justify the work [of building the church and parsonage] being at that time undertaken', and for the time being the matter lapsed.

About eight years later, in December 1852, the situation had changed. There were now fourteen farmhouses, with their complement of cottages, and all but one were occupied, albeit in some cases, transitorily; a mine had been opened on the banks of the Barle and nine miners were in occupation of cottage accommodation erected there; the equipment of more farms, and a great development of the mining enterprise, were in contemplation; the population had risen in seven years from 162 of all ages and sexes to no fewer than 281 on Frederic Knight's estate, and 376 on the Forest as a whole.[4] Application had been made to him for the use of some building on the Forest as a Methodist Chapel; and on 9 December 1852 he wrote to the Treasury that 'the want of a Church, and of a Resident Clergyman, is now seriously felt by the inhabitants of the said Forest. . . . I trust that your Lordships will therefore consider that the circumstances contemplated by the said Act of Parliament [the Exmoor Inclosure Act, 55 Geo III, c 138], and explained in detail in the sections 70 to 80 thereof, have now arrived, and that Your Lordships will be pleased to give your assent and authority for building a Church and Parsonage house, and for endowing a Minister, on the terms and in the manner laid down in the said Act. The approval of the Lord Bishop of Bath and Wells, of the erection of a Church on Exmoor, has been signified in a private letter from his Lordship's secretary.'

The Bishop, Lord Auckland, wrote, at the same time, 'to assure your Lordships that the application has my entire sanction and support'.

The matter took the usual leisurely course customary where Government action is involved. The Lords Commissioners of the Treasury referred it to the Commissioners of Woods and Forests; they passed it on to Mr Clutton, their Receiver for the district in which Exmoor is situated, and in May 1853 he reported favourably to the application. He added, incidentally, that there was an infant school in the village, provided by Frederic Knight, at which thirty children attended, but that it did not, for want of proper supervision, appear to be satisfactorily conducted. The Commissioners of Woods and Forests then consulted their legal advisers upon certain points involved in the application, and in September 1853 they laid all the facts before the Lords of the Treasury in a document which contained no expression of any opinion of their own upon them.

The Treasury decided that the time had come to carry out the provisions of the Inclosure Act for the parochialisation of Exmoor, and in 1855 work was begun.

A church to accommodate 209 people, dedicated to St Luke, was built on the site reserved, where formerly the annual pony sales had been held, and it was consecrated by the Bishop, Lord Auckland, on 21 October 1856, 'in bad weather'. The parsonage was erected at the same time, and the total cost was estimated to be £2,972 6s. The ecclesiastical parish of Exmoor, in the rural deanery of Dunster, thus created, was defined by the boundaries of the old Royal Forest, and in extent it is the largest parish in Somerset. The living is a perpetual curacy, valued then at £150 per annum, and in 1929 at £250 per annum, with 10 acres of

Page 229   (*above*) A 'Roman' surface working at Burcombe;
(*below*) Wheal Eliza mine and cottage

Page 230 (left) Entrance to the Main Drift at Cornham Ford

(right) Inside the Main Drift

glebe; and the first incumbent was a friend of Frederic Knight, the Rev W. H. Thornton, of Trinity College, Cambridge, then curate to the vicar of Lynton, who was presented by Lord Palmerston on behalf of the Crown. He was the author, in later life, of two volumes of reminiscences, which might have contained much of historical interest about the Forest during the four years of his incumbency, when development was very active, but the subject matter is mostly small-talk.

The difficulties of life for a young parson—Mr Thornton was only twenty-six years of age at the date of his appointment—with a rapidly growing family and the nearest doctor 11 miles distant, led to the resignation of the first incumbent after four years, but the Exmoor parsons have generally remained long enough to learn the necessities of their parishioners and to minister to them. By an exchange of patronage arranged in 1889, the living became the gift of Earl Fortescue. The present patron is the Bishop of Bath and Wells and the benefice is now worth £1,129 per annum. The parish church remained the only place of worship until 1929 when the Methodists built a small asbestos Gospel Hall opposite Jubilee Villas, where services were held for a number of years.

As regards the civil parish of Exmoor, there is no doubt that it was created at the same time as the ecclesiastical parish, by virtue of the Inclosure Act of 1815 (Sec 78), which enacted that this process should follow the consecration of the church. The Order of the Poor Law Commissioners for this purpose has not been found, but the first assessment of the parish, which still exists, was made in January 1858. It was sworn by Robert Smith and William Poole, 'both of Exmoor, surveyors of highways', before M. Fenwick[5] and Arthur Locke, justices of the peace for the county of Somerset, and the new parish was described as being in the 'division of Dulverton'. The gross estimated rental of the parish at this date, including the non-Knight properties, which were situated, for the most part, in the south-eastern corner of the parish, below Sherdon Water, and on the western side, beyond the river Barle, and amounted to some 20 per cent of the total area, was £5,147. Frederic Knight's estate was assessed at £4,336,

o

of which £3,072 was in respect of lands let, and £1,264 of lands in hand.

It does not appear that Exmoor was made a member of the Dulverton Union, and it would seem that for the first four years of its existence as a civil parish it administered its own affairs as an independent unit. William Kingdon, the blacksmith at Simonsbath, acted as parish clerk. In November 1861, however, the Poor Law Commissioners issued an Order under which it was to be added to South Molton Union from 25 December next ensuing, and so it remained, the only constituent member of this union outside the county of Devon, until the enactment of the Local Government Act, 1894, the Act which set up the Rural District Councils. These bodies were constituted definitely on the basis of county boundaries, and Exmoor, left high and dry by this principle, had to be dealt with by special provision. Accordingly, in November 1894, an Order was issued by the Local Government Board, which had been set up in 1871 and had absorbed the Poor Law Board, providing for the temporary administration of the parish by the District Council of the Rural District of South Molton, with which it was then united.

So things continued for a few months, when the Somerset County Council, acting in pursuance of powers given by the Local Government Act, 1888, (the Act setting up the County Councils) caused an inquiry to be made as to the desirability of transferring the parish of Exmoor to the Rural District of Dulverton, in the same county, following which an Order was made for the transference in April 1895, which was confirmed in January of the following year by the Local Government Board.

Since this date there has been no change in the status or grouping of the parish.

As regards the parliamentary franchise, the position of the residents upon the Forest, prior to the formation of the parish, was determined by the Reform Act, 1832 (sec 38), which provided that every place, whether extraparochial or otherwise, having no Overseers, should be deemed to be within the adjoining parish or township for the purpose of making out the Voters' List. Those qualified were included in the Exford parish list.

The amenities on the Forest were few, and though in 1814

Simonsbath farm was 'licensed and frequented as an Inn', this appears to have lapsed when John Knight occupied the house himself. The village seems to have been without an inn until 1855, when an existing house was licensed, doubtless to cater for the thirst of the newly arrived miners. Hannam says that at this time Robert Smith had drawn up plans for 'a Splended Hotell from the Premeses now used as workshops', while the inn would revert to a shop, but nothing came of this.

The first tenant was 'not keeping his House orderley but was continuley having Rowes and Fighting' and at Lady Day 1856 the tenancy was transferred to Hannam's brother-in-law, Samuel Gifford, who hoped to have an oven installed and to bake there. Henry Scale had similar ideas and, in July that year, 'applied for leave to erect a shop for a man at South Molton'. Frederic Knight stipulated 'that the shopman should live on Exmoor, and that the business should not be placed in the hands of a South Molton or Barnstaple tradesman, who would suck the money out of the property; further, that provisions should be sold at the same rates as the South Molton shops', which charged 2d per pound for flour and provided a 6lb loaf for 1s (against 3d per lb and a 5lb loaf, at Simonsbath). The bakery was built of wood and felt, and let to Gifford for £10 a year, but after some months, there was a disagreement (which Hannam relates) and Gifford left. On 19 February 1858, Scale wrote to his employers at Dowlais, 'I thank you for releasing me from the responsibility of the Shop Building—I can let it for you at a good rent', the company having had to make a contribution of £103 towards its cost.

Thereafter the bakehouse was again run with the inn, which it adjoined, and Gifford resumed possession until 1860, when he was succeeded first by John Hosking, and in 1862 by Robert Holcombe, but by 1866 James Fry had become both grocer and landlord of the Simonsbath Inn. The sale of beer and spirits was stopped by Frederic Knight about 1873, when the inn became a 'refreshment house' with only a license for wine, and the social advancement of the workers was attributed, by Mr G. C. Smyth-Richards, almost entirely to this, for men accumulated the money which would have been spent. Beer was, however, brewed in more than one of the Forest farmhouses, for home consumption.

James Fry 'helped when the additions were made, by hauling the materials in the year 1878', and by the end of the century, he was, 'thanks to his wife, a prosperous man', the inn having become The William Rufus Hotel in 1895.[6] Further improvements were made, and in 1903 the name was changed again to The Exmoor Forest Hotel, and in 1933 the tenant, who was Mrs Mary H. Elworthy, was granted a full license.

The only other inn on the Knight estate was at Red Deer, where John Knight had purchased an 'Allotment, Dwelling House and Premises' in February 1841. In the census return that June, it is referred to as Gallon House, with Richard Bromham as publican, while also on the Forest at that date was the Acland Arms, an isolated and supposedly disreputable hostelry at Moles Chamber. The first mention of the Sportsman's Arms at Sandyway was not until the 1851 census. The Red Deer had given up its license through lack of trade by 1883, and the Acland Arms soon after, while even the Sportsman's Arms relinquished its license, for that reason, for some five years until 1956.

The shop and inn at Simonsbath was also the receiving point for letters, and in July 1856 Scale was complaining, 'I have just found yours of the 15th on a dirty tea table in the Shop where the letters are taken in', though, as he was writing on the 16th, he had little to grumble at. Apparently a room was then rented, for in October he wrote, 'we have got a regular post office established at last but shall have to pay 1s per week in future'. At this time letters arrived, from South Molton, at 12 noon on Tuesdays, Thursdays and Saturdays, outgoing post being despatched at 1.30 pm, presumably after the postman had lunched. When the telegraph line was extended from Exford in 1898, the Post Office moved to the newly built Jubilee Villas. Always combined with the general stores, for a while it was in a now demolished cottage, adjoining Pound Cottages and facing the hotel, then it returned to the neighbour of the original Jubilee Villa, and in 1969 it was transferred to Simonsbath House, now a guest house.

The Local Government Board Order of January 1896 was the last act in the history of the inclosure of Exmoor Forest. Its evolution has been traced from the days when it was an uninclosed waste of some 20,000 acres; untraversed save by pack-horse tracks; uninhabited save by one family; untilled save for a few acres; unstocked save for summer grazing. A century later it was ring-fenced as to the major part; accessible from all sides by good roads; giving shelter and support to a population of 250 people working, for the most part, on the former Knight estate of some sixteen adequately equipped farms, comprised in about 5,000 acres of improved and inclosed lands; stocked with some 200 horses, 800 cattle and 10,000 sheep. The district was parochialised both for ecclesiastical and civil purposes. After 150 years, the achievement is even greater. The enforced neglect of the depression years has been made good, reclamation completed, buildings modernised, and new houses built, with the result that, in spite of a substantial decline in the general agricultural population, there were still 231 people in the parish, at the last census (only fourteen fewer than in 1931). Whereas in 1929 a good half of the cattle and many hoggs were wintered away, today the former Knight lands on the Forest can adequately support much the same number of cattle and 1,000 more sheep the whole year round, though, with the disappearance of draught horses, there are probably no more than a quarter of the former number of horses.

Some of the work undertaken in the process of this achievement may have been fantastic, other of it unfruitful, while much must have been unremunerative; regarded merely as an investment of capital, though the figure ultimately paid for the estate, by a knowledgeable local landowner, showed the Knights' venture to be far from the extravagant folly its critics supposed. More recent prices, when compared with the value of similar land elsewhere unreclaimed, confirm the increasing worth of the money and labour expended on the Forest. Here, and for all time, there has been created as the result of it a thriving community contributing in men and material, to the welfare of this country—and this, surely, is the measure of the success of the great work of the old iron-master and his son. Without doubt, the reclamation of the Forest by them was one of the greatest achievements, of its kind, that the nineteenth century has to show, and its completion in this century has been a worthy continuation of their pioneer work.

POPULATION OF EXMOOR

The census figures relation to the Forest, and later the parish of Exmoor, are listed below. A curious feature of the reports is that in each up to 1881 appeared a reference to a mythical part of Exmoor in Devon, which had neither houses nor population.

Year	Total Population (number of females in brackets)	Total Number of Houses (number uninhabited in brackets)
1821	113 (12)	not given
1831	52 (21)	not given
1841	163[7](47)	27 and 1 building
1851	275 (120)	69 (15) and 2 buildings
1861	323 (136)	64 (2)
1871	339 (not given)	56
1881	313 (not given)	53
1891	269 (not given)	50
1901	268 (not given)	59 (6)
1911	257 (113)	not given
1921	290 (not given)	not given
1931	245 (115)	52
1951	237 (111)	55
1961	231 (111)	58

(See pp 295–9 for notes)

WILLIAM HANNAM AND HIS 'HISTORY'

The Hannam family originated from the Wincanton area, where they had farmed for generations. William Hannam's father, also William, was born there in 1779 and having married another member of the family, Sarah Hannam, in 1803, lived at South Cheriton, in the parish of Horsington. Described as 'butcher and yeoman' he profitably combined dairying and stock rearing on between 400 and 500 acres with a butcher's business.

The younger William was one of ten children, five girls and five boys, and was born at Horsington in 1811. He was thirty-one when, in 1842, he married Elizabeth Gifford, who was the same age and came from the neighbouring parish of Blackford. Her father had died seventeen years earlier and she had little dowry to bring him, whilst William had three surviving brothers to compete for his father's land. He therefore rented a farm of some 70 or 80 acres, including orchards, at nearby North Cheriton, where his father also rented land, and here their first child, Charlotte Emma, was born in 1843. Unable to make a success of this venture by itself, Hannam suggested that he should take over the tenancy of his father's land to increase the size of his holding, but his father demurred, and it was then that the son had thoughts of moving farther afield.

William Hannam the elder had visited Exmoor regularly to buy store cattle and had spoken well of it, while in the early 1840s a number of farmers from the district south of Wincanton, where Somerset, Dorset and Wiltshire meet, were negotiating to take farms on the Forest. This aroused the son's interest, and he visited Exmoor for himself in September 1844, seeing it at its best after a warm, dry summer. He agreed to take Cornham Farm for twelve years from Lady Day 1845, but lacking sufficient capital to farm the 545 acres unaided, William Hannam was helped financially by his father, who became joint tenant.

The fine summer turned into a long, bitter winter which had not let up when the Hannam family moved in at Lady Day, and once at Cornham he attempted to carry on dairy farming at 1,250ft above sea level as he would have at Cheriton. The following year his second daughter, Mary Jane, was born at Cornham (the birth was registered by Dr C. P. Collyns, who conveniently acted as registrar as well as doctor), but Hannam was losing heart, and he suggested to his father that the farm be given up. Possibly knowing him to be a rolling stone, the old man would not agree.

In March 1847 his father died, the executors were not so kindly disposed and prices for agricultural produce were falling. Hannam already owed the money he had borrowed from his father, and was getting deeper into debt, even though he was to some extent acclimatising his farming to Exmoor conditions (Sir Thomas Acland remarked in 1851 on his 'herd of yearlings, crossed between Devon and Hereford, in as beautiful condition as any one would wish to see'). Eventually there was a forced sale in 1856 to meet his creditors' demands.

Hannam dragged on at Cornham until March 1858 (though probably because of these difficulties his wife had returned home for the birth of their son), having stayed longer than any of the original tenants save Matthews of Honeymead, but his experiences were already affecting his mind. His wife again stayed with her family during the winter of 1858, when he would not settle down to any job to keep them, and though she returned when Hannam agreed to take a dairy at Cothlestone, near Taunton, the following year, he soon gave this up and became a tramp, leaving his family behind. Three years later he was still on the roads, and his ultimate fate is not known, though his wife appears eventually to have returned to Blackford, and he is known to have been still living in 1868.

The 'History' is, in fact, Hannam's recollection of his life on Exmoor; it was written over a period starting early in 1858 and ending in October 1862, and despite its title actually covers a span of thirteen years on the Forest. Started in self-justification, the manuscript gradually deteriorates into a long, repetitive, series of grudges against Hannam's farm workers, relatives, neighbours, and in particular against Robert Smith, all written in the vernacular. By his own account Hannam cannot have been an easy man to live or work with, and towards the end he was on the border of insanity. The original manuscript, now in the Bodleian library, was sent to Dr Orwin by Mr Horace Stay, a descendant of Hannam's sister Charlotte, who had married George Stay, after the publication of *The Reclamation of Exmoor Forest* in 1929. The edited version now printed is little more than a quarter its length, largely due to the exclusion of many pages of incoherent diatribe, though the factual portions have been included as they were written and in the original spelling. Shorn of its verbiage the 'History' gives a moving first-hand account of the hardships and struggles of the early tenants and their often quite unsuitable attempts to farm Exmoor, while even allowing for his hatred of Robert Smith he gives a new insight into the character of Frederic Knight's agent and his tangled financial affairs.

A HISTORY OF TWELVE YEARS' LIFE ON EXMOOR

by William Hannam

1841–2   Reports of Exmoor

In the year 1845 I first occupied Cornham Farm on Exmoor—
For year previous my Father had attended Mr Knights Sales to
purchase Cattle—I had listened with attentive ear on many occasions to hear him relate the Particulars of the Countrey specifying
the fine crops of Corn he had seen the Beautiful Pasture the Land
produced and what he thought may be done with perseverence—I
have hird him speak of a fine lott of oxen he saw together in one
of the yards of Honey Mead Farm I believe it was over 100 a Cross
between the Scott and Short Horn. His [visit] generally used to occupye him a wick from the time he turned home untill his return
—He used to go by way of Durston—as in those days there was no
Railroads to South Moulton or Barnstable and it being verey bad
roads made it a verey severe journey to go through in two days.

After attending a Sale at Exmoor I think it must be in the year
1841 or 1842 my Brotherlaw Mr Hay and a first Cozen Mr George
Baker with my Father went to Exmoor to see if they should like
a Farm. My Father had bin to Mr Knights sale in the September
Previous and bt a lott of Cattle which I believe turned out rather
profetable. Mr Hay and Mr Baker went over the Forrest or a Part
but was in Treaty for part of Cornham Farm which with the part
called the Chains was estimated 1800 acres. It being a great
Quantity of it verey Ruff wett Land they were indused to decline
taking it.

1842–4   First tenants

I think it was the year 1842 Mr Mathews took the Farm called Honey Mead which consisted neerley 2000 Acres [Lady Day 1842] —Mr John Mathews took the Brendon Burton Estate of Mr Knight and 1000 Acres of the Forrest I believe in the same year— they then began to send down Cattle Horses and I believe boath began to lett large Dareys. Many Dareymen and Labourers were sent down from Dorsett & Somerset and there began to be a great Anxietey as to who should gett a Farm on Exmoor.

A Mr Wooldredge from Wilshire occupied Cornham Darey House and Milked a large Dairey[1]—In the following year Mr Godwin with his Brotherlaw Mr Light took Simmonsbath Farm which was then I believe 2000 Acres [Lady Day 1843]—They also took down a Darey woman & Labourers and a Quantitey of Sheep and Cattle. People felt more antious than ever respecting renting Farms on Exmoor. Mr Light Mr Godwin's Fatherlaw was indused to take Horsen Farm. Mr James Burge of Castle Carey whose son Maried Mr Lights daughter took Winters Head Farm Mr Hibbard about the same time took Emmetts Farm [September 1844]. In the same Autumn Messrs Dowding and Card took the Warren Farm Mr James Coombs took the Crooked Post Farm all from within a few Milles of each other.

It turned out to be a verey fine warm Summer the Crops in the upper Countrey were all but Burnt up—Butt on Exmoor the Crops of Corn & Grass was abundant and as fine a Harvest as ever was known. Mr Mathews that year attended Wilton Fair and bt I think it was 500 South Down Yews which answered his purpose I hird him say uncomernley well. I saw them in the Month of December [1844] at Honey Mead Farm and altho the Frost was so severe in the Room where I slept the Jug was Frozen to the Bason they were looking remarkably well and altho I think Mr Mathews had but a scanty crop of Turnips that year I believe he Bread a Lamb to a Yeo and I think he told me sold 300 at L1. 5s. Each and the remainder at L1 or L1 1s. per Head the following October.

In the year [1838] I had bin renting a Farm at North Cheriton [near Wincanton] of Mr Bewley the Term taken for seven years expired at the Ladey day following—It was rented at a high price

neerley L3 per Acre as there was a Quantitey of Yong orcherds on
it which I was unfortunate with not having but one Cropp during
the seven years—It was a small Farm of about 70 or 80 Acres and
land that prodused but a scantey Crop in a dry summer.

September 1844   A first visit to Exmoor

In the year [1844] in the Month of September Mr Knight had
a large Sale of Cattle at Exmoor and Mr Mathues also had one
coming on the Following day—There being so much conversation
in the Neighbourhood respecting the Exmoor Farms through so
maney Parteys takeing and about to take Farms I had a great
inclination to see it.

A Freind and Neighbour of mine at that time and a Person
being a dealer in Cattle having dealt largely with the Messrs
Mathues—by Name Mr Arthur—felt a great inclination as well as
myself to see Exmoor—We arranged to putt my Mare in the Gig
to take the Jurney. We started of the Sunday Afternoon as the
Sale was on Tuesday and gott to Taunton—The following day we
gott to Exford or rather I think to Mr Mathues at Honey Mead
where I think we spent the Evining and slept the Night There was
a deal of conversation during the Evining and princaply in favour
of the Exmoor Farms and the favourable Prospect Peeple connected at that time seemed to entertain. As I before said I think
Mr Mathues was then occupying 2000 Acres and report said he
was in Treatey for the Warren Farm of many hundred acres more
—The following day we attended the sale at Cornham held there
by Mr Modgridge then the Appointed Steward for Mr Knight
[J. Mogridge of Molland (see page 78)]—I forgett the Quantitey
of Cattle to be sold but I believe it was several hundreds and a
great maney hundred sheep. There was a large attendance and I
believe the most part was sold altho not at high Prises—I looked
out a Bullock to kill for the sale. The Cattle was in first rate
Condition. I believe most of the before named Tennants that had
taken Farms I have named before were preasant at the sale and all
seemed Highly taken up with the Contrey and the apperence of
the Crops—In the evining we returned to Mr Godwins at Simmonsbath Farm to spend a few ours with him and his Friends
from Dorsett which then bid fair to poppulize the Forrest of

Exmoor—I recollect on our way from Cornham to Mr Godwin Mr Knight came up with us. Mr Godwin made the remark heare are the Dorsetshire Farmers Sir—Mr Knights reply was I wish I could gett more of them Godwin. Mr Arthur and myself spent the Evining at Mr Godwin's and then returned to Mr Mathues for a Bedd whose Sale was to take place the next Day at Winstichen Farm [at that time included in Honeymead]—Mr Mathues had an Auctineer from Dorsetshire which did not gett through the Buseness verey well altho I believe Mr Mathues did not like to submitt to the Prises of the Day Preveious and not many were sold—We then returned to Mr Mathues and Mr Arthur the following day Bought I think it was 30 of their princaply Scotch oxen and also bt at Mr Knights sale 12 or 14.

After hearing the favourable oppinion Mr Mathues Messrs Godwin and Light and the maney Darey Peeple who were daring under Mr Mathues and Godwin seeing the Beautifull Crops of Corn they were just beginning to harvest and everything looking so prosperes—I was indused to ask of Mr Knight or Mr Modgridge or it may be boath If they had a Farm they could lett to mee. Mr Modgridge I Believe inquird in what part of the Forrest I should like a Farm—I believe I told him I should like a part of Cornham—Mr Modgridge named it to Mr Knight who I believe said from Knowing my Father through attending his sales he should be quite agreeable to do so—I was to communicate with my Father and write to say what day wee would attend.

After our return the following Morning I saw my Father and informed him of our Journey and what we had done—He then inquird how I liked Exmoor—I told him from what I had hird and seen I had a verey good opinion of it and I had purposed to look over a Farm if he thought favourable of it—He said it would require more Cappital than I had to take so large a Farm as they would like to lett but he thought wee may be able to take a Farm for him to have a part and no doubt some Money could be gott as he was in a large Buseness and a deal of Monay out in his Trade He could not assist mee much in that way at the Present time—he said he would think it over and would see mee again before writing an answer to Mr Modgridge—In talking the matter over Mr George Gifford and Mr Samuel Ritchards [Hannam's brother-in-law, and a relative of his wife, respectively] said they should much like to see the Contrey—It was then aranged they should Accompinney my Father and mee and the Day was Fixed when we should start and Mr Modgridge was writen to accordingley.

25–28 September 1844   A second visit

I believe it was the Wednesday following we leaved with the Intention of getting to Taunton that Afternoon and with the intention of being at Wivilscombe Fair the following day—But it turned out to be on the same day as we leaved which Account was given wrong in the Almanack in the list of Fairs. We gott to Taunton that Evining and the Next Morning started by way of Wivilscombe as we hird at Taunton it had not bin a verey selling Fair my Father thought there may be some sheep near unsold which turned out to be the case a Person living close by the Town A Butcher by the name of Hill having about such a lott of Yeos as My Father wished to buy—We watter and fedd the Horses and they Dealt—We then sped on our journey a diferent way from what I had before bin and gott to Simmonsbath in the Evining where we had everey kindness showen us for the Night—Mr Knight had several Gentlemen with him whose companey we were taken into to take some wine with and we spent a verey Pleasant Evening—Mr Card of Gillingham was preasant and I believe had just made an arrangement for the Warren Farm.

The following Morning when we had Breakfased we started to look over Cornham some on Horses and some Walking but I think my Father took his Gig—Cornham Farm was then estimated to be Two Thosand Eight Hundred Acres. We went over a great part of the Farm as far as Mr Modgridge knew as he had not bin long with Mr Knight but he happened to ask of some meen working how fare it extended when we found we had leaved several Hundred Acres behind we had not seen and had to retreat back again—We then bent our way back to Simmonsbath took some Dinner and Rode over the South Forrest Farms which was then lett to Messrs Hibbard Light & Burge we then returned to Simmonsbath and spent a Pleasent Evining talking over matters again My Freinds Mr Gifford and Mr Ritchards after seeing Mr Gooddwins Farm the Crops of Corn he was then Carieing and the

Condition of the Stock were highley taken up with the appearance and in the Corse of the Evining Named to Mr Knight what other Farms he had to lett us they should have no objection to take a Farm. Mr Knights reply was he had other Farms of good Qualitey on Badger Ley and diferent parts of the Forrest but he did not think he must lett aney more that season as he thought he had lett Quite as much as they would be able to gett the Buildings up in preparation for the Ladey Day following which turned out to be the Case as they had five Farm Houses & Buldings to contend with and could finish none having sett in a verey severe winter a deal of Frost & Snow there was but little done.

The following Morning we leaved for Home—It being Sadderday it was Taunton Great Market Day—the last Sadderday in September we got to Taunton and I sopose stoped two ours fedd the Horses and had some Dinner—We then gott on our Journey so far a Bridghampton having driven near 60 Miles we halted at Mr Browns who wished us to feed the Horses and take supper as he wished to hear a little about Exmoor. We halted about an Hour—Had the Horses putt to and intended soon to gett Home but after getting a few Miles Mr Giffords Poney altho having bin driven near 60 Miles Made a Start [they would have travelled from Taunton through Langport and would be near Sparkford]—it made a Bound upon the Arm of the Gig My Fathers Side and Tipped the Gig over in the Road. I gott round in time to take it by the Head and stop it and as happened nothing was hurt but the Poney was so much disturbed and frightened we could putt it in no more and was oblidged to draw the Gig on to the nearest Farm. Having gott Home thus ended our Second Journey to Exmoor.

October 1844   Negotiations for Cornham
My Father then wrote to Mr Modgridge to know if they would lett a partt of the Farm and what Quantitey—I believe he had a reply to the effect they would lett a part but wishing him to come down again—Accordingley we started on a Sunday Morning and gott to Exford and stoped at Mr Browns [the White Horse Inn]— The following Morning we started to Simmonsbath. I believe we then went over part of the Farm and it was aranged for us to have

Page 247   (*above*) The Porlock railway at Elsworthy;
(*below*) Simonsbath bridge after the 1952 floods

Page 248　(above) Simonsbath village; (below) Exmoor parish church

the Preasent Part I now occupye with Titchcombe which was
estimated to be about 1000 or from that to 1100 Acres the First
Year—The following Year we were to have Half the Chains
suposed to be about 500 Acres More which was to be divided with
a Fence by the following Year—The Matter was gone into what
more Buldings would be requird which was to be a Dwelling
House Barn & Waggon House and cirtin alterations made to the
Buldings then up—A specefied time was stated for the New
Buldings to be compleeted and a plan was prepared in what
manner they were to be bult—My Father said he did not like the
Plan of some of the buldings he had seen in the Forrest He should
like the Barn to be Bult so as to Drive a Load of Corn in to unload
and the Waggon House to be suffient Height to driven in and
House severall Load of Hay or Corn. Mr Knight verey kindley
replyed He may have it his own Plan. Matters being so far aranged
and the Farm taken we leaved for Home the Agreement was to be
Drawn by some future day[2]—It was also stated that a House
intended for a Darey was to be bult on Titchcomb with Cow
Stalls and Piggery as soon as requird or when the Land was
Broken and gott into Grass. This must be I think some time in
October the Farm was taken.

December 1844–March 1845   Preliminary work
I did not go to Exmoor again untill about the Middle of
December. Mr Arthur then went with mee having some buseness
with Mr Mathues—We then made a stay several Days and Mr
Arthur then had a great inclination to take a Farm and looked
over something of Mr Mathues which he had Bought and some he
was renting of some other partey—called Verney Ball—We went
to South Molten Market on the first Sadderday in December and
on our return went to Cornham and Mr Arthur Bt 150 Hogs sheep
of Mr Modgridge that were reserved at the Sale in September.
Spent the Sunday with Mr Mathues and part of Monday and went
to Cornham I lett the Little Cornhams to a Person to Plow by the
Acre and lott a Quantitey of Land to pare and Burn on part of
Titchcombe to different Parties—On Monday Evining we drove
to Taunton. It was verey severe Frostey weather. We leaved
Exford about 5 oclock got to Taunton about Half Past Nine the

P

following morning. We leaved about five and gott Home to Breakfast as Mr Arthur had to attend a Market that Day at Stalbridge—and to show the Qualitey of the Mare I do not believe the whip was taken in Hand the whole of the Distance or did we feed but twise on the journey.

I did not go to Exmoor again untill after Crismass but began to arange by selling of my stock I had at Cheriton as I thought it to good a Qualitey to take to Exmoor and to forward in Calf and as Hay was likely to be verey Dear I wished to return as much as I could to sell in the Spring which by so doing I was enabled to sell a Rick at L42 which more than paid for what I requird at Exmoor. After Crismass I again visseted Exmoor, Took down some Horses 2 Carts and Carted out the Manure as there was a large Quantitey about the Yards—I remaind and assisted myself for some days and was Treated verey kindley at Simmonsbath House by Mrs Harvey then the Housekeeper—Between Crismass and Ladey Day I was Down maney Times and always took up my abode at Simmonsbath—I then began to prepare to settle Down on Exmoor. Sent two more Horses with a Load of Darey Utensels and different things.

March 1845   A bad spring

Ladey Day now was near and Mr Modgridge advertised a Three Days Sale at Cornham, First Day for Beast second for Poneys and sheep the third for Plant Tackell & Mashinarey which with Drills Chopp Cutters and one thing and the other I should think would spread over two Acres of the North Field—It turned out to be verey Cold severe weather and there being a great scarcetey of Keep in the Contrey there was not a verey large attendance or a Brisk sale the first Day for the Beast the seccond Day for the Poneys and sheep was still worse it being so Cold people could scarceley live there being a strong freesing Eastley Wind The Third Day no one attended the sale and it was given up there was a Quantitey of the Stock and scarceley aney of the Implyments Sold.

The time was now neerley arived for the different parties who had taken Farms to enter on them—There was to be a certin part of the Buldings on each Farm to be gott readey by Ladey Day but it turned out such a severe winter nothing scarceley could be done to Bulding—Things now had quite a different apperence from the September preveos—there had bin a Deal of Cattle lost During the winter and a great Deal that was living was looking misabrly Bad There had bin a great deal of Stock putt out to keep by Mr Mathues Mr Godwin and Mr Hibbard which came back in Missabrly bad Condition the Forrest was looking verey Barren not a Green Blade to be seen—Several of the Parties that had taken Farms coming on to take Posession of there Farms and nothing prepared for them felt much dissattisfied and gave up their Farms but still offerd to take them on if Mr Knight would make them an alowance of Half a Years Rent to meet the Ill-convenience which he would not concede to do—They would have to contend with Mr Knight through the Rimision of Modgridge. Acordingley Mr Light gave up Harson Mr Burge Winters Head & Messrs Dowding & Card Warren Farms and saccrifised what they had spent in Labour which I believe amounted to from L40 to L50 Each—Mr John Mathues and Mr Knight having had some little altercation respecting the Damage of the Deer and Rabbets and Mr Mathues remarking he wished he had never takin it was told by Mr Modgridge He may if he Choose gaive it up to which Mr Mathues assented and at the following Ladey Day gave notice. Mr Godwin and Mr Light at the same time desolved Partnership and Mr Light leaved soon after Ladey Day.

24–26 March 1845   The journey to Exmoor

I now returned to Cheriton and prepared to leave for Exmoor—I must say I did not return in very good Spirts after witnessing what I had and hearing of Four Tennants giving up it rather putt a damp on mee as I thought it rather to large an undertaking but knowing My Father generaley paid nerley the Rent of my Farm yerley for keep for stock Extra of his Farm in one way and the other I thought he would not require to do so but would send a Quantitey with me the Summer and make a greater Provision thrue the winter and he would if I had not pirswade him out of it have taken a much larger Quantitey. It was a Great Anksiatey on my mind for a long time—Wee had a great maney of the most respectable Peeple wishing us every success in our undertaking.

We gott Loaded on the Sadderday and started Monday—We had three Waggons with three Horses each and two Carts with one Horse each. Had two Horses come to meet at Handey Cross and two more of Mr Knights at Rawley Cross [Raleigh's Cross. They were travelling from Taunton via Bishops Lydeard, Handy Cross and the Brendons]. I had a coverd Carr with my wife servents & Child with which we intended to gett to Exmoor the same Day but could gett no farther than Exford as the Roads were in such a State after the severe Frost the Horses could scarce gett along we gott to Simmonsbath the next morning where I leaved my Family and returned to meet the waggons which I expecded to mett about Cutcombe or Exford as the were going to Travell all Night. I Rode to Rawley Cross when I found they had arived some little time having had such a difficultey to assend Elwrthey Hill. Having now 15 Horses and the Stables but small there was not room for more Than 4 or 5 Horses to Lay Down or feed some were feedding in Buckkets and some out of the Bedds of the Carts about the Yard—It was then five oclock and A tremendous Misk or thick Fog—I said to the Men it is no use staying long here as there is no accomadation for the Horses and night is coming on we shall not see our way over the Hills our better way will be to gett as soon as we can to Cutcombe. Neither of the Men knew the least part of the Road and before we gott Half the distance it was so dark we could not see a yard—The Roads were in such a state after the Frost and having verey Heavey Loads the wheels Cutt over the Fellows nearley every step the moved so that we could but just make a moove onwards—I now began to ask myself a few Questions what busseness I had to be where I was and it being Easter Tuesday it occured to my mind it was Wincanton Fair where I had spent so maney happey hours in my Life time—I had begun to think in my mind I was going from Home but still I thought it was no use putting the Hand to the Plow and look back. I thought in my mind the Crops I had seen grown there the summer before and the oppineon Mr Mathues and Mr Godwin entertained of it with perseverence a Person may yett do well—We gott on to Cutcombe about Nine oclock where I found also there was no Accomadation for the Horses or not but three or four—I said to the men it is no use staying heare we must gett to Exford as soon as we can or they will be gone to Bedd gave the meen some Beer and I went on as fast as I could to gett the Peeple to await up untill the came—The White Horse at that time was kept by Mr Brown a Person from the Higher part of Somersett whom I knew and he verey kindley made Room for the Horses and Meen and the laid down a few hours—The following morning we mooved on again to Exmoor or I may say to Cornham with part of the Goods.

There was no House but the Cottages at Cornham at that time in one of theese we were to reside the first six months whilst the present Farm House was Bulding we staid with our servents and Little Girl at Simmonsbath a few days whilst the Cottage was cleaning up and we could gett things a little in place—Mrs Harvey then the House Keepper at Simmonsbath was verey kind in doing every possable to make us comfortable to assist us on and wished us to remain longer but my wife and servents were antios to gett to their Home be it ever so Homeley and as Mrs Harvey had two other Fameleys coming to reside with her whilst their Houses were being finished we thought the sooner we were away the better.

1845   Richard Hibberd of Emmett's Grange

Mr Hibbert then arived to occupye Emmets Farm [in March 1845] no house being readey for him he remained at the Simmonsbath house the first month or two. Winters Head Farm was then lett to a Person by the name of Ilett from Ilminster who also staid at the Simmonsbath house with his fameley for two or three Months—Mr Hibbert soon gott sickened having lost maney Cattle was alowed to give up part of the Farm and was abated the greater part of the Rent the first year. He then went on with Spiret for a time but having Ill luck with his horses and not feeling sattesfied with the Fences and Buldings He commenced a Law Suit against Mr Knight which was caried into Court at Bridgwater [in 1847] and I believe thrown against Mr Hibbert— And then Mr Knight had two cross Actions against Hibbart for alowing Straw and Turnips to be caried of the Farm [see page 79]. I believe the Law Suit was caried on by Mr Hibberts attorney for near two years which ruined him and his. Every thing was taken to and sold with the Exception of a Bedd on the Flower and a few things for their use and he was depending wholely on his Freinds for the support of his wife and Fameley—I assisted him in maney respects—I lent him severall Pounds Cheque to Change in Cash Pd for Bread at South Molton—lett him have a Pig about four score weight live at the Butchers when my Cart went with Butter then and after His Horses and Tackle were disposed of sent My Horses and Men to take his Corn in the Barn from the Ricks—He was verey unfortunate but since leaving he has bin one of the most fortunate Meen I sopose ever Hird of.

1845-6   Other tenants

Mr Ilett then went to the Winters Head Farm but not remain above one Year and Half. He Brought an emence Quantitey of Plow Tackle of every description Hay Potatoes Cidur and things to Numerous to mention—He had some verrey good Horses and was Halling for maney wicks from White Lackington Farm near Ilminster. He neerley filled all the Simmonsbath Buldings and a Quantitey at other Places—He had scarceley aney stock on the Farm and I do not believe he paid aney Rent. Mr Coombs that occupied the Crooked Post Farm had Down five Hundred sheep which he Bought of Messrs Dowding and Card that had taken the Warren Farm and given it up—They Bt them in at a verey low price the autom previos—About seven or eight shillings Each in the Auttum—and there was a great Scarcetey of Keep the winter they gott verey Poor I have hird they were scarceley able to walk down in the Spring—He had onley 400 Acres of Land and not a Foot of it Cultivated or fitt for that Class of Sheep—The Concequence was the whole of them gott in such a weak state they Died—I believe he went out the Morning after Showing them and found 60 Dead—He would not be pirswaded to putt them out to Keep—He kept on the farm I think four or five Years and lost the whole he possesed [James Coombes remained at Crooked Post until 1851]. Mr Godwin at the End of two Years gave up about Half his Farm Mr Light having withdrawn his son as a Partner and I expect the Cappetell with him. Mr Godwin then kept the other part of the Farm on the first Term of six Years and gave it up at a verey great Sacrifice and loss of Capitell.

1842 onwards   Honeymead

I will now return to Mr Mathues being the first to occupye a Farm on the Moore and the onley one leaved from my Neighboured. In [1842] as I before said Mr Mathues began with Milking and Letting Dareys out in one Season I think he had as maney as 180 Cows in Milk—He then Changed from the South Down sheep to keep Exmoor Horns and Summer them on the unbroken land and Milk Daireys on the other. Butt the fences not being up in a proper manner soon beat him on thatt sistem as the sheep would consume the Best pasture from the Cows and he found he could make butt little from them. He used to complain as well as Mr Godwin they could not make more then L6 pr Cow of them (the Cows) and wondred that my Cows made and prodused so well and would not or were hard to believe that we made so much more per Cow—For the first 5 or 6 Years I kept no sheep through seeing how the were teased with the sheep through the Fences—Mr Mathues also suffered a deal through putting out to maney Cattle to keep on straw the winter I hird him say he thought he was L200 the worse for putting out in one season beside the expence of the Keep I believe he had 7 or 8 at a time that could not Raise up without help in the spring following—I no doubt this was partley the reason Mr Mathues was indused to give up the Dairey sistem as in the corse of a few Years he declined to keep aney—His brother John putt a lott to Keep the winter—Mr Mathues then turned his attention to keep all sheep and Horses and took a Farm at Wivilscombe and occupye the Farm on the Moore as a summer Farm.

1845-7   Tenants leave

As I before said Mr John Mathues had bin occupying the Brendon Barton Farm and 1000 Acres of the Forrest (Brendon Barton Farm over 400 Acres) up to near L700 pr Year Rent which was given up at the same time as Messrs Light Burge Dowding and Card gave up the other Farms [1845]—Brendon Barton was not lett for two Years but kept in Hand and the greater part of the scotch Beast and sheep were sold belonging to Mr Knight on the Forrest and for two Years there was butt little stock on the Moor on the Farms that was not lett I think not more than from two to three hundred Beast of a season the Grass grew up on a Great maney Thousand Acres and wasted down again and was made nothing of—Mr Meadows then took the B Barton Farm. Maney Parteys came to see other Farms but I believe none was lett. Mr Modgridge then leaved the stewardship and I think Cpn Edward Knight was steward for a time—Mr Ilett leaved Winters Head Farm and I have hird paid no Rent whilst there—Mr Howchin[3] then undertook to take in the Cattle and went on with it for severall years and I think gott a fair Quantitey for severall Years and gave good sattisfaction to the Peeple sending them—Mr Godwin was alowed to give up the Duerdown part of his Farm About Half the Farm by giving something more for the other.

1845–8   Improvements at Cornham

There is on Exmoor everey thing that Nature need provide to bring it into Cultavation—There are the Hills and the Valeys for shelter the Beautifull Streems of water for the Cattle Stone wherever or within a verey short distance it may be required for Bulding Fencing or Draning and the Land I found verey Gratefull for what ever Manure was putt on it as a Dressing on the Grass I found it improve the Pasture. The Field 45 Acres the west side of the House which the first season I enterd I mowed and it was scarceley worth Raking together it apeard as if it was exhausted with growing Corn as long almost as one Corn would Bear another the Pasture was nothing scareceley but Heather and Colts-foot. I however dressed it on the Grain severall times which verey much improved it after which I have commenced to Cutt a fair Cropp of Hay verey soon after Midsummer.

The piece ajoining 32 Acres when I enters the Farm was maney Acres of it coverd with Rushes—The streem of water from the Yards was flowing over it from two large Gutters at the Topp where the Grass was verey Rank and Rushey—I had 6 Large Gutters Cutt down across it to take the water to the Bottom in its Foul State and a lott of other Gutters cutt at the Bottom on the Dead Leveall which made the Bottom of the Field neerly as good as the other. By paying attention to the water and woishing the Dung down over it Brought [the Redd Clover] up a thick as it could come and by alternateley Mowing it cleened it of the Rushes.

The three Fields on little Cornham 50 Acres had bin sown with Corn as long as it would bear aney thing and it was leaved a Mass of Couch and Coltsfoot and not a Grass seed sown in it—I first comenced on them to Plow and Clean them altho Mr. Knight himself pirswade me to leave them as it would onely bring mee in debt having spent L50 in Bone Dust Manure himself to grow Turnips and gott none. I however saw if I cleened them and gott them to a proper Grass I could improve it with Topp Dressing which I continued to do altho at a Great expence as they were 50 Acres.

I pared and Burnt and Broke 100 Acres or there about that had not bin Broken before which with Paring and Burning Liming and Grass seedding cost mee over L500. I never sold L5 worth of Corn of the present Cornham Farm during the Term—I have Bt and Brought on to consume with Pigs and Cattle from 30 to L50 worth pr year which with cutting up the Rushes and ?straw for Bedding made a Quantitey of Manure which was all carried on the Grass Land and it not being Broken by mee but alternateley mown was the reason it was so much improved and had such a diferent apearance from the other Farms on the Forrest—I think I can safeley say for maney years I Manured 100 Acres pr Year. Maney Peeple I have hird raise a great objection to Mowing Land thinking it injurios to it—I think with regard to the Exmore Land it is a great improvement to Mowe alternateley and topp Dress.

I was on the Moor 13 years and never found the season but I made a deal of sweet Hay at some time of the summer—We may spoil a part some seasons which is the case in other places but very frequent for want of Hands to attend to it. In the year 1848 we had a verey wet July and part of August and there was a deal spoilt not onley on the Moor but around there was Hundreds of Acres caried to the Dung Heap—I that season made about 20 Acres verey well in June and a deal more sweet the last wick in August and September—32 Acres I spoilt as for six wicks there was not two dry days following.

1847 *Illness*

In the year 1847 I had a severe attack of the tipheis Fever and was laid up for maney wicks. At that time I had near 1100 Acres which I found was to much as I began to find there was a great outlay before there was aney return from it—As I was laying ill it was a great Anksiety on my Mind and partickulerey as My Mrs was laid up at the same time—It was in the Month of June and July we were then Milking from 40 to 50 Cows—We were fortunate in having a Mrs Stay to assist us that year in the Darey and Mrs Sister and one of my Cosens came to our assistence During my ilness—Mr Lee our Medical Man paid me every kind attention during my ilness—Mr Knight was verey antios on my behalf and wished partickalerey for Dr Collens [Dr Charles Palk Collyns of Dulverton] to attend mee also to give his opinion.

1847   Tenants' vicissitudes

The letting Farms went on verey slowley for some time untill three Peeple came out of Dorsetshire from near Weymouth 2 Brothers by the name of Dulley and another by the name of Henditch. One of the Dulleys took Winters Head Farm, the other Duerdown and Henditch took a Farm at Dryford [Driver] where a House was to be emedateley Bult—It was about Mickalmass time they took the Farms and to take on the Ladey Day following Henditch and the one at Duerdown made some Hay the same Autom and sett on to pare and Burn and during the winter to Plow—March came on and the one at Duerdown sent in a lott of Cattle from Bristoll Fair Bt oats and Diferent things and began to sow was down there a Deal himself for a time—Untill a few days before Midsummer. He came of a South Molton Fair Day and took everey thing of boath Live and Dead stock went by way of South Molton to Taunton and sold it and leaved for America—He owed a good bitt of Money to diferent Peeple which he wished to wrong them out of but they followed him to South Molton some of it they goot out of him by threats and stopping him on the Road —Mr Godwin and mee followed Him to assist to make him pay John Brown and others. The other Dulley anterd on the Winters Head Farm staied there a few days and comensed a little work— All of a sudden he took up his Traps and leaved by Moon light and no one knew it for a time—Henditch sent on some Horses to Dyford and putt in the oats and came on to Live soon after Ladey

Day and gott on and improved the Farm verey much. He had a long Grown up Fameley and they were verey Industrios Peeple.

March 1848   Robert Smith arrives

It must be about this time Mr Smith came on as a Steward [Lady Day 1848]—We had hird there was such a Person coming on—I had bin to Simmonsbath and in the Road gott in Conversation with him (Mr Smith) and learnt who he was—I told him I expected Mr Mathues up to spend a few hours with mee and envited him to meet him which he felt verey Pleased to Do and accordingley baoth came and we spent a verey pleasent Evining— He was then staying at the Simmonsbath House and verey soon after he came there to reside and commensed Farming Emmetts Farm and when the House was put in order went there to reside— He now began to putt advirtisments in the Mark Lane and diferent Papers to lett Farms and stating the great advantages in taking Farms on the Moor—a great maney strangers came on to see Farms and they were all taken over My Farm to see the Pasture the Dairey and what was worth their Notice—Verey soon after Mr Searson Mr Smiths Brother Law came and he was taken by Mr Smith to Cornham—I found by Mr Smiths conversation he was endeavring to gett him to take a Farm—I reccolect a remark Mr Smith made with respect to Mr Searson having a sunney Spott already I fancied he could not verey easey gett Mr Searson to take with him.

Robert Smith's management

There is not the leist Doubt but Mr Smiths was intended as a Modell Farm to induce others to follow his steeps and this was intended to help on theese new Tennants that were Drawn by theese advertisments in the London Papers and writing Essays which Mr Smith was assistieng Mr Ackland to do and took him over my Farm and to my House maney times whilst it was in hand to write an Essay with respect to the Best Mode of Farming the County of Somerset for a Prize of L50⁴ which was contested for by Mr Ackland and one or two others from Somerset and Mr Ackland obtained it—Boath Parteys were taken over my Farm severall times whilst it was in hand and to inspect the Dairey as at that time Mr Smiths Farm was not in much of a State of Cultava-tion and but few of the others were either as they had not bin long on.

I also reccollect of Mr Shaw the Edditor of the Mark Lane Express being took on the Moor by Mr Smith and went round to the diferent Farms and remained on the Moor for severall Days after which there was a long Letter in the Mark Lane Express representing the advantage to be derived by renting the Exmoor Farms and the numereos Tennantrey from Diferent Conteys and the extencive Farms that was then lett and the advantages and improvements to be made by the Catch Water Meadows and what may be seen on Mr Smiths Farm at Emmetts Grange but nothing said about the enormeos Expence he had bin at to make those Meadows or whose Cappitell he was expending in making them. I think Mr Knight in time will see that Mr Smith has spent scores of Pounds usesley in Cutting Gutters to take water on that is a Newsance to the Land instead of a Benifitt—I do not think that the Bog water taken of the Hill that have never bin Broken or Limed and turned on the Land that has been Limed can be of aney Benifitt—I know maney hundered Acres in the Higher part of Somersett that used to be Flooded that is now made dry as peeple that had a deal of expeirence in Water Meadows saw it was an injurey.

I believe Mr Smith made a great mistake in neglecting the Fences to Drayn the Bogs and spending a deal of Money in Cutting Gutters for Catch Meadows—I believe to the spending such a sum of Money about serching for the Iorn ore which was wonted so badley to gett up the Fences had a deal to do with driving away the Tennants—There never was a Man come on Mr Knights Propertey yett that made so maney mistakes as Mr Smith in the First place to sell away a Quantitey of fine Beach and thorn Plants with the intention no doubt to gett a little Money together which could be but a small sum after all and to think to subtitute wire and Gorse instead which was no Fence as it was and in two years was decayed and down in the Ditch again and the stock running the Fences from one end to the other And the Horn Sheep Ranging the Cuntrey back to where they were Bredd and maney lost and never recoverd again.

Robert Smith's farming

Mr Smith when he first came on and Mr Searson as well said there was no Nessitey of making Hay as oats to Cutt to Chaff were much better. They boath found however that a little Hay was usefull. Mr Smith when he first came on the Moor Commenced to Farm after Mr Huxtable and Mr Meecheys sistom by stocking his Farm with Pigs—I Believe he at one time had over 200 He soon gott sickned of Pig Farming as I expect he found he had the greater part to Buy for them and to fetch from Barnstable as no doubt he found out the Corn he grew on the Forrest would not feed them altho he tryed maney Maxems such as the Proliffick Barley Flax seed and severall Acres of Potatoes but all to no purpose—It must have Cost him a large sum in erecting Piggereys to the extent he Caried it—He also had a Mill and Steemer on the Newest Principle but it was all failuers.

Mr Smith began to Attempt things that was Quite unreasonable for the Climate He attempted to Grow Wheat several seasons I hird him say one Year he had 20 Acres and not a small concern for Exmoor his reply was—I was at his House repeatedley and I never saw a Loaf of Bread made with it neither have I in the 12 Years I have bin on the Moor seen a Loaf of Bread fitt for aney one to eat altho I have seen Mr Mathues and Godwin and maney others attempted to Grow it—Mr Smith attempted to grow Mustard Seed Rape Seed Flax Seed Peas Barley several Acres of Potatoes and maney other things to numeros to Mention but all Failures it onley ledd others to attemp the same and misslaid them—I made one attempt to grow the productive Bareley he told so much about but it was not worth doing—I also did attempt 2 Acres of Spring Wheat but good for nothing but Pigs altho Boath the Barley and Wheat was Grown in as Favourable spots of Land as the Moor can produce being a Southeren Aspect and much below the greater part of exmoor.

Robert Smith's finances

It appears that Mr Smith when he took on the Stewardship and Farm of Mr Knight was possesed of but little or no Cappetal but was depending princaply on his Brother Mr John Smith—He then aplied to a Mr Lovebond of Bridgwater who advertised to lett out Money on aproved securetey—It appears he wrote to Mr Lovebond who came down—I sopose Mr Lovebond would not advance it unless he gott some other securitey beside himself and he took him to mee of a Morning about Eight oclock—He called me from the Room we were in to the ajoining and asked mee to join him for three Hundred Pounds—Mr Smith said he did not require it but a few Months untill he gott his Salerey as Mr. Fowler came down and took away all the Money and leaved him destitute.[5] I went and named it to my wife who had a great objection to it at first but we thought it over what power he had in his hands to do us a deal of good or injurey I was induced to assist him with my signature.

It went on past the given time then it was renewed again and again maney times for Years—I think it was in the year 1854 in May It appears that neither Princaple or Interest was paid the Interest over L40. Mr Lovebond sent his assistant from Bridgwater to Exmoor with a request that the Money be emedateley paid—Mr Foster the Persons name that was sent wheather he knew Mr Smith was from Home I cannot say but he came direct to my House—He gott to us about 8 oclock in the Morning.

I asked him to take some Breakfast which he did—We then walked to Emmetts Grange and as I said before Mr Smith was not home—We had just gott outside the Gate when a second person was sent direct from Bridgwater and Posted from South Molton and to inform Mr Foster he was to emedateley take steps to recover the whole sum by taking suffient stock of his Farm to mine and emedateley sell it to mee or some one else. It appears they had an oppertunitey of getting a Knowledge of his Debts from some Redgester office a List of which was sent by the second person up to the amount of over L4000. (Mr Lovebond told me since he gott a List over L7000) Mr Foster then insisted on emedateley taking away the stock to secure mee. After a deal of pirswasion I prevaild on him to go with me untill Mr Smith returned. The(y) then sent boath Careges back to South Molton and went with me to Cornham where they remained untill the next Morning—Mr Foster entreated me not to think of renewing the Bill again He said Mr Smith was not justified in asking mee or

I in doing it as he had Brothers and he ought to refer to them—He
said Mr Smith nor aney one else could afford to pay the enormous
Interest he was paying it would Ruin aney Man (It was neerley
20 pr Cent).

The following Morning Mr Smith came over—Mr Foster went
out and gave him a Meeting—They withdrew to the Field at the
West of the Yard and there they held a long Conversation. Mr
Foster then showed him the List of Regesturd Debts he had
against him—He was then verey much alarmed, and Begged him
to renew the Bill once more for a few Months—At last Mr Foster
concented to do so if he gott another Bondsman to join with
mee—He could not think on aney one for some time at length he
said he would ask Mr Minnett. Mr Foster and him then went to
Mr Minnetts and gott him to putt his Name to the Note of Hand
and then returned to mee to do so—Mr Smith then ashurd Mr
Foster and myself it should be paid of the following autom when
he gott his salerey through which I was induced to join him again
with the expectation it would be so.[6]

1849–54   Tenants come and go

I will now return to Mr Smith respecting the Harson Farm
which he lett to Mr Searson [1849]. A great maney others came to
see Farms amongst them was a Mr Chambers who took the
Winters Head Farm—He was a smart spicey looking Person and
Quite a Ladey for his wife appeared to be resentley Maried—They
drove in a fine Dog Cart and for a time took up their abode at the
Fortesque Hotell at Barnstable untill the House was putt in order
which took a deal to do—I have hird they wished the Roof of the
House to be taken of and the Rooms rose Higher and made more
Loftey but Mr Knight verey Prudentley declines to do so I hird
through the Pirswasion of John Smith who was then Master of
the Bulding then going on—He did not however require it long
at the end of six months or thereabout after getting about L400 in
Debt in the Neighbrud of Barnstable he Drove of in his Dog Cart
and putt the Key under the Dore—He gott about L100 in for
Furniture to a Mr Gribble which he did not take away with him.
Mr Gribble gott news of it and went and took it away but was
stopped on the way and it was taken and sold for Rent by Mr

Smith a verey hard case for Mr Gribble. Maney other Tradesmen in Barnstable were taken in as I say up to the sum of L400. Thus ended Mr Chambers at Winters Head Farm.

Maney others now came to take Farms—Mr Spooner took Winters Head [1852] Mr Harrold took the Warren Farm [by 1850] Mr Meadows took Lark barrow [1849]—Barwell Tomshill. Mr Groves took a Farm on Pinkrey [1849] and a Person by the name of Sharp took the Crooked Post Farm [1854]. Mr Godwins term of six years [from 1843 of Simonsbath Barton] was now expired and he made up his mind to leave—the Farm was not lett for a year it was then taken by a Mr Pople—About the same time Mr Bullass took Duerdown Farm [1852]—Barwell did not occupye the Tomshill Farm but a few months from Ladey Day till November but sufficent time to gett indebted to maney Peeple and left them unpaid—Mr Meadows sold a verey good Propertey in Leastershire took his poor Father down near 80 years old. In about three years he spent the whole of his property and leaved indebted to the Neighbroud. He bought 80 beast in the Spring to go on the Farm to Eat Rushes and Heather. Meadows had no land Cultivated. Poor old Mr Groves who was quite an Invaleed and we may say almost one Foot in the Grave and ought to have bin pirswaded by some one that he was not a sutable Person to occupy a Farm on Exmoor—He had some property which was in his Brothers Hands who had a long Fameley and he did not like to distress him for it. He occupyed the Farm about twelve Months. Peeple begun to press him for Payment of what he owed them and being of a weak mind he destroyd himself by Blowing his Brains out by the Road side not far from his own Dore. What things he had was taken to and sold and Mr Smith had the greater part of the Proceeds for Rent.

Mr Harrold went on with great spirt with Farming for a time gave up his Trade as a Master Tayler and Liverey stable Keeper in Lester Town into the hands of his forman. In two or three years he gott tierd of it and returned into Lester again and putt Barwell to manage the Farm which Turned out a Bad Speculation as he gave himself up to Drinking and was near the Buseness some times for a wick or fortnight. This of Corse ended Bad as I will relate hereafter.

There was two Peeple that rented the Farms at Lark Barrough & Tomshill when the Buldings were putt up—one a Fr Hays from Exford and a Fr Stribling from near Barnstable neither of then continued but a little time—Mr Meadows took on the Lark B Farm after Fr Hays and a conciderable deal more on to it I believe to the Extent of 900 Acres—Mr Meadows comenced to Buy in a lott of Steers and verey good Cattle about May and June from the Inland Contreys up to the number of 70 or 80. He had no Land or verey little that had bin nearley Seeded out and his Land in genaral was produsing verey indiferent pasture. The stock was going back in Condition instead of Forward and not having a provision for the winter was oblidged to be sold in the Autom at a great sacrifice I believe at a deal less than Cost Price—He took 60 of them to Bridgwater Fair but could not sell them. He then returned Home and Bt a lott of sheep on the Toms Hill Farm and sent up with the intention of taking them down again but they were sold. Mr Meadows Bt the little Hay and straw on Toms Hill Farm as Mr Barwell was oblidged to give up. The Toms Hill Farm then was not lett for severall years.

Mr Hedditch about this time leaved the Dryford Farm he had spent a deal of Labour and cappitall and improved the Farm verey much—The House was locked up for a time then it was lett to a Mr Allen from Derbeyshire who did not occupye it but one Year. It was then lett to a person by the name of Minnett from Lincolnshire [in 1853] who Mr Smith gott to take it of Mr Allens Hands— and to take what Hay and Corn he had there at a valuation of himself which caused a dispute and illfeeling betwin Mr Allen and Minnett—Mr Poppell onley occupyed the Simmonsbath Farm about a Year and Half—I believe he was indebted to a Person before coming to Exmoor who was about to putt on him for the Amount. His Fatherlaw came in before the Person he was indebted to and sold all he had—I think Mr Poppell would or may have done well if he had bin allowed to continue as he began to have his Farm verey well stocked and seemed to be improving it.

Mr Mathues first Term of 12 years now having or was about to expire (He paid verey little or no Rent whilst there) He had taken a verey good Farm at Wivilscombe when he had a severe attack of Ilness. He was indused to take on the Farm at Exmoor for another

Term [1854]. Mr Mathues began to keep mostley sheep and Grow but little Corn. His confidential Man or that ought to have bin depended on gave up to Drinking and was not near the Bussiness for severall Days following so much that he was indused after discharging him severall times and taking him on again was oblidged to discgarge him altogether—Mr Smith then represented that Mr Mathues intended Living a deal on Exmoor himself and had a deal done to the House and Pillers to the Gate Entry—I think he Mr Smith expected to gett a lott of Gentleman Farmers Resident as Farmers to join with him I sopose with his Hounds and Keep him Companey regardless at whose expence it may be or whom he ruined.

1850–6   Sheep

I was pirswaded by Mr Smith and maney others to keep some Sheep and less Dairey which indused me to do so—I had seen how my Neighbours had bin Teased with the Horn Sheep through the Fences—(I scarceley ever see Mr Godwin but he had lost some of his Sheep and we could stand on my Farm and see Sheep all over his Farm among the Cows and in the Mowing Ground) (Sheep that he had Bought in the previos season in small lotts and would return across the Cuntrey to where they were Bredd).

Through seeing Mr Mathues keep the South Downs with such success (Having 50 yeos to Lamb in a Previos season) I was indused in the year 1850 I think it was to Buy 100 South Down Yeos (I Bought them of young George Neal) I put them to a nott sheep [one without horns] and the Bred me a good lott of Lambs 106 and I believe in the season I lost 4 Yeos I sold 100 of the Lambs in August at 16/- a Head droped in March and Appril as a proof they were not verey Bad ones they were sold the following Appril at 37s pr Head and wintered without Turnips or Hay.

Through being so succesful with them I was indused to go into a larger lott Mr Leblance [Charles Le Blanc was tenant of Simons-bath House] had Bought 200 at Britpord Fair the year Preveos and was now going to Change his Flock to keep Horns—I had the oppertuntey of Buying them and I thought verey Cheep.

I Bought 170 at L1. 1. 9 pr Head about a Month after I drafted the worst of them boath as to age and Qualitey and the worst of

my own 100 also I drafted 60 and sold them at 23 and 25 pr Head
the greater part at 25 I then had 200 good Matching Yeos that I
believe a little time after would made 28s. or 30s. pr Head and I
no doubt I should have taken them up and sold them had they not
bin taken down in the Foot Rott which I had over 100 at one
time—they seemed to be doing as well as sheep could do and as
I had Abundence of Grass Hay & Oats and a Chaff Cutter to go
by water I depended I could do well for them—I had them begin
to drop their Lambs in the later part of Febuarey and through
March and April [1853]—I should think near Half of them had
Dubble Lambs which was so much the worse as they had not Milk
for one the weather was so severe and such a Quantitey of Snow
as had not bin known for years which laid on the Ground and the
Roads were blocked up for maney wicks we were oblidged to keep
them in the Yards and Houses with hay and water for maney
wicks—I believe I lost near 40 Yeos and 150 Lambs we had maney
Cows in full Milk which we milked Night and Day and attended
them with but all to no purpose as it matterd not what sort they
were the winter was so severe I believe neerley Half the Lambs on
the Forrest Dyed that winter.

Mr Spooner Lambed a Quantitey of the Scotch Sheep which
are concidred the moast Hardey Class of aney (He said they would
do best on the native Grass Nought but Powder and Shott will
kill them) I believe he lost a Quantitey of them—(He did not
Lamb his untill Aprill and May) It was a verey late Spring and the
Stock gott verey much out of Condition. The following winter I
did not keep so maney and it turned out a Mielder winter but a
verey backward Spring and I do not think stock paid aney thing
for the Keep—I believe I reared about a 140 Lambs from 150 Yeos
I sold the Yeos in September [1854] (at 34s. pr Head) in the same
Autom there was a great scarcetey of Keep in the upper Cuntreys
the Land was Burnt up and scarceley a Green Blade to be seen—In
the month of November sheep was verey low in price there was
scarceley aney Sale for them we had an abundence of Keep I went
to a Fair at Blandford in Dorsetshire and Bought 200 Lambs
which Cost mee home with the expences about 16s. pr Head the
expences getting them down was about 6d pr Head—I did not
Lamb aney Yeos this season and well I did not as it turned out one

of the severest winters that has bin Known for 40 Years—It mattered not what sort they were or what we gave them we could not Keep Life there was an emence Quantitey of sheep and Lambs lost not onley on the Forrest but on all high exposed Farms I lost over 100 sheep and I believe if I had not taken some Keep near South Molton I should have lost neerley all. I putt 160 out which I was prety fortunate to save and with what I kept Life they made a verey good profitt 9s. pr Head beside the wool and I sold them in August. I lost more of my own Breed than those I Bought it Cost mee over L100 in Keep that winter and I do not think the stock was worth so much money in the Spring as it was in the Autom. I had 28 yerlings that I was obligded to gett oil Cake for or they would not have lived—I believe in Truth I was L400 sacrifised that winter and spring through the severe weather.

The winter of [1855–] 1856 was much more favourable altho a verey backward spring and had the stock bin obligded to be sold in the Month of March it would not have Fetched the Price it was worth in the November previos—I was verey fortunate this season I believe I reared over a Lamb to the Yeo about 150 in Number I was verey fortunate this season taking it altogether I did not lost a Bullock the whole of the Summer Season neither had I an ocasion to (?) one from 150 to 170 Head I had during the Summer of my own and Keeping stock—I had near 100 Beast to Keep at L1 10s pr Head and a Quantitey of Sheep at 2½d pr Head pr Wick and Horses at 2s and 3s pr wick a price that Cattle had not bin taken in on Exmoor on aney preveos Season—maney over stocked and gave a deal of dissattesfaction.

1850–6 Produce

In the Year 1850 we had to contend with Bad times and for a year or two previos our Cheese we could not gett more than 5d; or 6d. to retail there was such a Quantitey of Americen Cheese Brought over—I advertised a Sale by Auction in Barnstable and tryed it on severall wicks in the Month of April and in aney could not make more than I name and I no doubt at the present time the same Qualitey would make 10d pr lb we had over one Hundred Cheese in number that avareged over 56 lbs Each altho we did not make a Sattisfactorey price then I believe the Publick Auction did

good as I think it established the thing it gott into maney Peepls
Heads and that reccommended others and since or in the last
three Seasons we have sold none less than 8d pr lb at aney time of
the Year and if it had bin kept to the age of what I sold by Auction
no doubt it would have made 10d. Sold a deal of Butter at 7 and
7½ pr lb Could gett no more than 7 s. per score for good Fatt Pigs
I killed a lott of Pigs and salted and dryed the Baken and Hams.
I could gett no more than 6d pr lb for Baken Hams or Lard. The
following spring I took neir 30 hundred weight into a Room at
the Golden Fleese and Tryed it wickly I sold about 10 cwt weight
by retail I sold the reminder to Mr May about a Ton weight In the
year of 1856 and for maney years before and after it would make
8d and 10d pr lb I supplyd over 400 diferent Peeple with Cheese
at 8d pr lb all the respectable Inhabbetents of the North and South
of Deaven.

Farm labourers

In the autom of the Year 1854 I putt an advertisment on the
Sherborne Journall for a Laborer with a Fameley to work on the
Farm and his wife to assist in the Dairey occasionley I had onley
three applications one of the Three was from Kington Magnan A
Person by the Name of Dowding.

I engaged this Person by the name of Dowding and two of his
Boys aranged what Day to send two Horses and a Cart to Taunton
to Meet them which took them I believe three days and two
Nights. I gave them everey assistence and encouragement I Pd
him and his Boys from 25 to 30s pr wick They had a verey good
house and a good Garden and their Firing cost them but little I
lett them have wheat I Bought at a verey low Price I found the old
man natuley a lasey inclined old fellow and as fast as he could gett
a few shillings he was away to spend it—The Boys were willing to
do what they were able or had bin accustomed to do and would
have suited mee verey well had not their Minds bin sett against it.

The same winter which was one of the most favourable known
for maney years in the Month of Januarey or February we had a
little Frost[7]—he was then Loading Trenching Sodd with a Pick he
must be a Notorios Lasey Fellow to stick up and gett his Fingers
Frost Bitten and was oblidged to have the Tops of severall of them

taken of—He was now laid up the rest part of the winter and at North Molton to live and under the Docters Care and living from the Boys Earnings untill he gott better when he went about with a Breef and gatherd a subscription to pay the Docter—I then imployed him again and told him I would give him what he erned which was but verey little when he was well and I leave Peeple to Judge still less with the Fingers taken of—I Bore with his lasey ways as long as I could at last I was oblidged to discharge him— He then went with one of the Iorn Companeys and they gave him 15s pr wick.[8]

I the said to the oldest Boy now John you can see I can do with your Lasey old Father no longer—I want you to be about late and erley and studey my interest and I will give you 1s pr wick more untill Mickalmass which was then 11s per wick—The Boys went on verey well for about a Fortnight—I then could see there was a Change in the manner of the eldest Boy—I had requested him to gett my Poney in and saddled as erley as half past five or from then to six that I may see round all the Cattle—Of a Morning about a fortnight after I had occasion to complain to him the Poney was not in it was nearley half past six—I told him then what to go about until I returned and went round to see the Stock on my return I went to Breakfast and made inquirey where he was— My Wife said he is leaved you have bin Grumbling with him or finding fault—I said I see I have Enemeys (some one has Pirswade him to Leave) his mind is poisened by some one to try to do mee injurey—

My Mrs said wont you Ride after John and gett him Back I should be sorrey to part with him he is a quiet willing Ladd—I rode on to Exford (I made inquirey at Simonsbath)—At Exford I saw him just enter an Inn (Coombs at the Swan)—I leaved my Poney and went in He had just ordered a Pint of Beer—I told him I would give him one shilling pr wick more which was 12s if he went back and did his best and looked to the stock erley and late and I would also give him some Licquer—he would not return then but some time in the Night he came back—The next day he came on to work and I continued to gave him 12s pr wick untill Ladey Day—He had also 12 or 15s given him by the Peeple that had their Cattle with mee.

Maney a Time have we had neither Mann or Maid My Wife and Children oblidgēd to do the work instead of my Children being putt to shool. I have maney a time Milked 20 or 25 Cows before Going to Barnstable Market my two little Girls before the were 11 years old have milked 10 and 12 at a Milking and at the same time paying Meen 2s and 2/6d pr day for about 8 or 9 Hours work—(It was not so untill after Smith came on as Steward I had no difficuly to gett Peeple to do work at a reasable Price before—I had no difficulty to gett my Hay made or Grass cutt and gave all Parteys sattisfaction I the first two or 3 years gott my Grass cutt at 1/–d pr Acre and give them sometimes a Bottle of Sidur and I could gett aney Quantitey of Meen to help about the Hay by giving them a little Bread & Cheese and sidur).

Mining

Mr Smith I think about the year 1850 or 51 began serching for Iorn Ore. I had often picked up large Pieces of Iorn on the surfice which is sopposed to have bin taken up (In the time of the Romans) a Sentry or two since—He now commenced serching on diferent parts of the Forrest and got out little Quantiteys of diferent sorts which no doubt he thought and was verey sanguine was going to turn out a wonderfully proffetable specculation. He went on serching for severall years Bult a Larbertory to put the Diferent specimens in putt his son with a Mr Nisbett a Noted Chemist in London to learn Chemestrey to assaye the Qualitey of it—His plege was often when he came to solisett mee to join his Bills that he was spending so much money in serching for the Iorn ore which kept Mr Knight and Mr Fowler short of Money and he could not gett his salerey—He said Boath Mr Knight and Fowler had maney times wished it to be given up but he was cirtin it would turn out a good speculation—After advertising it in the Mining Journall and a deal of expence and Pirseverence he gott some partey to commence to work it.

1856   Mining lodgers

When Mr Smith had the Mining Parteys coming on to commence working he wished to gett accomadation for some of them to Board and Lodge—He applied to us if we could take in the Cpn and Purcer belonging to Mr Snider called the North of England Company. Mr Smith said this Mr Snider was a most Liberal Gentleman to Pay everey one he had to do with after a deal of pirswsion we were indused to say we would give it a Tryall— Accordingley of an afternoon they Drove in the Yard in a Chaise from South Molton one by the Name of Phillips called a Captain the other by the Name of Rotherey as Purser. There were with us about three wicks a Deal of the Time Filps was ill and obliged to send for the Docter who attended him by Night as well as by Day. When they wished to have their Bill as soon as I gave it in their hands they began to find fault it was an Over Charge. They now begin to Pack up with the intention of Leaving—I locked the Dore where they had packed up their traps—They felt much anoid at my doing so and was Quite impudent I told them I knew a little what belonged to Travelling as well as them and I was not going to be done by a scool boy which one of them had the apperence of—He then leaved and was going to London in a few days the other came and pd the Bill and took the things away— One of them then took Lodgings at South Molton and took a Cupple of Females with him [the 'brace of doxies' referred to by Frederic Knight (page 199)]. I mereley relate this little matter as being the onley Transaction I had to do with the Mining Companeys and I do not think but verey few have done themselves aney good by it.

1855-7   The shop and inn

About the time it was about to commence my Brother Law Mr [Samuel] Gifford was out of Buseness and came to pay us a Vissitt and stay a few wicks at Cornham—There had bin no Bake House or oven for the Publick up to that time and as the talk was they Mining was going on so extencive and there was to be a Tram Road out of Hand there was to be an oven Bult which had bin in Contemplation I should think for a Twelve Months—I had the frame work Bt to Cornham with the intention of having one there—My Mrs happened to say something to her Brother about it when he said he should not mind going into that himself—He told Mr Smith what he thought of Doing when Mr Smith said their intention was to Buld an oven at Simmonsbath where the

Present Inn now is with the intention for that to be the Bake House and Shop to sell all kind of Provisions—And his intention was to Fitt and Buld up a Splended Hotell from the Premeses now used as workshops—He had a specimen of the intended Buldings on a sheet of Paper which he produced to us and which was to be commenced verey soon. The present In had bin Licenced about a twelve Months and was Kept by a Person who had bin complained of severall times by Mr Leblanc with respect to his not keeping his House orderley but was continuley having Rowes and Fighting through being complained of by Mr Smith. He said he would not remain there and more than once Mr Smith said had given Notice to leave it—Mr Smith said he should at Ladey Day expect him to do so. Mr Gifford said he did not mind taking that the In as well for a time it was what he had not bin acustomed to but he could gett a Yong Man he was aquainted with to assist him.

Mr Gifford then took the In of Mr Smith with the Expectation of an oven being emaudately Bult—It was drawing near Ladey Day [1856] he returned Home to prepare to take down his Goods and came with it I believe the Ladey Day—The Person then occupying it was verey unwilling to leave—He however at last made up his mind to it by Mr Giffords taking a few of his things of his Hands and I believe sold the remainder and leaved for America. Mr Gifford now commenced Quite a new Line of Bussiness from whatever he had bin acustomed to. He however seemed to have made up his mind to it altho I should think it was no verey envios Position to contend with the Partey that he generley had around him—There was nothing said or Done to-wards Bulding an oven for maney Months. I think it must be over a twelve Months—It was then proposed for the Master of the Dowlass Iorn Companey to Buld an oven and putt up a Temporey House with Board and Felt—As soon as it was Compleated Mr Gifford was asked if he would like to commence the Bussiness to Bake—He said he had no objection provided they could agree what was to be the Rent of it Mr Gifford enquird of Mr Scale[9]— His reply was Half the Proffetts Mr Gifford—I should go into nothing of that kind said Mr Gifford as it is verey uncertin weather that may be aney thing or nothing—Mr Scale then said the Rent will be this Lunchen we are partaking of Mr Gifford which was himself Mr Smith and severall others—Mr Gifford then commenced to Bake employed a Baker and I believe gave him 12s. pr wick beside his Board also commenced a Shop to sell all kinds of Provision and Grocery—He caried it on for severall Months and had just established a good Bussiness—Mr Scale and Smith putt their Heads no doubt together to endeavour to gett him to Buy it and named it to him which he declined to do—He said no but he had no objection to Rent it at a Fair Rent—Their object seemed to be to sell it. He then asked them what they expected for it Mr Scale said L100 Mr Gifford said it did not suit him to Buy it— He then offerd it to maney other Parteys at Barnstable South Molton and diferent parts of the Neighborud but no one could see their way clear to have to do with it—He then gave Mr Gifford a wick to leave it and he gave up the Key which I believe he had no occasion to have done—It has laid now near twelve Months and made no use of it and seems likeley to continue so. And often at Simmonsbath there is not a Loaf of Bread to be gott at either Shopp.

Money troubles

The Rent days came on and I was not prepared with the Rent— Mr Knight was then in the sistom of having Messrs Rowcliff the Attorneys to take the Rents and aney that could not meet the Rents a Bill was drawn on the old Bank at Barnstable—at the Tennants Expence, which caused the Arears of Rent to be laying back in the year 1850 and which Mr Smith then no doubt began to press them the Exetars to come forward to pay up and to putt more stock on the Farm.

Coppey of Letter from Mr Knight

Woolverley March 16 1851

Hannam,

I haven writen to Mr Smith to tell him that on the recept of L400 from your Fathers Exetors I will cancell my Claim to all farther arears up to Ladey Day 1851 I will make you a present of Cows to the Amount of Half the sum I receve L200 not in Money but Cows—I will then agree to receve the incressed Rent of L40 Rent on your Farm in Lime Bills at Challicombe Kiln in the next

two Years the Lime to be applyd to your Grass Land. If this offer
be not axcepted by the Exetors and the L400 be not paid by them
leaving you your present stock—I shall instruct Messrs Rowcliff
to proceed instantley against them for the whole amount due.

My Lease was now drawing to a Close and being so mixed up
with others through my Father being Joint Tennant Mr Knight
held his Exeturs responsabe to fulfill the Lease and I had a
Concidrable sum of Money belonging to them and other Freinds
invested in the Farm—I begun to feel myself in an unpleasant
situation—I owed a good Bitt of Money to different peeple in the
Neighbourwod but they verey kindley did not press mee for payment—I named the Situation to Mr Smith repeatedley that I was
in for severall years before and told him it was impossible for me
to meet the increased Rent that was intended to be putt on as I had
lost the whole we were woth and spent it in improving the Farm
and the Farm had alreadey bin to dear—he said I had better to see
Mr Fowler and if I like He would see him with me at his Ressi-
dence and appointed the Day to meet mee at Birmingham as he
was then about to leave for his Brothers in Lincolnshire to stay
for a time. Accordingley we meet the appointed day I took with
me a statement of what I owed as near as I could Judge and a list
of what I thought the Stock and what was on the Farm was worth.
I saw Mr Fowler and also Mr Smith and showed Mr Fowler a
statement of how I was situated and I was antios that something
should be done to ease my mind and to place me in a position to
continue the Farm as it would be a hard case for mee to leave more
than our own propertey which was from L1500 to L1600 and 12
Years Labour of the prime of our Life in the Farm and not be
alowed an oppertunitey to recover it again. Mr Fowler said he
felt my situation verey much but had not gott it in his power to
settle aney matters himself it rested a deal more with Mr Smith and
Mr Knight and it was a pittey I should have come such a distance
an expence and loss of Time to no purpose—He said I may depend
on not being pressed for the Rent due neither should he think
aney one else would press me for a time as it appeared my Farm
was well stocked—I may depend on his doing everey thing in his
power to assist us—I leaved Birmingham again the same afternoon

and gott home the Next day it occupied me near three days and two Nights.

It was now near Midsummer [1856] things seemed to look a little more cheering I shorn my sheep and Sold the wool which mett a payment at the Bank I soon had 100 Lambs to sell and some Beast with which I payed of other sums and Bt in 8 or 10 Cows which made up a Drove of 15 or 16 Cows the Keeping Cattle was doing well and everey one that came to see it was highley pleased with the apearence of it and the Farm was looking well we made a good lott of hay with the exception of 8 or 10 Acres which through the negligence of the Labourers was spoiled—My prospects now seemed to look better and I fancied luck was taking a Turn in my behalf I still felt antios for something to be settled it was now gott to Sepr and the Rent day was drawing near I saw Mr Smith and wished to know what was going to be done—He said he thought the Exetors my Brother and Brotherlaw [his eldest brother Thomas Hannam of Horsington, and Thomas Richards of Wincanton, husband of his wife's sister Jane] should come down to meet Mr Fowler He would write to them for that purpose —the Rent day was within a few days of South Molton Fair I took some sheep to the Fair and the evining preveos to the Fair mett them at South Molton.

29 September 1856   A meeting with Mr Knight

Mr Knight gott to Exmoor the Monday and called at Cornham appointing to Meet at Mr Smiths. We then leaved for Mr Smiths to Meet Mr Fowler—We gott there about six or half past and after waiting in the office a little time was taken to the Room to Mr Fowler—We had a deal of Conversation Mr Knight was in the ajoining Room and Mr Smith went two and from to him as Mr Smith remarked that Mr Knight felt so much for mee he could not enter the Room to see mee—The buseness was talked over betwin Mr Fowler and the Excutors with respect to the Rent then due and when it could be paid up—Mr Fowler Kindley asked mee by what time I thought I could make up the Rent—I told him by the reley part of November as I had a lott of steers Beast that I intended selling at North Molton Fair but as I had a deal of Keep I did not wish to part with them before that time and they were making great improvment I had also a deal of Keeping stock that would become due by that time which would bring in a Concidrable sum to meet the Rent then due and the Cows and Heafers Poneys and Colts I thought would be better to remain untill the Usuall time of my having a sale the 8th of December. Mr Fowler remarked that would be Quite sattisfactorey and if I requird longer time I could have had it Granted—Mr Fowler then enquird if I had a wish to continue the Farm I said I should like to do so as I did (not) see in what way I could recover myself in aney other way— Mr Fowler then inquird of Mr Smith if he thought there was a possibilletey of my doing so to make the Rent and pay my way. Mr Smith replyed he thought there was as I had adopted taking in keeping stock and was likeley to give sattesfaction at the price I was getting he thought it would pay. Mr Fowler then replyed I may continue the Farm—I said at the same Rent I sopose Sir. Yess he replyed I may.

After we gott Home to Cornham they began to make inquireys about different matters respecting my affairs I had furnished them with an account of what I owed with respect to Rent and other Peeple as near as I could judje—I found they were verey dissattisfied and the next morning looked over and talked over matters again and made remarks that I was not justified in paying aney more money to aney one. My Wife named to them if they had not better lett her Aunt Coward [Mrs Anna Coward of Compton Pauncefoot, with whom his wife had lived for eleven years after the death of her father] know how matters stood but it appeard it was their whole wish to keep it from hir as we had L300 of hir Money (and Mrs Giffords) which they were affraid would induce hir to putt in before them. They then leaved for Home—I rode out round the Farm after they were gone. I satt on my Poney on Little Cornham and where I had a sight of the Farm and a feeling came over mee I must confess I shedd maney Tears.

The same day the Rent day was at the Gallon House.

October 1856   *Levying execution*

Of an afternoon one of my little Girls came Running up to me in the Fields to say some one was come in a Carrege to see mee my wife was gone to Simmonsbath to see hir Brother. I hastened down and found one Person in the House and two in the Field who informed mee their Busseness was to take to everey thing on the Farm boath within dores and without and they were to take everey Head of Cattle into the Home Fields Keeping Cattle as well as my own I will leave aney one to guess my feelings—I emeadateley went to [Mr Smith] with the sherreffs officer expecting he would have Compremised the matter in some way but instead of which he said he thought it had better take its corse.

At the time they putt in the Execution I had a Quantitey of Cattle on to keep the season not being up for over a Month and no doubt maney would have lett it continue the Winter but they directley took it away. Mr Knight at the time I was putt on had just leaved England but Mr Charles Knight happened to be staying with Capten Knight at Linmouth and boath Mr Charles Knight and Cpn Knight called on us the Sadderday Morning. Mr Charles Knight remarked it was unfortunate his Brother should be from home and inquird if I should not like to reserve part of the stock. I told him as it was gone so far aney thing that would make its value had better be sold to make up the sum requird but I should like to reserve a few of the Cows and two or three of the Horses and the Dairey utensells and Furniture as I did not expect it would make Half its value.

Some time previos it may have bin three wicks or a Month—I was in Conversation with Mr Knight at Simmonsbath in the Road respecting the unpleasant situation we were in Mr Knight asked mee what preposeal I could make or what could be done—I named to him whether he would axcept a Partener—By all means he said Hannam if he has Money—I replyed the Person I thought of had no want of that—I said the Person I had in my Mind to name to was Mr Crang of Challicombe [William Crang of Challacombe]— Mr Knights reply was by all means Hannam I do not want a better Man.

I then went to South Molton and there meet Mr Maunder[10] and had some conversation with him respecting taking part in the Farm and I found he had bin talking with Mr Smith respecting it and had aranged to come out to go over the Farm on the Monday following—In conversation with Mr Maunder he said he would go into no partnership in the Farm but what he should like to himself and he only requird two or three peeces to summer his Flock of sheep and Poneys.

On the Monday following Mr Maunder and Mr Smith came and went over the Farm a good part of it before I knew they were come one we then went over the remainder and Mr Smith had aranged for Mr Maunder to have rather over Half the Farm exclusive of Rexey Ball and which ever had that to take it at Half price—I did not like giving up so much of it as if I could not stock it myself I could gett plenty of stock of others and repay mee much better.

Mr Smith and him then leaved but before leaving said they thought I had better see Mr Charless Knight that evining and tell him how I was situated and I should find what he was inclined to do—Accordingley I took my Poney and Rode away to Linmouth to see them—they treated mee verey Kindley wished mee to take something to eat and they would see me as soon as they had Dined—I had not bin long satt doing to a part of a Cold Leg of Mutton and a Jug of Strong Beer when I had a piece of warm Rost Beef and part of a Decanter of wine sent out. After I had taken what I please I was sent for to meet the Mr Knights. Mr Charles Knight made a Memerandom of what Information I gave him with respect to my being in a Position to make the Rent of the Farm and said he would see Mr Smith the following Morning only as he intended being at Simmonsbath to meet the Stag Hounds. I was intreated by boath Mr Knights and their Sister not to leave that Knight but at aney hour the next Morning the House keeper would gett me Breakfast as it was a verey Ruff Dark Night. I leaved about six oclock the next Morning. Mr Knight saw Mr Smith and told him he would lett mee have L50 to lay out in what I thought proper to reserve which reserved 3 Cows 2 Horses and Plow tackell sufficent to carey on the Farm.

8 October 1856   Forced sale

Soon after I returned from Linmouth the Auctineer Mr Watts from Yeovell arived and the Sheriff offecer and Clark three of them. We then numberd the Beast and gott things readey for the Sale the following Day—Mr Crang kindley came out and renderd everey assistance in his power with respect to reserving what we requird and aney other assistance he could render—I then named to Mr Smith I should like to reserve part of the Sheep and Hay He replyed he would not reccommend me to do so but would lett it all be sold I then asked him how I was to Keep two or three Cows and Horses if I Bought them or How I was to support my Wife and Fameley During the winter as I thought the Sheep would be sold verey low and I could make something from it by taking in Cattle—I gott Mr George Gold [George Avery Gould, tenant of Simonsbath Barton] to Reserve it for mee A few Fields of the Grass and part of the Hay to the amount of L54. The House Hold Goods and Darey Utensells were valued over in Conversation with Mr Smith before the Sale. We receved a few Bills I believe about 100 to circulate there was no advertisement putt in aney paper so that had I not perseveird and gott a Quantitey more Bills printed and circulated in the Neighborwood verey few peeple would have atended—I gott 2 pieces of Beef a Ham and 2 Legs of Mutton which no doubt ledd a great maney to attend and stay at the sale that would not have done so otherwise.

As it was we had a prety good attendance I should say near 400 peeple. The Horses was an amence sacrifice I had a beautiful lott of Poneys—Mr Smith Bt severall of them at concidrable less than their value they were from the Breed of Mr Fisher of White Chapple—Mr Maunder Bt a Horse at L13 10s that I refused L23 for when 3 years old warented in everey respect and never was the leist the matter with it.

The Winter Feed on the Farm was sold in the sale for L54— except what was Bought for Mee.

1855–8   Warren Farm changes hands

Mr Harrold term being up at Ladey Day 1855 He was preparing to leave and gave Notice to do so the Michalmass previos and was representing that he should make a sacrifice of severall Thousand Pounds on the Farm when he leaved—the next account we hird was that the Farm was Lett to a Person from Yorkshire and he was intending to take of all Mr Harrolds Stock Implymets and every thing on the Farm at a Valuation with the Exeption of the weather sheep and Hogs which Mr Smith should have Bought—No one had seen this Person Mr Wood that had taken the Farm but it appears the meen were Bribed not to lett him if possable go near aney other of the Tennants and Mr Harrold would present them with a great coat each if they kept him from the other Tennants untill after he was gott fixed and paid down the Deposett on the Valuation of three Hundred Pounds—It appears that Mr Harrold had for a long time bin urging this Mr Wood on to take the Farm —He told him he may Lamb the 370 yeos, Milk from 20 to 30 Cows and Make L15 pr Cow of them, grow maney Thousand Bushells of Oatts. In fact there was everey thing prepard for him that he may clear his three Hundred pr Year and almost sitt in his Arm Chair—He told him up such a fine storey that he indused him to take the Farm and agree to take of the Stock at the Valuation of one Man which was to be an Auctineer from Lestershire. He was to pay hin down L300 as a depossett and the remainder by instalments—This person was now took down by Mr Harrold and the Valuation gone into which was up to the Amount of L1240, 10s.—The 370 Yeos valued at L1 6s. Each one hundred of them Broke Mouthed. Poneys that cost him about L3 or L4 Each valued at 10 the Plow Tackell fitt for nothing but the Fire—The Corn Fairley Heated and Rotten the Hay that was made the Previos Summer good but for little and a lott old Rushes that had bin cutt for Bedding mixed in the Middle of the Rick and I think it was near or over L200 for Tennant Right.

It now began to be rumerd about him he was taken in. He then gott Mrs Wood down just in the verey severe weather in Januarey [1855] and 2 or three Meen and Horses—There was not a Turnip or the liest provision of Grass for they 370 Yeos as the winter commenced began now to drop their Lambs and I believe he lost from 40 to 50 during the Lambing. Poor Mrs Wood was there alone for a long time as Mr Wood was away when the verey severe weather was and had the Care of the whole of the stock. The Land was several feet coverd with Snow and the Roads blocked up for a long time.

Mr Wood then returned and he asked Mr Gold and Bullass [George Gould, tenant of Simonsbath Barton, and John Bullas, tenant of Duredon] to put a valuation on the stock and the Corn and Plow Tackell which they did and at the outside value they could putt on it was L680 which to him was valued at L1240 10s.

R

—I believe Mr Wood had to pay a sum of L200 some time in April—Through the pirswsion of his attourney and Frends he refused to pay it but commenced selling of the stock and I believe sold the whole which after putting the Keep and Labour and risk to it I believe did not make over L500—They then commenced a Law Suit which was caried into Court in London—The Suit came on and was thrown against Mr Wood There was L300 Expences and over which it appears Mr Wood had not the means to pay it. (Caried to a Tryall in London Bullass and Gould and severall others up as witnesses.) He returned and sold up the Corn and the Remainder of the Plow tackell and Traps he had there and leaved. What the result of it will be or where it will end peeple fancey it will ruin Boath of them. (Wood went through the Insolvent Court, Harrold was made a Bank Rupt soon after.)

Mr Smith then advertise the Crops of Grass on the Farm for sale by Auction—Maney Peeple attended the Sale to Purchase but it appears the Possession of the Farm was not given up by Messrs Wood and Harrell that they could not venture to sell it—Therefore the Pasture of the 530 Acres I believe it to be has not bin stocked the whole of the Summer or is it likeley to be as it is now the Month of September 1858 and it is still as it was when Mr Wood leaved it—There was several Acres of Corn Sown by Mr Wood which is now standing uncutt and the House and Premesies are beginning to look in Quite a Delabbidated State like maney others in the Forrest.

Winter 1856   Attempts to obtain a new lease

The sale was now past and nothing or verey little was said to Mr Maunder the sale Day or mee respecting the Farm. I hird nothing more respecting the Farm for some days when in conversation with Mr Smith in the House and in my wife's presence he said why should you have aney connection or partnership with aney one in the Farm but take it yourself. I hird no more neither did I see Mr Maunder to have aney thing to say about the Farm but about that time he Mr Maunder told Mr Crang he had declined to have aney thing more to do with Cornham and throughed some refelction with respect to my not being to my word—Nothing more was hird about it now for some days when Mr Smith was going towards Simmonsbath by way of the little Cornhams I took my Poney and Rode with him and on the way gott in Conversation with him about the Farm when he replyed you may depend you have lost continuing the Farm through not axcepting Mr Maunders preposal. He said he had a Letter from Mr Knight to lett the Farm by Tender and Mr Knight should request him to gett some Devonshire Tennants.

The same wick the Farm was advertised on the North Deaven Journall to be lett by Tender—I think it was severall wicks before aney one applied to go over it—In the mean time I saw Mr Crang and we had some talk about the Farm and wheather there had bin maney applycations. Mr Crang said Mr Maunder told him he would have nothing to do with Cornham—Mr Maunder that year had bin renting an alottment of Mr Spooner and the Time was nerley expird to give it up—Mr Maunder was then in treatey with Mr Smith for an alottment of 7 or 8 Hundred Acres called Mr Mathues Alottment. In riding from South Molton with him of a Sadderday evining in the Month of Novr he told me there was 6d. pr Acre diference betwin them and he was to have an answer the following Monday.

Some time after in conversation with Mr Maunder he said he receved a Note in reply from Mr Smith that he was to await or not be in haste for a few days as Cornham would be advertised to be lett—It appeard there was not more than three applycations or Tenders outt in esclusive of Mr Crang on my behalf and Mr Maunder—There was maney Peepple would have putt in for the Farm no doubt had it not bin out of good feeling on my behalf understanding I had everey wish to continue it.

Some time before the last day of the Tenders were to be given in Mr Crang was gott the better of his Ilness and said to mee he should like to see Mr Knight respecting the Farm and wished me to be possetive wheather I was to have the Farm at the past Rent—Mr Knight was then at Simmonsbath Mr Crang then arranged to come to Cornham the following Morning.

Mr Knight and Mr Crang then went into a Conversation respecting the Farm—Mr Crang said to Mr Knight I hear Cornham is advertised sir—Hannam has given mee to understand he is to continue it at the former Rent provided he gott some one to assist him—I have no objection to take the Farm without giving a Tender Mr Knight I will take the Farm see it managed see it stocked and see the Rent paid for three Years I think by that time he will be in a position to go on with the Farm again without assistance—Mr Knight said he thought it had better be tendered for—Mr Crang gave way and said he would putt in a Tender the Following wick.

Mr Knight and Mr Smith then leaved. Mr Crang said he thought we had pretty well secured the Farm and I believe from Mr Knights Conversation and the manner he receved him he had as good as taken it—At last after I should think it must be the relaps of a fortnight—a Letter was sent by Smith to mee to give to Mr Crang to say Mr Maunders Tender was axcepted. I never saw a Man so much stricken as Mr Crang was when I read him the Letter I believe if a dagger had penetrated him he would scareceley have Bledd. Mr Crang remarked well I am deceved in Mr Knight.

I think it must be the following Sadderday I was at South Molton in the Parlor at the Barnstable Inn—Mr Maunder came in and began to boast he had taken Cornham Farm—I said Mr Maunder there will be a deal of dirtey work to be done before I am gott out of Cornham—He gott verey warm with Pastion took his Coat of and threw it across the Chair damed my Eyes and said he would Strike my Bloddey Neck of—I then to passifye his anger gave him a song, the Coress of each Verse tosting the Heart that can feel for another. Mr Maunder putt on his Coat and Leaved.

The 25 of March [1857] was now drawing on I had writen maney Letters to Messrs Fowler and Knight respecting continuing the Farm My wife also wrote to Mr Knight and Mr Maunder—I had maney Kind Letters from Mr Fowler I wrote to him to be alowed to continue part of the Farm with Mr Maunder I also saw Mr Maunder and named it to him and he seemed to fall in with it and told mee he would write to Mr Fowler on the subject—I believe he saw Mr Smith after and he Smith prevaild on him not to do so as the next time I saw him he Mr Maunder was Quite averse to it and about the same time I had a Letter from Mr Smith to the effect that Mr Fowler had writen to Mr Maunder and he had declined it.

I think it was the 17 of March the Exeturs mett at Emmetts to settle up the Rent—When I was with them at Emetts I was scareceley alowed a Voise in the matter. If I began to relate aney thing to Mr Fowler they would cry Hush and prevent mee from speaking if Possable. They could not gett mee to say I would give up possesion so they leaved as they came and not in verey good Temper.

25 March 1857   A year's grace

In the time these Letters were passing betwin Mr Fowler and mee the 25 of March came—Mr Smith had bin representing to peeple he was sorrey to say he should have to turn us out of Dores if we were not gone out and I believe he thought he was going to frighten mee to that effect—the 25 of March he sent three or four fellows who remained waiting about several Hours in the Yard and stable—They then decamped with some Horses I had to Keep of Mr Knights and Mr Tors [the Rev J. Torr, curate at Simonsbath] It so happened we had a Deal of snow the previos Night—About one oclock Mr Smith came to the Front Dore—I went to the Dore and took him in the Parler—Mr Smith was looking verey Chopp fallen and beaten—He asked me if I intended to leave or what was to be done—He said Mr Maunder had taken the Farm and his stock was ranging over Harsen which would be a serios thing for Harsen Farm—I told him they would not do so on my account as I did not intend to leave—I told him it was a most raskeley thing to wish to gett mee away after being on so maney years and spent such a sum of Money as I had—He looked as if he was regulerley Beaten—His teeth did almost Hacker.

A few days after Mr Crang had a Letter to know if he would take the Farm for one year for our continuation—Mr Crang verey kindley came forward to do so with the expectation to putt us in a position to continue it for the future Mr Knight then mett Mr Crang at Cornham and the Farm was taken for one year—There was an agreement drawn up (For Mr Crang and Mee to sign) that there should be no Plowing or Mowing—with respect to Plowing I did not care about but I told him we must have some Hay—I had to depend Chifley on Keeping Cattle this season.

As I before said there was maney parteys that had Cattle out (to keep) the previos Summer and had it used so bad they would not risk putting it out this season—I was at Tiverton the Great Market the 21 of April and gott on pretty well I think I booked up 70 Head of Beast and Horses—I was at Credditon Market (a few day After) and I found I could not gett on so well altho I had several Friends who were doing their best for mee but I afterward lerned out the reason there was several Peeple sent out by some one to Circulate the report that I should take in everey thing I could regardless whether I starved it or not as I had the Farm onley but a few Months until Mickelmass then Mr Mander was to have it in posetion.

I had a Piece of Meadow 32 Acres I kept unstocked which had a fine piece of Grass—I had at last a Letter from Mr Fowler who gave me pirmision to Cutt it. It apeard that a wise provedence would smile on us or use what ever stratagems they may—It turned out all in our favour that it was not cutt earlier as we had a deal of Rain in July and through being delaid we had a Deal more Hay and a fine time to make it we made it in about 10 days and without the least Rain. I myself asked the faver of Mr Knight to alow us to sell the Hay of the Farm and he verey kindley granted it to be sold to aney one on the Forrest—we sold a quantitey of it in small parsels at 2/10 pr Tun before the 25 of March 1858.

In the Month of Januarey 57 the Roof of the Cheese Room was taken of with a Huriken and the Rafters laid Bare so much so that it Rained down through near Half a Land Yard. Mr Smith was spoken to repeatedley about it—it had bin in that state over a twelve months. The onley Boy I had to do a few jobs and look to the stock was inticed away from mee Not a Carpenter or aney one could be gott to even repair up the Dores and Gates about the yard. In the severe snowey weather we had not a Dore to maney of the Howses.

Some time on the erley part of March [1858] Smith had wrote to Mr Crang wishing to gett they Possession of a Cottage for Mr Mander—I begged Mr Crang not to give up the Possession of aney part—He however agreed to Meet Mr Smith there of a Morning. I felt a determination he should not gett Possession—I gave him a meeting in the Yard and they excitement being more

than I could Bear I was compeled to give him a thorough blowing
up and tell him the rights of my mind.

March 1858   Cornham is given up

Ladey Day was now past and Mr Knight did not come near us
or I do not think I should bin oblidged to leave the Farm. Smith
and Mander came on the Ladey Day Mr Crang was there and took
away his sheep Smith Loiterd about there for a long time—There
was I sopose 20 or 30 of the Miners and other parteys looking out
about the Yards expecting to see us Turned out of Dores by Smith
who had represented maney times he should have to do so and
Mr Thornton [the Rev W. H. Thornton of Simonsbath] as well
who was verey officios—I had bin up to Sandford and on my
return I found Mr Crang had given up Possession to Mander of
the Land—I saw now that unless we leaved it would be putting
Mr Crang to an Expence—We had a deal of Goods and the Dairey
Utensils three Cows and Horses—It was preposed by Mr Gold
and Mr Crang to have a sale which was fixed and took place and
about L30 sacrifice made.

Mr Knight in the first onsett held out he would be Librall to
mee after the affair was settled with the Exetars to continue mee in
the Farm—He then held out through Smith he would give mee
L150 to leave the Farm Quietley. Mr Thornton held out to mee
what an advantage it would be to me to take the L150. I told him
it would be of no use to mee, I could not carey it away and Cheat
Peeple. He then said I had better go into Dorsett and take a Dairey
or Emegrate which I sopose they expect me to do before the L150
is fourth coming as it is now the 8 of October [1858], just two
years since my Beautifull lott of Yong Stock was made a sacrifice
of L200 and L100 expences and the L150 is not fourth coming
yett.

1857–8   More changes of tenants

I have hird they old meen on the Forrest remark who must have
seen and Noticed all the Tennants that had bin on the Moor they
could see it answerd Mr Knights purpose to go a cirtin distance
up the Cuntrey for Tennants say the Higher part of Somersett or
Dorsett but he must not go farther—I do not believe at the

Present time there is but few that will occupye their Farms seven Years Leice—After the Tomshill Farm had lay by for severall Years it was lett to two Brothers by the name of Dixen [1857] but they seem to be doing but little on it—they Crooked Post Farm was taken by a Person by the name of Sharp who continued it one year after F Coombs leaving it but I believe Paid no Rent it was then after laying by a Year or two lett in pieces and alottments to diferent Peeple—Mr Minnett leaved the Dryford Farm but altho it had bin talked about for near a twelve months previos to Ladey Day he did not leave untill the later part of May [1858]. The Farm was not lett or but little made of it for the Year—Mr Leblancs Farm was lett in pieces and alottments and a part lett with the House to Mr Torr[11]—The Lark Barrow Farm no one has Taken since Mr Meadows leaved it. I think in the end [Mr Knight] will see it is not a lott of Gentlemen Farmers that live maney Milles away is going to improve it much but are more likeley to bring some of the old Mens words True that they should see it Exmoor again and as before a sheep walk and the Farm Houses occupied by Shepperds and Herdman.

To present apperence at all events it does not look verey prospereos or improving neith(er) will it I think with the present maneger—I do not know but one Farm on the Moor that looks improving or aney thing like a Tennant likeley to continue which is Mr Georg Gold who may be reaping some of the Cappitell Mr Godwin Leaved—Mr Poppell was on the same Farm I think two years and I believe in the Time paid one Half Years Rent I believe the others was spent in improvmets of the Farm as was the Case with Mr Spooners Mr Bullass and Minnett as I have hird them Boast of not paying aney Rent the first Year and Half.

April 1858   Leaving Exmoor

Mr Gold was so kind as to take a little place six Mills out of Barnstable [at Loxhore] which I may have had—(It was about 30 Acres at L50 pr year) there was not the liest thing done to the House or the least preparation made and I thought my wife would be quite Missarable and as nothing was settled up that we could putt any stock on I went to Barnstable to a little House that was all readey to putt the few things down in and I thought as comfortable little place as could be I thought the Children could go to scool My Mrs could have an oppertunitey to see hir Frends for a time and myself I thought would do a little Dealing for a time—I was again doomed to dissapointment I had no means to gett on with Dealing altho it was held out to me what I may expect if I gave up the Farm Quietley—my little Girls have neither scarceley known what a days Health has bin since partickalerey the one who has bin laid up in the whooping Couff and inflamation on the Chest to almost tear hir to pieces and break up hir constitution.

I have since bin in the most Missarable state myself not having aney thing settled or knowing where to go—Frequentley we have not had scarceley a Loaf of Bread except being beholding to a Neighbor and not a Bitt of Meat for days together.

Sometimes when I lay thinking it is almost more than my mind will bear to think and look back how I have strived and to see what I am brought to.

I lived at Barnstable rather over a Twelve Months—The Children went to Scool and through the Kindness of Mr J Gould & Mr King to the Wesleyin Day Scool.

It gott on to the Month of November [1858] of an Evining Quite unexpected we had Mr and Mrs Ritchards [Mrs Hannam's sister Jane and her husband Thomas Richards] of Wincanton come in they had passed through Barnstable the Day Preveos to Ilfracombe (No doubt they were writen to by Smith or Thornton or some one) They came by the last train in the Evining and leaved by the first in the Morning—I Believe the came for no other purpose but a Spy and to entice my wife and little Ladd away.

A few days after I found my wife more sett against mee than before and she began to Pack up hir things to go up the Countrey among hir Friends and upbraided mee verey much of a Sunday Afternoon about getting up the Cuntry to take something—A few days after she leaved, and took my little Boy with hir thinking no doubt I should soon follow (I saw by Hir Manner of Leaving I should have a deal to contend with) She remained I think near four Months and whilst she was up maney Letters passed and all on the same terms Pressing Mee to come up to have a Dairey or gett a Situation which I did not feel much inclined for—Lady Day [1859] came and as we had notice to leave the House wee were then In I was oblidged to look for another—We had just removed the things which took the Children near a fortnight to putt it in place and clear up the house which kept them from Scool to do it—My wife and little ladd now returned I anktiosley expected she had come to some arrangment with hir Freinds to Meet the few Peeple that we were indebted to and then I should have Freinds to assist mee to gett into Bussiness I found just the same independent Spirit still worretting mee to gett into something up the Cuntrey.

Postscript

The remainder of Hannam's account is a sad story of his deterioration until he reached the border of insanity. After leaving Barnstaple he heard that there was a vacancy on Lord Portman's estate at Yeovil for a bailiff to manage a dairy and applied for the job asking a salary of £100 a year. On learning that a working bailiff was wanted at a wage of 14s per week he declined this as beneath his dignity, although he was penniless.

He then learned that Mr Henry Stuckey of Drayton, near Langport had a dairy to let at Cothelstone Farm, near Taunton, and in the summer of 1859 he agreed to take this at a rent of £152 pa, aided by an advance of £30 from his relatives. He had scarcely taken over the dairy before he decided that he could not make it pay, and the good-natured Mr Stuckey agreed to employ him as working bailiff at 16s a week. This did not last long as he was sacked for neglecting his duties. Even now Mr Stuckey had pity on his family and let his wife and children remain in the house and provided them with food, while Hannam stayed on as unpaid handyman in exchange for his keep.

Leaving his family at Cothelstone he now wandered back to North Devon, staying much of the time with the long-suffering Mr Crang at Challacombe, and while there he learned that his brother-in-law, Samuel Gifford, was giving up the Inn at Simonsbath at Lady Day 1860. From time to time he returned to Cothelstone where he was less and less welcome, until in May 1860 Mr Stuckey turned him out, though he continued to shelter his family. His wife considered divorcing him and taking a job as a housekeeper, but this came to nothing, and after outstaying his welcome at various friends and relatives Hannam returned to Cothelstone in October with 'no shews to my Feet or Cloaths to my Back'. He stayed most of the winter while his eldest daughter was sent to relatives at Wincanton, but in the spring returned to Mr Crang. It was there that Hannam heard of the dismissal of Robert Smith.

25 March 1861   Robert Smith is dismissed

Smith was turned out of the Stewardship at Lady Day 1861. I think he was Beat and all Power was taken out of his Hands. He then putt an Articall on the North Deaven Journall Puffing up What he had done on the Moor and that he had resined the Agencey and a Deal to Praise Himself in the Eyes of the Publick— Mr Knight the following wick in a few words gave him a flatt Contradiction and to say he felt it Necessary to dismiss him from the Agencey.

The summer of 1861 was spent with a Mr Dibble near Bridgwater until he fell from a rick and broke several ribs. After convalescing at Cothelstone he went on his travels once more, and his story ends inconclusively in October 1862.

(See pp 295–9 for notes)

THE KNIGHT ESTATES IN DEVON AND SOMERSET

Sir Frederic Knight's Exmoor Estate, 1886

Number	Allotment Original holder	Acquisition	Area a. r. p.
32 to 41	The King's Allotment (including 12 acres reserved for a church)	Purchased 1820, £48,922	10,262 1 6
	Simonsbath Farm	Purchased 1820, £1,200	108 2 0
42 and 77 to 81	Sir T. D. Acland, Bart. (including 15a. 1r. 25p. by Porlock road at Larkbarrow reserved by the vendor)	Purchased from him, 1819, £16,415. Mineral rights purchased 1829 and conveyed 1855, £492 2s.	3,298 3 7
128 to 225 (131 and 158 duplicated)	Sir C. W. Bampfylde, Bart.	Purchased from him, 1821, £7,985 2s. 92 life tenancies purchased 1819–20, £547 18s. 4d. Mineral rights purchased 1829 and conveyed 1855, £270	1,881 2 3
43	The Earl of Carnarvon	Purchased from him, 1829, £940	246 3 4
281	Sir Arthur Chichester	Purchased from him with Brendon Manor, 1820	9 1 35
277	Charles Chichester	Purchased from Robert Chichester, 1839, £78 15s.	15 2 20
68	John Hill	Purchased from him, 1828	133 3 22
100	Phillip Hancock	Purchased from Francis and Phillip Hancock, 1841, £450. Included a dwellinghouse	42 2 0
101	Phillip Hancock	?Purchased from him, 1828	21 3 21

292

Allotment Number	Original holder	Acquisition	Area a. r. p.
75	Henry Studdy	Purchased from Amelia Warren Griffiths, 1838, £58	29 0 5
54	Thomas Thornton and Hugh Greenslade the lessee	Purchased from Francis Hooper, 1828, £80	36 3 18
55	Thomas Thornton and William Moggeridge Stawell the lessee	Purchased from W. Stawell, ?1829	20 1 19
48	J. P. Chichester	Purchased from him, 1839, £221	36 3 15
			16,144 1 15
Munckham Manor (Exford Monachorum) Three cottages and enclosed waste of the Manor		Purchased from Bunce Curling, 1824, £155	83 2 0

Sir Frederic Knight's Brendon Estate, 1886

Property	Acquisition	Area a. r. p.
The Manor of Brendon Cheriton and Cheriton Woods Farm, yard, and buildings. Garden, orchard, arable, meadow, pasture, wood, road, and Bridge Ball Stream	Purchased from Sir Arthur Chichester, 1820, £20,000 plus £3,225 for the timber	102 2 24
Barton and Hallslake Farmhouse, pond, buildings, garden, pasture, meadow, Scob Hill, Scob Hill Wood and Barton Wood		629 3 32
Bridgeball Cottages, gardens, arable and meadow		3 2 1
Cranscombe House and wood, garden, meadow and pasture		46 0 37
Tibbacott Cottages, meadow and arable		3 0 38
Glebe House and yard, garden, arable, meadow, pasture and wood		57 2 22

Property	Acquisition	Area a. r. p
Badgworthy Black Hill, Badgworthy Lees, Holcombe Hill and Badgworthy Wood		875 3 36
Common inclosures at Farley Hill, Tibbacott, Shilston, Woolaway, Slocomslade and Churchcombe Cottages, buildings, yard, garden, orchard, arable, meadow, pasture and wood		108 3 16
Inclosures taken from Brendon Common since 1839, at Woolaway, Tibbacott, Sherdon Hill, Shilston Hill and Higher Churchcombe		103 1 14
Brendon Common		3,399 3 26
		5,331 1 6
Farley House, garden, meadow, arable, and Cliff Wood	Purchased from the executors of Richard Hobbs, ?1829	30 1 21
Farley Farm, yard and buildings, garden, meadow and pasture, Farley Wood, Cliff Wood, and Higher Farley Wood	Purchased from William Fry, 1821, £3,000	102 1 4
Cheriton Farm, yard and buildings, garden, arable, meadow, pasture and wood	Purchased from the executors of John Nott, 1871, £1,560	51 0 1
Cheriton Arable, meadow, pasture and wood	Purchased from John Squire, 1869, £2,150	70 1 37
Malmsmead House, shed and yard, orchard, arable, meadow, pasture and wood	Purchased from George Frost, 1822, £750	44 0 4
Malmsmead Wood, Southern Wood, and Ashford Wood		9 3 18
Part Southern Ball		8 3 25
Scores Down Pasture	Purchased from David Richards, 1869, £400	17 1 32
		5,665 2 28

NOTES

NOTES TO C. S. ORWIN AND EXMOOR (*pages* 18–22)

1 Another reasoned advocate of land nationalisation was Prof R. G. Stapledon who for similar reasons was 'reluctantly driven to the conclusion' that only by this means could hill farming provide an adequate livelihood.

NOTES TO CHAPTER I (*pages* 23–36)

1 The British Museum Act, 1963, abolished family trustees, including that of the Knight family, the last trustee being Richard Ayshford Knight.

2 The estate was first mortgaged for £16,000 in 1826, increased to £36,000 in 1848, to £91,000 in 1864 and ultimately to £123,060 in 1877.

NOTES TO CHAPTER II (*pages* 37–56)

1 'An Act for Vesting in His Majesty certain parts of the Forest of Exmoor otherwise Exmore, in the Counties of Somerset and Devon; and for inclosing the said Forest' (4 July 1815).

2 As a result of further research, after his *History* had been published, Mr E. T. MacDermot became convinced that the Inclosure survey did not, in fact, include the whole of the ancient Forest, and that the curious indentation in the boundary at Kittuck, between Badgworthy Water and Chalk Water, was due to the boundary stones having been moved, in anticipation of the inclosure, in order to appropriate this area into Oare Common.

3 For a full account of the final inclosure of Exmoor Forest, see MacDermot, ch xv (pp 406–40), from which this brief summary of the principal events has been abstracted.

4 At a later date, Mrs Jack Russell once pounded the field at the boundary fence by Red Deer, when hunting with the members of the South Molton Hunt Club.

5 Where the roads cut the wall, gates were placed to prevent the straying of livestock. Between Red Deer and Honeymead, on the Exford road, and on the Forest boundary on the Brendon road, if

not also at other points, ingenious double gates were erected. They were hung on opposite sides of the same hanging-post, and they closed, without fastening of any kind, against the same clapping post. Thus, they were easy to pass, and a wind that might blow one of them open would keep the other closed. Honeymead Two Gates were removed long since, when the fields adjacent were fenced; Brendon Two Gates were only abolished during the widening of the road from the Exe Valley to Lynton.

NOTES TO CHAPTER III (*pages* 57–72)

1 This was not the present farmhouse, which was not built until 1845, but would be the earlier farm manager's house and cottages.
2 The inclosure award was made three years later on 1 May 1841.
3 'The Shepherds have hitherto stolen most of the Fawns; Howchin [the factotum at Simonsbath] detected two of them walking off with a fine Red Deer Calf', *Letter from John Knight to his Wife*, 28 July 1841.

NOTES TO CHAPTER IV (*pages* 73–97)

1 The action was carried to the Court of Exchequer the following year on an obscure point of law. Although Hibberd was awarded 40s damages he had to pay the costs, and according to Hannam this ruined him.
2 Hannam refers to Robert Smith as being 'possesed of but little or no Cappetal'.
3 It was not until more than a generation after this date that the *Agricultural Holdings Act*, 1883, secured to all tenant-farmers such equitable conditions of tenure as were provided, on Exmoor, by Frederic Knight, under the lease which Robert Smith had drafted for him.
4 From (Sir) Thomas Dyke Acland's prize essay on 'The Farming of Somersetshire', published, in 1850, by the Royal Agricultural Society. 'Young Acland is going to publish an account of the farming of Somersetshire; he has been several times to Simonsbath and has, I believe, changed his opinions of the Forest. Previously his ideas were obtained from old Ralph, of Exford, and other people of the same description, but now I fancy Smith, the agent, has talked him over, and he thinks everything doing well.' *Letter from Lewis Knight to his sister, Margaret, at the Palazzo Bracci, Rome*, 17 January 1850. 'Old Ralph' was the Exford parson, the Rev Joseph Ralph, the son of a Cumberland statesman, and 'as great with his woolly flock with his parishioners'.

NOTES TO CHAPTER V (*pages* 98–114)

1 Although much of John Knight's real property was left jointly to Frederic and Charles Knight, the estates, in Devon and Somerset,

had been willed solely to Frederic, other beneficiaries being left substantial legacies.

2 Howchin, who was officially butler at Simonsbath House, seems to have been employed in a variety of capacities. His letter is evidence of the good relations which existed between Frederic Knight and his servants. He inquires after 'Mrs. Knight and Baby'; tells his master of the sport his neighbour Sir Arthur Chichester had enjoyed, in the previous season, with grouse and deer in Scotland, and remarks that he was married in November 1847, and has four children, all born in the month of November in the four following years, 'which is rather a singular circumstance'; he retails the local news, such as the death of 'old Mr. Litson, of Willsham'. When Simonsbath House was let, he and his wife, who was the cook, 'and a very good one', started a hotel in Dover Street, Piccadilly, known as Howchin's Hotel.

3 Parson Jack Russell figures as depasturing horses on the Forest in the accounts for the year 1851.

NOTES TO CHAPTER VI (*pages* 115–29)

1 The first tenant of Larkbarrow was 'old Farmer Hayes of Exford, the herds father. He bears a very good character and is a very good farmer for the country'.

2 The Challacombe Commons were inclosed by agreement in 1862, but Smyth seems to have been given possession of part, and started work some five years earlier.

3 John Gourdie, the shepherd who brought down the last consignment of Cheviot sheep to Exmoor, was, from 1898 until his death in 1931, tenant of Wintershead, the farm on which Gerard Spooner had once before experimented with Cheviots and Blackfaces. Little, another of the original shepherds, brought down by Frederic Knight, was living in retirement at Castle Hill in 1929. His descendents were employed by the Fortescue estate on Exmoor, as they are today.

4 Four of these in 1876 were grey French mares [Percherons], drafts from the General Omnibus Company's stock, bought by Samuel Sidney for Frederic Knight, lame from London stones, and worked sound on Exmoor.

5 About 33s 6d per acre. But, as Earl Fortescue pointed out, this cannot have represented the whole of the cost of turning the moorland into pasture.

NOTES TO CHAPTER IX (*pages* 149–55)

1 He had had only two predecessors; William Scott, bailiff until about 1880, followed by William Brian.

NOTES TO CHAPTER X (*pages* 156–69)

1 Hill sheep subsidy increased to 16s a ewe, though as flock numbers returned to normal it dropped again to 2s 6d by 1951–2.

S

2 Recently there has been a heartening improvement in sheep prices, helped in part by purchases by cereal farmers using sheep as a break from monoculture to keep their land healthy.

NOTES TO CHAPTER XI (*pages 170–221*)

1 Mr E. T. MacDermot suggests that either Michael Wynston or James Boevey, who held the Forest of Exmoor, 1653–95, may have been the 'Roman' in this case.

2 It is referred to by this name in the 1851 Census return.

3 A full account of these events is given in Chapter I of *The West Somerset Mineral Railway and the story of the Brendon Hills Iron Mines*, 1952.

4 George Templer, of Stover, near Newton Abbot, formerly master of the South Devon Hounds. 'Scholar and sportsman, poet and wit.'

5 Robert Smith had a dual interest in the cottages, for as well as being Frederic Knight's agent, he was employed by the Dowlais Iron Company at the mines until February 1856 as agent and subsequently as cashier.

6 Henry William Schneider, Member of Parliament for Norwich City, 1857–60 (in which year his election was declared void for corrupt practices), and Robert Hannay, of Ulverston.

7 They had, in fact, already spent over £8,000, not including the rent of £1,750, but, for this expenditure, had raised only some 2,000 tons of ore.

NOTES TO CHAPTER XII (*pages 222–36*)

1 Tenant of Honeymead.

2 Tenant of Simonsbath Barton.

3 Tenant of Brendon Barton.

4 The figures quoted in the application are so much higher than the 1851 census, that they must have included labourers who worked on the Forest, but lived in adjoining parishes.

5 Mordaunt Fenwick, who later added the name of Bissett, by which he is well remembered as Master of the Devon and Somerset Staghounds from 1855 to 1880.

6 There was a legend that 'Exmoor was afforested by William Rufus, some seven hundred years ago'.

7 A number of agricultural labourers were temporarily absent, having returned to their homes outside the Forest for the weekend.

NOTES TO
A HISTORY OF TWELVE YEARS' LIFE ON EXMOOR
(*pages 240–91*)

1 The original buildings at Cornham had been constructed some twenty years before, and the farm had always been in hand. George Wooldridge had been bailiff of a large Wiltshire farm until he went

to work at Honeymead, and he was appointed bailiff at Cornham in 1841.

2 This agreement provided for Hannam to take 545 acres, including the house, homestead and three cottages, from Lady Day 1845 (see page 75). He seems to have had an additional 500 acres of rough grazing on the Chains.

3 General factotum to the Knight family (see note 2, page 297).

4 This was published in 1850 (see note 4, page 296).

5 William Fowler, surveyor, of Waterloo Street, Birmingham, the receiver appointed by the Court of Chancery (see page 99).

6 Hannam was in no position to guarantee money to anyone, as he already owed rent. Later he did not renew the bill, and ascribed his differences with Smith and Minett to this. Minett was tenant of Driver.

7 February 1855 was in fact outstandingly cold as Hannam himself complains on pages 267–8.

8 He became the first tenant of the Cornham Ford cottages in March 1857. According to Henry Scale he 'had some turf for fuel and was turned out of his house by the landlord at Cornham Farm'.

9 Superintendent for the Dowlais Company. Scale provided the shop as a private venture (see page 233).

10 Edwin Maunder, woolstapler and farmer, of Heasley Mill, North Molton, and later to become tenant of Cornham, Duredon and Titchcombe.

11 Charles Le Blanc gave up Simonsbath House and its land in 1858, the house and 128 acres being let to the new curate, the Rev J. Torr.

BIBLIOGRAPHY

Acland, Thomas Dyke. 'On the Farming of Somersetshire', *Journal of the Royal Agricultural Society of England*, 1st series, vol xi, 1850

Ashton, T. S. *Iron and Steel in the Industrial Revolution*, 1924

Bentham, Edward George & Lindley, John. *Selections from the Physiological and Horticultural Papers published in the transactions of the Royal Horticultural Society by the late T. A. Knight, Prefixed by a Sketch of his Life*, 1841

Billingsley, John. *General View of the Agriculture of the County of Somerset*, 1795

Bleasdale, A. & Douglas, C. K. M. 'Storm over Exmoor on August 15, 1952', *The Meteorological Magazine*, December 1952

Blathwayt Papers

Bradley, A. G. *Exmoor Memories*, 1926

Burke's Landed Gentry

Butler, Josephine E. *Memoir of John Grey of Dilston*, 1869

Cantrill, T. C., Sherlock, R. L. & Dewey, Henry. *Special Reports on the Mineral Resources of Great Britain*, Vol ix, Iron Ores

Can Exmoor Survive?, 1967

Castle Hill Estate Office Papers

Census Returns for the Extra Parochial Area of Exmoor

Collyns, Charles Palk. *Notes on the Chase of the Wild Red Deer*, 1862

Dictionary of National Biography

Dixon, Henry Hall ('The Druid'). *Scott and Sebright*, 1862

Dowlais Iron Company Papers

Duke, Brian. 'Winter at Warren Farm', *The Exmoor Review*, No 5, Winter, 1963

Evered, Philip. *Staghunting with the Devon and Somerset*, 1902

Parish of Exmoor Rate Books

Fitt, J. Nevill. 'Waste Hill Lands; How they may be utilized by Pony Breeding', *Journal of the Royal Agricultural Society of England*, 2nd series, Vol xv, 1879

Fortescue, Hon John William. *Records of Stag Hunting on Exmoor*, 1887

Hall, H. Byng. *Exmoor; or the Footsteps of St. Hubert in the West*, 1849

Hamilton, Archibald. *The Red Deer of Exmoor*, 1907

Hayes, John. 'Galloways on Exmoor', *Journal of the Galloway Cattle Society*, December 1968

Healey, Charles E. H. Chadwyck. *History of Part of West Somerset*, 1901

Henriques, Robert. *Sir Robert Waley Cohen 1877–1952*, 1966

Horsington Parish Registers

Macdermot, Edward T. *The History of the Forest of Exmoor*, 1911

Mackie, J. M. B. 'Galloways on Exmoor', *The Exmoor Review*, No 2, Summer, 1960

Miles, Roger. *Forestry in the English Landscape*, 1967

Mining Journal, 1846–55

Page, John Lloyd Warden. *An Exploration of Exmoor and the Hill Country of West Somerset*, 1890

Pell, Albert. *The Making of the Land in England*, 1899

Prothero, Rowland E. (Lord Ernle). *The Pioneers and Progress of English Farming*, 1888

Rawle, Edwin John. *Annals of the Ancient Forest of Exmoor*, 1893

Reclamation in Exmoor National Park, 1967

Roberts, Charles Gay. 'Sutherland Reclamation', *Journal of the Royal Agricultural Society of England*, 2nd series, Vol xv, 1879

Royal Commission on Agriculture Report, 1882

Sidney, Samuel. 'The Ponies of Exmoor', *The Illustrated London News*, 22 Oct, 1853

— 'Exmoor Farming', *The Illustrated London News*, 19 Nov, 1853

— 'Exmoor Reclamation', *Journal of the Royal Agricultural Society of England*, 2nd series, Vol xiv, 1878

— *The Book of the Horse*, New Edition, 1893

Smith, Robert S. 'The Cultivation of Moorland', *Journal of the Royal Agricultural Society of England*, 1st series, Vol xvii, 1856

— 'Irrigation', *Journal of the Bath and West of England Society*, Vol iv, 1856

— 'The Exmoor Cottages', *Journal of the Bath and West of England Society*, Vol vi, 1858

Smyth, Warrington W. 'On the Iron Ores of Exmoor', *Quarterly Journal of the Geological Society*, 1859

Smyth-Richards, F. G. 'Exmoor Agent', *The Exmoor Review*, No 11, 1970

Snell, F. J. *A Book of Exmoor*, 1903

— *The Blackmore Country*, 1906

Sporting Magazine 1824, 1860

Thornton, W. H. *Reminiscences and Reflections of an Old West Country Clergyman*, Vol i, 1897

Tozer, Edward J. F. *The South Devon Hunt*, 1916

Victoria County History of Worcestershire, Vol iii

Whitton, T. H. F. 'Good Estate Management, a Devon and Somerset Estate', *Agriculture*, 1954

Wilson, Woodrow. *The Cambridge Modern History*, Vol vii, The United States, 1903

Wolverley House Papers

INDEX

Page numbers in italics indicate illustrations

Cornwall, Duchy of, 150
Cost of cultivations, 84, 87; of equipping a farm, 83, 96–7, 99, 100, 138; of fences, 83; of reclamation, 96–7, 126, 133, 297; of running the estate, 98, 101; see also Value of land
Cottage building, see Housing
Countryside Act, 1968, 165, 169
Coward, Mrs Anna, 277
Cow Castle, 172
Crang, farmer, 66
Crang, William, 278, 279, 282, 283–4, 285, 286, 287, 290, 291
Crawshay, Robert, 198, 201
Crick, Richard and Thomas, tenants of Warren, 100
Crooked Post, 75, 78, 79, 99–100, 115, 116, 117, 149, 242, 254, 264, 288
Crop rotations, 60, 71, 74, 101, 105, 106–7, 109–10, 132, 135, 145–6
Cullen, engineer to the Porlock railway, 210
Cultivations, 84, 87, 126
Cumberland, land reclamation in, 63
Cunynghame, Daniel, 28, 31
Cutcliffe, Federata, 42

Dairying on Exmoor Forest, 74, 79, 95, 98, 99, 154, 161, 169, 238, 242, 244, 249, 250, 255, 258, 259, 266, 267, 269, 271, 278, 281, 287
Dartmoor, 150, 169, 171
Davies, Llewellyn, 220
Davis, E. P., 218, 219
Day, John, 47
Deer, Fallow, 54, 110; Red, 61, 107, 110–11, 164, 173
Deer, damage, 98, 101, 110, 151, 251; park at Simonsbath, 54, 62, 110; stealing, 65–6, 111, 173
Deer Park mine, see Mines
Devon Cattle Breeders Society, 162
Dixon, Henry Hall ('The Druid'), 107, 197, 300
Dixon, William, 218
Dixon, William and Ford, tenants of Tom's Hill, 100, 288
Dowding and Card, tenants of Warren, 242, 251, 254, 255
Dowlais Iron Company, 16, 114, 180, 182, 183, 186, 187, 189, 191, 192, 195, 196, 198, 199, 200, 201, 204, 207, 208, 209, 210, 213, 214, 217, 218, 223, 233, 273, 298, 299, 300
Downton Castle, 27, 29, 30, 34, 73

Drainage, 56, 59, 60, 82, 90, 101, 126, 133, 168, 256, 298; see also Subsoiling
Driver, 36, 54, 79, 93, 100, *104*, 117, 150, 151, 159, 163, 166, 219, 226, 258–9, 265, 288, 299; Gate, 152
'Druid, The', see Dixon, H. H.
Drybridge, *68*, 220
Dudley, 179; Iron Works, 218
Dulley, tenant of Duredon, 258
Dulley, tenant of Wintershead, 258
Dulverton, 231; Rural District, 232; Union, 232
Dundas, Lord, 69
Dunstan, William, 177, 179, 204, 210, 213
Duredon, 36, 79, 83, 93, 100, 117, 119, 123, 129, 135, 142, 147, 159, 166, 168, 215, 219, 226, 256, 258, 264, 281, 299

Ebbw Vale Company, 179, 201
Ebrington, Lord, see Fortescue, 4th Earl
Eddy, Stephen, 205
Electricity supply, 155, 156, 168
Ellis, Joseph, 218, 219
Elworthy, Mrs Mary H., 234
Emmett's Grange, 36, 60, 76–7, 78, 79, 82, *86*, 92, 95, *103*, 113, 114, 146, 159, 163, 164, 166, 242, 253–4, 259, 260, 262, 285
Epsom, 93
Ernle, Lord (Prothero, R. E.), 52, 301
Evans, John, 187, 188
Evans, William, 207
Exe Cleave, 149, 164, 165; mine, see Mines; Head, 215, 219; river, 57, 107
Exford, 80, 115, 142, 151, 165, 169, 225, 232, 234, 246, 249, 252, 253, 265, 270, 296, 297
Exmoor and Porlock Railway, see Railways
Exmoor Forest, allotments on, 39–42, 46, 48, 51, 52, 53, 141, 292–3; see also King's Allotment; boundary, 45, 52, 58, 67, 143, 215, 222, 228, 295; history before 1818, 37–9, 222; inclosure, 37, 38–42, 222, 223–4, 228, 231; Mining Syndicate, 219–20; National Park, 162, 163, 165, 166; Society, 162, 165

Falkirk Fair, 63
Family farmers, 131, 143–4, 146
Farms and farmhouses, construction and equipment of, 71, 72, 74, 75, 78, 79, 80, 82, 83, 90, 91, 97, 99, 100, 101, 132,